THE INORDINANCE OF TIME

Northwestern University
Studies in Phenomenology
and
Existential Philosophy

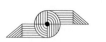

THE
INORDINANCE
OF TIME

Shaun Gallagher

Northwestern University Press
Evanston, Illinois
1998

Northwestern University Press
Evanston, Illinois 60208-4210

Printed in the United States of America

ISBN 0-8101-1581-6 (cloth)
ISBN 0-8101-1582-4 (paper)

Library of Congress Cataloging-in-Publication Data

Gallagher, Shaun, 1948–
    The inordinance of time / Shaun Gallagher.
       p. cm. — (Northwestern University studies in phenomenology
and existential philosophy)
    Parts of this book have been read at various conferences and
colloquia.
    Includes bibliographical references and index.
    ISBN 0-8101-1581-6 (cloth : alk. paper).—ISBN 0-8101-1582-4
(pbk. : alk. paper)
    1. Time. I. Title. II. Series: Northwestern University studies
in phenomenology & existential philosophy.
    BD638.G33 1998
    115—dc21
                                                98-4435
                                                  CIP

For Laura and Julia

Tá a fhios agat gur leat a bhfuil agam,
Tír na nOg, san iarthar buí,
Ar chladach na mara goirme.

You know that what I have is yours,
Land of Youth, in the golden west,
On the shore of the blue sea.

—*Eachtra Chonnla Fhionn*, The Adventure of Connla the Fair

עולמך תראה בחייך ואחריתך לחיי העולם הבא
ותקותך לדור דורים לבך יהגה תבונה
פיך ידבר חכמות ולשונך ירחיש תנח
עפעפיך יישירו נגדך עיניך יאירו במאור תורה
ופניך יזהירו כזהר הרקיע שפתותיך יביעו דעת
וכליותיך תעלוזנה מישרים ופעמיך ירוצו לשמוע
דברי עתיק יומין.

May you live to see your world fulfilled, may you be our link to future
  worlds,
and may your hope encompass all generations yet to be.
May your heart conceive with understanding, may your voice speak
  wisdom,
your words enlivened with sounds of joy. May your gaze be straight and
  sure,
your eyes lit with Torah's lamp, your face aglow with the heavens' radiance,
your lips expressing words of knowledge, and your inner self alive with
  righteousness.
And may you always rush in eagerness to hear the words of One more
  ancient than all time.

—*from the Talmud*

"Quercie grande da ghiande piccole crescono."

Contents

Acknowledgments   xi

1. Introduction: Time-Consciousness: Modern Problems and
    Postmodern Aporias   1

Part 1: The Perfection of the Phenomenological Paradigm

2. The Specious Present and Associated Perplexities   17

3. Husserl and the Specious Present   32

4. Reinterpreting Time-Consciousness   53

Part 2: Three Studies of Prenoetic Effects

5. The Theater of Personal Identity   73

6. Disrupting Seriality: The Idea of a Post-Husserlian Temporality   86

7. Time and Alterity   108

Part 3: Post-Husserlian Temporality

8. Intentionality and Interpretation   129

9. Beyond Intentionality   152

10. Inordinate Temporality   179

Notes   203

Works Cited   221

Index   235

Acknowledgments

I am grateful to Rudolf Bernet, John Brough, Philip Buckley, and John Burkey (Husserl scholars all, in strict alphabetical order), as well as Richard Cohen, Jonathan Cole, Martin Dillon, John Drummond, Lawrence Hass, Andrew Meltzoff, Brian Miclot, Dorothea Olkowski, and Stephen Watson for critical comments on earlier versions of some of the chapters, or for helpful and timely information when I really needed it.

I have learned a great deal in truly stimulating conversations with Tony Marcel. I have also benefited from the guidance of George L. Kline, who nurtured my interest in the philosophy of time; and especially from Elaine DeBenedictis Gallagher, who constantly challenges my philosophical presuppositions about time, and, as my wife, makes life much less abstract.

Certain institutions have supported my research for this book. I am grateful for the opportunities afforded by a sabbatical at Canisius College, a stay as Visiting Scientist at the Medical Research Council, Applied Psychology Unit in Cambridge, England, and a brief visit to the Husserl Archives, directed by Samuel Ijsseling, in Louvain, Belgium.

Parts of this book have been read at various conferences and colloquia at Mansfield College, Oxford; Muhlenburg College; University of California, Berkeley; University of Toledo; and Villanova University. I wish to thank all who commented at those forums.

An earlier version of chapter 5 appeared in *The Personalist Forum* 8 (1992): 21–30. Thanks to Thomas Buford for permission to incorporate it here. Thanks to Daniel Dennett for permission to use his diagram in chapter 10 (fig. 10.1). The figure originally appeared in his *Consciousness Explained* (Boston: Little, Brown, and Company, 1991), 136.

1

Introduction:
Time-Consciousness:
Modern Problems and
Postmodern Aporias

I t is ironic that just as researchers in the philosophy of mind and cognitive psychology have been resurrecting the concept of consciousness from the theoretical grave prepared for it by behaviorists, a diverse group of poststructuralists, in reaction to the phenomenological tradition that championed a philosophy of consciousness, have been burying consciousness beneath anonymous patterns of linguistic and historical processes. This simultaneous rise and fall, rebirth and death, centering and decentering of consciousness as a theoretical entity is documented in a variety of research agendas.

Over the past several decades, theorists in cognitive psychology, the neurosciences, and the philosophy of mind have lamented the fact that in their fields consciousness has rarely been the subject of serious investigation. Wholesale arguments against Cartesian dualism, from Watson to Ryle, had either dismissed or implied dismissal of the concept of consciousness, so that its recent retrieval cannot avoid appearing as a "historical reversal" of theoretical attitudes (Marcel 1988, 121; also see Pope and Singer 1978). During this same time period, however, the concept of consciousness has been decentered and deconstructed in philosophical movements on the European continent. Theoretical works by structuralists and poststructuralists like Lacan, Foucault, and Derrida have challenged the phenomenological privileging of consciousness that, Heidegger aside, had dominated continental thought from Husserl to Sartre.

A similar tale could be told about the related concept of intentionality. Just as interest in intentionality was dawning in psychology and philosophy of mind, it was sinking on the *abendländisch* horizon of continental European philosophy. Indeed, one could argue that most of the recent interest in Edmund Husserl's phenomenological concept of intentionality has been motivated, not by a concern to develop the tradition of continental thought, but by the appropriation of this concept in Anglo-American philosophy of mind (see Dreyfus 1982; Langsdorf 1984).

Husserl and phenomenology elicit a mixed reception in the context of mainstream cognitive science (see Gallagher 1997a). In some cases they are called upon to provide different and sometimes critical perspectives (e.g., Dreyfus 1982; Petitot, et al. 1997) but often they are dismissed as irrelevant or misguided (Churchland 1984; Dennett 1991; Haaparanta 1994). The new scientists of cognition more readily find their roots in a different ground. More precisely, to the extent that they look back, cognitive researchers like to reconstruct their theoretical connections, temporarily cut off by behaviorism, to the philosophical-psychological tradition stretching from John Locke to William James (see, e.g., Baars 1994; Crick and Koch 1992; Strange 1978).

In truth, however, outside of important methodological differences, Husserl and James are not often far apart. In one important respect they agree perfectly: consciousness has a temporal structure. They both take this to be a fundamental and essential characteristic of consciousness. Temporal structure is, moreover, a feature of consciousness that needs to be accounted for because it is ultimately tied to the concept of rationality and the very possibility of doing science and giving accounts. The ability to provide a scientifically organized account of something depends on organizational principles of cognition that run deeper than logic. Cognitive organization depends in a fundamental way on temporal order. Whether or not the world is rational in and of itself, our access to that world, and to rational order—even our access to relatively permanent laws of nature or the permanent laws of mathematics—depends on the temporal order of mental experience. Thus, both Husserl and James, continuing a tradition that extends back to Locke (1694), recognized the importance of providing a phenomenological account of time-consciousness.

It is precisely in relation to this concern about temporality, however, that Derrida (1973) effects a deconstruction of Husserl's notion of consciousness. More generally, the displacement of consciousness in poststructuralism is linked to a displacement of time. It is frequently noted, for example, that in poststructuralist theory metaphors associated with space replace ("displace," "decenter") concepts associated with time (see Flynn 1991; Jameson 1992). As a result, not only consciousness but temporal aspects of conscious experience are often ignored or take on the status of unresolved aporias in post-Husserlian thought.

The situation is no less complicated on the side of cognitive psychology and the analytic philosophy of mind. Despite the rediscovery of consciousness, discussions of time-consciousness are rarely found in mainstream cognitive science.[1] It has been remarked that in cognitive psychology, and more generally in the various cognitive sciences, Newtonian assumptions about the linearity and universality of time are simply imported into explanations of consciousness.[2] After all, if the temporal structure of conscious experience helps us to order the world, or helps us to gain access to the order of the world, then, when we start to examine the principles of that temporal structure and our experience of time, we simply do not expect to find an inordinate phenomenon.

Even those discussions that take their inspiration from the complexity introduced by parallel processing and neural connectivity do not question the temporal structure of consciousness. In recent discussions of temporal experience, research on the *phi* phenomenon, and Benjamin Libet's neurological discoveries of a backward referral in time are used to demonstrate that consciousness quite often involves an experience of temporality that is not properly ordered to objective sequence (Dennett 1991; Dennett and Kinsbourne 1992; Libet 1985b; Libet, et al. 1979; Penrose 1989, 1994). "Notoriously," as John Searle remarks in a more general context, "phenomenological time does not exactly match real time" (1992, 127). This fact appears as a surprising anomaly just because the scientific expectation is that phenomenal sequence should match objective and physiological linearities. The problem is not resolved, however, simply by positing a nonlinear relation between what remains a linear stream of consciousness and a complex system of nonlinear neuronal processing (as one finds, for example, in Dennett 1991; Dennett and Kinsbourne 1992; Baars 1987; Newman and Baars 1993). What remains unquestioned in such accounts is the phenomenological sequence, the Jamesian stream of consciousness, or what Dennett (1991) calls the "Joycean machine" (see Johnsen 1994).

Even for Penrose, who moves in an orthogonal direction to mainstream cognitive science, a central aporia of consciousness hinges on what he takes to be the obvious temporal flow-structure of experience. The phenomenal unity of consciousness through the passage of time, he argues, not only undermines the now standard account of consciousness as a product of parallel processing in the brain, but is quite at odds with standard physical accounts of time (Penrose 1989). In this respect, the modern Einsteinian concept of space-time is not so different from the poststructuralist spatial metaphor: both seem to deny validity to the flow of time-consciousness. To this aporia Penrose makes two suggestions. First, we may have to rethink the physical concept of time, taking into account certain still undeveloped aspects of quantum theory. Second, and closer to what I aim to do in this work, we need to reexamine what seem to be the "striking and immediate" temporal features of consciousness (1994, 384). In this regard, he guesses "that there is something illusory here too, and the time of our perceptions does not 'really' flow in quite the linear forward-moving way that we perceive it to flow" (1989, 444).

Is it possible, then, to revisit the problem of time-consciousness, to explore it in a way that recognizes the fundamental temporality of experience, and to do so in a way that opens up the problem within the fields of cognitive science without closing off the challenges of post-structuralism? This is the complex question that motivates this study. At the intersection of phenomenological, cognitive, and poststructural approaches I will examine a system of problems concerning the relationship between human experience and temporality. Although the problems I address receive their first significance in John Locke's account of time and consciousness, my focus will be on philosophers and psychologists of the twentieth century.

I develop this investigation along the lines of a clear argument that challenges both phenomenological and cognitive approaches to temporal experience. The argument can be stated, perhaps too succinctly, in three parts.

First, Husserl's account of time-consciousness not only develops within a broader phenomenological tradition, the history of which can be traced from John Locke to William James and thence to a number of contemporary theorists, but is the best account to be found within this tradition. In contrast to James and many others, Husserl solves a central paradox involved in most accounts of time-consciousness, including James's concept of the specious present. For reasons outlined later, I refer to this as the "cognitive paradox," and it is summarized in two assumptions. (1) The perception of succession requires a momentary and indivisible, and therefore durationless act of consciousness. (2) The perception of succession depends on the persistence of sensations or memory-images. Thus, the cognitive paradox involves the idea that succession can only be represented in momentary simultaneity. Husserl's concept of intentionality allows him to escape the limitations of these assumptions and to solve the cognitive paradox. His account thus puts to rest a number of objections and perplexities associated with the concept of the specious present developed by James, C. D. Broad, and others. These considerations are taken up and developed in part 1.

Second, despite Husserl's success, a number of problems remain, and these problems are related to the limitations of the phenomenological model itself. Such problems and limitations, explored in part 2, have been pointed out by a variety of post-Husserlian philosophers, including Heidegger, Merleau-Ponty, and poststructuralists like Levinas, Derrida, and Lyotard. These thinkers develop two basic sets of objections to Husserl's model. One set consists of objections that are theoretical in nature. (1) Contrary to his best intentions, Husserl's phenomenological analysis introduces structures that are not strictly phenomenological. Phenomenological reflection transforms conscious experience into something more reified than it is. This same criticism of phenomenology is also developed in analytic philosophy of mind. (2) Husserl introduces a concept of presence that is supposedly foundational for consciousness and that excludes nonpresence. But his phenomenology actually shows that presence depends on and is infected by a form of nonpresence connected to the retentional-protentional functions of time-consciousness. Thus, Husserl succeeds in saving his model only by illegitimately denying the alterity involved in presence. Another set of objections is based on the inadequacy of Husserl's model, and of phenomenological models in general, to provide an account of certain experiences. These are experiences that outstrip the lawlike structure of intentionality and that rely on "prenoetic" factors connected with embodied existence and hermeneutical dimensions like language and historical effect. Prenoetic processes constrain the operations of intentionality in ways that Husserl fails to recognize.

Third, it follows that to develop a more adequate model for the explication of temporal experience one must go beyond Husserl and phenomenology. In part 3, then, I pursue two strategies. The first is a conservative strategy that involves revising and expanding Husserl's analysis of intentionality in order to take into account factors connected with human embodiment, language, historical effect, and intersubjectivity. The second involves recognizing that no one discourse, even the enriched intentional model, captures all aspects of existence that affect temporal experience.

The remainder of this introduction provides a brief and incomplete overview of the problems that phenomenology solves and fails to solve in its account of time-consciousness. This will serve to indicate the direction followed in the remainder of the book.

A Brief History of the Cognitive Paradox

Prior to Locke, of course, one can find many finely detailed discussions concerning the relationship between human experience and temporality.

None of them, however, formulate the problem in precisely Locke's way. Both the Aristotelian and the Neoplatonic traditions provide metaphysical accounts of time and human subjectivity that become the "standard interpretations" defining categories by which we still think about time (Heidegger 1982, 231). Aristotle indicated the central question in precise terms. "Whether if soul did not exist time would exist or not, is a question that may fairly be asked" (*Physics* 223a21, Ross translation). His answer is less precise, but still definitive for the direction of Western thought on this problem. Time, as the measure of motion, depends on an entity that is capable of measuring, and further, upon an unspecified motion in the soul. As a result he contends that when there is no change in our own minds we fail to realize that time has passed; but if some movement does take place in the mind we do have some sense that time also passes (*Physics* 218b21–24, 219a5). Aristotle, however, does not offer a precise definition of what the relevant movement in the soul actually is.

Augustine provides an alternative model of temporal experience, although he nonetheless follows the Aristotelian idea that time is somehow "in the soul." On his account, however, there is no requirement of motion. Rather than an unspecified motion, Augustine identifies specific cognitive functions that account for the experience of time. Memory provides a sense of the past; perception directly delivers the present; expectation bestows a premeditation of the future (*Confessions*, XI, chaps. 18–20).

Locke, and other modern theorists, combine the concepts of *motion* and *cognitive functions*, in an attempt to form a coherent theory. When they do so they confront a difficult paradox involving succession and simultaneity. Although this paradox and its resolution will be examined in detail in the first part of this book, we note two things for now. First, the modern version of the paradox resembles in some ways a paradox that is already discernible in Augustine's account. Second, this fact suggests that the paradox is connected with the concept of cognitive function rather than with motion. For this reason I call it the "cognitive paradox."

Something like the cognitive paradox shows up in Augustine in the following way. His famous reduction of past (by way of memory) and future (by way of expectation) to the present entails his characterization of time as involving "a certain kind of extension [*distentio*]" (XI, chaps. 23, 26). Yet he also contends that "the present has no extension [*spatium*] whatever" (XI, chap. 15), for if it did have extension it could be divided and at some point one part of it would be past and another future. So a preliminary version of the paradox states that although time is reducible to the present and the present is not extended, time itself is extended in some fashion. Augustine resolves this issue in favor of the notion of a *distentio animi* but this only leads us, his readers, closer to a clear recognition of the cognitive paradox. The *distentio* of the mind, one might say the "mental space" in which we make judgments and comparisons with regard to the measurement of time, is made possible because memory retains an image, impression, or sign of the past in the present moment, and expectation projects a future by means of a sign of what is to come (XI, chap. 27). This means that images of successive pasts and futures are made simultaneous in the present. The paradox that remains unanswered in this solution is how the past comes to be represented as past by an impression that is completely present; or how the future comes to be represented as future by a sign that exists only in the present.

Accounts of time that employ cognitive functions such as memory, perception, and expectation, inevitably end up in similar paradoxes. In such accounts, what is needed is some sort of integrative function over and above memory, perception, and expectation, an integration that ties the past, present, and future together in the proper order. In most theories this integrative function is performed by a comparative judgment that represents the original experience of temporal sequence. It has been argued that, inevitably, in a cognitive representation of time the logical effect of the act of judgment is not to represent the subject and the predicate in their succession, but to attribute simultaneity to both (Khersonsky 1935/36). In effect, the experience of time that depends upon cognitive functions must represent succession within simultaneity, as Augustinian consciousness must represent the past and future within the present.

The modern version of the cognitive paradox takes a similar form. It can be found in many philosophical and psychological accounts of the subjective experience of time, including those given by Herbart, Drobisch, Waitz, Volkmann, Brentano, Lipps, Meinong, Guyau, Strong, Wundt, Ward, and James.[3] Lotze states the paradox quite explicitly. In order to be aware of the succession of two objects, A and B, "the two presentations of A and B should be objects, throughout simultaneous, of a relating knowledge, which itself completely indivisible, holds them together in a single indivisible [cognitive] act" (1887, § 154). Successive objects can be represented qua successive only if they are made simultaneous within an act of comparative judgment. In some cases this cognitive paradox is recognized as such and motivates some attempt at resolution. Lotze, for example, turns to a theory of temporal signs derived from objective time relations to resolve the paradox. Other theorists, such as James, ignore the cognitive paradox or even embrace it as the solution to other problems. The cognitive paradox and its resolution constitute part of the system of problems that I study in this work.

Two Lockean Problems and Two Sets of Solutions

Locke returns to an emphasis on motion in his modern explanation of what Aristotle had called motion in the soul. Locke introduces, for the first time, the conception of the mind as a *stream of consciousness*. Although Locke does not use this phrase—it belongs first to James—he does provide us with precisely that concept. He describes it as the "succession of ideas." "It is evident to anyone who will but observe what passes in his own mind, that there is a train of ideas which constantly succeed one another in his understanding, as long as he is awake" (1694, I, 239). Of course, the radicality of this conception of the mind is not adequately expressed by Locke, and it takes David Hume to capture it more precisely. It is not simply that there is a stream of ideas *in* the mind; rather, the stream of ideas *is* the mind. The mind is the flow of different perceptions "which succeed each other with an inconceivable rapidity, and are in a perpetual flux and movement" (Hume 1739, 252). To put this into perspective, and to give Locke his due, we should say that his introduction of this concept into the epistemological-psychological account of time is, in this field, comparable to the displacement of the Aristotelian concept of physical motion by the Newtonian one in physics—in effect, the establishment of a paradigm that was to be accepted and refined over the course of several hundred years. In the Lockean, phenomenological paradigm the mind is construed no longer as substance or primarily as a collection of functions, but as a flow, an unending movement that may change velocity, but can never stop altogether.

The radicality of this notion may be measured by the fact that philosophers have been able to explicate two problems that, prior to Locke's analysis, were never clearly defined as problems. The first, which for simplicity I will refer to as *the problem of objective synthesis*, can be expressed in various ways. It has to do with how the mind is able to perceive the change or persistence of temporal objects. How is it possible for an object to appear to be either changing or identical through change when the act of perception itself involves a continuous flow? How is consciousness itself tied together so as to represent an identical object? Another, more general way to explicate this problem is to note the fact that the succession of ideas is not the same as the idea of succession. Prior to Locke this was not the problem. Rather the problem had been an ontological one: what accounts for the identity of the thing itself? The traditional answer was substance. The problem that comes along with Locke's notion of conscious flow pertains to the experience of the thing as object of knowledge rather than as thing in itself.

The second problem is what Locke and every philosopher since Locke call the *problem of personal identity*. The concept of the succession of ideas or flow of consciousness introduces time itself into the very heart of subjectivity. Human existence is nothing other than this very flow of consciousness, this movement that constantly passes away. How is it possible to discover an identity *in* or *of* the temporal flow itself? Hume gives the most famous and most astonishing answer to this question: it is not possible; personal identity is a fiction.

Although one can contrast Locke and Hume on the details of their answers, it remains clear that they employ the same phenomenological model of subjectivity that involves the flow of consciousness. Within this stream-of-consciousness model a number of different answers to these two problems have been developed. I want to explore, in the first part of this book, those approaches that stay with this phenomenological paradigm of consciousness, for it is this same model that is at stake both in poststructuralist displacements and in current scientific discussions of consciousness. In particular I focus on two closely linked traditions that attempt to resolve the problems encountered in this paradigm, the first associated with James, the second initiated by Husserl.

That James's conception of the stream of consciousness develops the Lockean phenomenological paradigm is obvious to anyone who has read his *Principles of Psychology*. Still, it is also obvious that despite his employment of the Lockean model, he disagrees with Locke on numerous points. He takes issue with the "Lockian School" concerning the possibility that ideas are unchanging. In contrast to Locke's view that we can repeat simple ideas, James maintains that no idea "once gone can recur and be identical with what it was before" (1890, 230). He also sides with Thomas Reid against Locke concerning the sense of duration (1890, 609). He cites James Ward's evaluation of Locke in this regard: "recent experiments have set this fact in a more striking light, and made clear what Locke had dimly before his mind" (1890, 634 n.). James himself employs similar phrases to summarize his view of Locke: in contrast to the light thrown on these matters by modern psychology, Locke saw things in a "dim way" (1890, 609 n.).

Although the unhappy fact of chronology does not allow Locke to comment on James's work, at least one of Locke's editors does not hesitate to introduce James into the 1897 edition of Locke's *Essay*. Alexander Campbell Fraser cites James at certain strategic points in Locke's text. Where Locke fails to develop the idea of retention as immediate "contemplation," Fraser stresses the very Jamesian notion of the blending of past and future within the perception of the present (Locke 1694, 193 n. 1). He explicitly quotes James's notion of the specious present at that point in Locke's text that speaks of our sense of duration (1694, 241 n. 1), and several times he views James as filling out or enlightening Locke's account (e.g., 1694, 133 n., 222 n. 2, 245 n. 1).

James not only develops in great detail the notion of the stream of consciousness, but, in his concept of the specious present, offers his own resolution to the problem of objective synthesis.[4] The notion of the specious present, however, as it is developed by James and others in the Jamesian tradition remains problematic. I will show in later chapters that the numerous perplexities that infect this Jamesian doctrine can all be traced back to a certain acquiescence in the face of the cognitive paradox briefly explicated above. In effect, the specious present, as developed in the Jamesian tradition, is simply a restatement of the cognitive paradox, an attempt to make the paradox operate as a solution to the problem of objective synthesis.

Within the phenomenological paradigm the task is to find a way to explicate a notion of the specious present that escapes the cognitive paradox and all the perplexities associated with it. The concept of the specious present can be redeemed only if it can be explained so as to avoid the cognitive paradox. To do this one requires the concept of intentionality as it is explicated by Husserl. I want to show that although Husserl does not explicitly examine or employ the doctrine of the specious present, his analysis of time-consciousness does provide a way of explaining the specious present that avoids the cognitive paradox and the perplexities associated with it. As a result, Husserl's account genuinely solves the problem of objective synthesis within the Lockean-phenomenological model.

The problem of personal identity is also addressed by both James and Husserl. The former identifies the problem of personal identity as a special case of judgment. "As a mere subjective phenomenon the judgment [of personal identity] presents no difficulty or mystery peculiar to itself. It belongs to the great class of judgments of sameness; and there is nothing more remarkable in making a judgment of sameness in the first person than in the second or the third" (1890, 331). In these cases the cognitive functions are, he says, "essentially alike." To establish the objective or real identity of the person simply requires sufficient evidence to show that the present self is the same as the past self. The evidence consists of the sense of "warmth and intimacy" that James associates with one's own body. This sense is an "organic emotion" due to physiological alterations, or a sense of "general bodily tone." Thus, the present self is always accompanied by a feeling of the actual existence of the body at the moment. Not only are our own past experiences thought of as imbued with past feelings of warmth and intimacy, but the present thought of them "infallibly brings some degree of organic motion" (1890, 333). Our judgment thus "assimilates" to each other the present and the past selves within the warmth and intimacy that we feel as we judge. Warmth and intimacy operate not only as objective evidence, but as subjective markers, tokens of identity.

James adds to this the continuity of consciousness. In contrast to Hume who finds "nothing but Diversity, diversity abstract and absolute" among the succession of ideas, James finds in the stream a real continuity that forms a basis of personal identity (see 1890, 352). "The sense of our own personal identity, then, is exactly like any one of our other perceptions of sameness among phenomena. It is a conclusion grounded either on the resemblance in a fundamental respect [pertaining to warmth and intimacy], or on the continuity before the mind, of the phenomena compared" (1890, 334).

It is important to note two things about the problem of personal identity. First, it is a problem that concerns the temporality of the stream of consciousness. We are motivated to pose the problem precisely because the self finds itself or loses itself in a temporal flux. The task is to establish identity through change from present to past. Second, in James's resolution we ascertain identity by a comparative judgment that synthesizes the past and the present. James's solution to the problem of personal identity, like his solution to the problem of objective synthesis, depends entirely on the possibility of time-consciousness bringing the past and the present, successive states, into the simultaneous synthesis of a single cognitive act. In this respect we would have to ask whether James's solution to the problem of personal identity is viable if, at bottom, it involves us again in the cognitive paradox of representing successive states within a simultaneity.

One could respond in a Lotzean fashion to this problem. In this case, one would not only insist upon markers, tokens, or signs of personal identity ("warmth and intimacy"), but also on objective *temporal* signs that would signify "pastness-presentness," "earlier-later" even within the simultaneity. I plan to show, however, that such a solution is predicated on assumptions about the way consciousness works—assumptions that lead directly to the cognitive paradox. If, in this context, James does not adopt Lotze's solution to the problem of time-consciousness, he nonetheless holds to the Lotzean assumption that past states of consciousness (sensation, memory images) really continue to persist in present consciousness. A more basic question, then, is whether this Lotzean assumption is justified. Husserl's answer is no. He avoids the cognitive paradox by rejecting the assumption that leads to it.

Here we come close to the heart of the matter. What saves Husserl from the cognitive paradox and allows him to perfect the phenomenological paradigm is his ability to make a distinction between the real (*reell*) contents and the intentional contents of consciousness. Everything

hinges on his concept of intentionality, of which the most general formulation—"all consciousness is consciousness of something"—is not precise
enough to demonstrate its explanatory power. We need to investigate the
"of" in that formula; how precisely there can be a presence *of* something that does not amount to a *real* presence. We also need to see
how intentionality functions in a double way on the microlevel of time-
consciousness. With this concept of intentionality Husserl is able to explain how the past can be present, and yet avoid the cognitive paradox
that translates the flow of succession into a static simultaneity. In this way,
we'll see, Husserl genuinely solves the problems of objective synthesis and
personal identity within the terms of the Lockean paradigm.

Post-Husserlian Aporias

The details of Husserl's analysis are explored in later chapters, but if all of
this is correct it would seem that Husserl has set everything aright. The
Husserlian model provides the most adequate and systematic account
of personal identity and objective synthesis. It avoids perplexities and
paradoxes at every turn. So it is not surprising that his phenomenology
of time-consciousness has been called "his finest piece of philosophical
investigation, and one of the finest pieces in the whole history of philosophy" (Findlay 1975, 3) as well as "the most subtle such analysis ever
performed" (Casey 1977, 200; see Blumenberg 1986). Nor should it be
so surprising that his conception of intentionality has been put forward
as a model with an explanatory power that may be useful for cognitive
science (Dreyfus 1982; Miller 1984).

Still, Husserl's description of the formal structure of intentional
consciousness, especially with regard to its temporal aspects, does not
fit into the mainstream reductionist programs of cognitive science very
well, insofar as it requires an intentionality that is seemingly irreducible.
Moreover, from a different perspective, Husserl's most adequate phenomenology appears to be inadequate, insofar as it cannot account for
aspects of experience that outstrip the intentional and temporal structure
of consciousness. The limitations of his phenomenological model have
been explicated by various authors, from Heidegger and Merleau-Ponty
to the poststructuralists. In part 2 of this study I examine their complaints
in detail. Here, however, I want to assert in the most general way that
Husserl's account of time-consciousness is interesting and important, not
only because it succeeds in perfecting the phenomenological model of
consciousness, and not simply because it has the potential to make the

cognitive sciences face up to certain irreducible dimensions of personal intentionality, but also because in its limitations and in what it fails to account for, it both provides an indication for further thought, and suggests that there is no unique and final discourse capable of delineating time.

In the poststructuralist view, our conceptions of time are necessarily metaphysical constructs produced within a dualistic, subject-object framework. Modern analyses of time-consciousness, from Locke to Kant to James and Husserl, are conducted under the aegis of the "philosophy of the subject" and as such they are closely related to modern conceptions of the mind, unmediated introspection, and incorrigible subjectivity. At the same time these analyses claim a certain objectivity that would deny the limitations imposed by their metaphysical assumptions. Derrida's deconstructive reading of Husserl shows this in precise terms. Husserl's account of time-consciousness hinges on the concept of the "living present," the now-phase of consciousness, a structure that Husserl describes as the phenomenological (and purportedly nonmetaphysical) foundation of human subjectivity and personal identity. Derrida's reading reveals that on Husserl's own account the living present is composed of a complex system of nonpresence, a nonidentical system of differences introduced by the retentional and protentional structure of consciousness. In order to solve various problems concerning the identity and unity of consciousness, Husserl is required to deny the alterity introduced by difference. Because of that denial his account of time-consciousness remains limited in a variety of ways. For example, he excludes certain linguistic aspects that constrain perceptual experience, he ignores the role played by other persons in the constitution of the individual sense of time, and he suppresses the possibility of a certain kind of reversibility in the experience of time.

For the post-Husserlians it is important not only to notice the limitations found in Husserl's account, but to notice that Husserl himself fails to notice them. If Husserl has perfected a particular paradigm, he nonetheless fails to recognize that it is only one particular paradigm— one among other possible paradigms. In Husserl's view, his account would be *the* account of human experience. Phenomenology easily turns into a metaphysical metadiscourse that claims too much authority, too much adjudicative power.

The post-Husserlians thus suggest that Husserl's account can be deconstructed, or displaced, together with the traditional metaphysics of subjectivity. But this is interesting only to the extent that it shows the limitations of the Husserlian model. We note that poststructuralist approaches cannot and do not pretend to show that Husserl's account is wrong, so much as wrongheaded; nor do they propose a better account. They do a good job of showing that Husserl's analysis is limited and that one should recognize its limitations. Once we recognize these limitations, however, we are presented with a challenge. Is it possible to overcome such limitations by fixing or expanding the Lockean-Husserlian theory, or do we need to shift to a radically new theory?

The post-Husserlian complaints are not without foundation (if I may put it that way), and the response they elicit seems to rule out a simple return to or defense of Husserl. Still, the response to such complaints is not difficult to articulate, although carrying it out represents a new challenge. It involves recognizing the Husserlian account for what it is— the perfection of a particular model, the best account of one particular and limited discourse among other possible discourses.

To go beyond Husserl and phenomenology I pursue two strategies. The first, a more conservative strategy, involves expanding on Husserl's account of intentionality to include prenoetic and hermeneutical factors connected with human embodiment, language, historical effect, and intersubjectivity. The second involves recognizing that even a hermeneutically enriched model does not capture all aspects of existence that affect temporal experience. One needs to consider a variety of metaphors developed in the cognitive and social sciences, as well as in art and literature. More specifically, the exploration of various extra-intentional dimensions of existence and the constraints they impose on intentionality suggests that no one discourse, no grand theory will be able to integrate all of these dimensions. This is a conclusion generalized from a growing consensus found in cognitive psychology. It entails a consideration of a multiplicity of discourses and metaphors, and suggests that only a disparate set of disciplines, a set of cognitive sciences and arts, can formulate appropriate agendas for the investigation of temporal experience. This realization helps to indicate a number of directions that phenomenologists, cognitive scientists, and others might take in order to deal with the complexities and aporias outlined by the post-Husserlians.

PART   1

THE PERFECTION
OF THE
PHENOMENOLOGICAL
PARADIGM

2

The Specious Present and Associated Perplexities

William James's famous discussion of the specious present in his *Principles of Psychology* (1890), and C. D. Broad's exposition of the same concept in *Scientific Thought* (1923) have been the targets of numerous criticisms and the sources of continuing controversy. The most influential objections raised against this concept can be found in J. D. Mabbott's (1951) seemingly devastating analysis of Broad's diagram of the specious present. Since then, there have been a variety of attempts either to defend the doctrine of the specious present or to defeat it. In response to a defense by Mundle (1954), for example, Plumer (1985) categorizes it as myth. In this chapter I intend to demythologize the specious present in order to understand the problem it was meant to address and the perplexities it has caused.

The Specious Present in the Jamesian Tradition

William James finds the notion of the specious present in an account of time perception provided by E. R. Clay (1882). As Clay describes it, the present to which conscious experience attends "is really a part of the past—a recent past—delusively given as being a time that intervenes between the past and the future" (cited in James 1890, 609). He names this present, which is really the just past, the "specious present." For Clay the specious present is clearly the referent of a conscious act, a given "part" of time. James expands the concept by introducing the future dimension. Like Clay he describes the specious present as the given referent of a conscious act, i.e., a duration through which passes a changing parade of objective contents of which consciousness is aware. Thus, James calls it a "duration-block," an "interval of time" that we perceive (1890, 610).

> In short, the practically cognized present is no knife-edge, but a saddle-back, with a certain breadth of its own on which we sit perched, and from which we look in two directions into time. The unit of composition of our perception of time is a *duration*, with a bow and a stern, as it were—a rearward- and a forward-looking end. (1890, 609)

Conceived in this way it seems possible to measure the specious present by the standards of objective time. James cites psychological experiments conducted by Wundt, Dietze, and others to show maximum and minimum intervals of time that we can sense. These experiments indicate no general agreement on the length of the specious present, but suggest that it varies between individuals, and even within an individual depending upon state of alertness or fatigue, and, perhaps surprisingly, between different sense modalities within the same person. James averages things out and writes: "These figures may be roughly taken to stand for the most important part of what, with Mr. Clay, we called, a few pages back, the *specious present*. The specious present has, in addition, a vaguely vanishing backward and forward fringe; but its nucleus is probably the dozen seconds or less that have just elapsed" (1890, 613). The specious present is more or less this amount of "intuited duration" which is "*pictured fairly steadily in each passing instant of consciousness*" (1890, 630).

In the tradition that follows James the specious present continues to be understood as a sensed or immediately experienced duration. But the sensing or experiencing act of consciousness, the content of which has the specious present structure, is itself not understood as enduring. C. D. Broad, for example, clearly recognizes that the doctrine of the specious present as a sensed duration does not imply an enduring act of awareness. Rather, according to Broad, it requires, for its very definition, the conception of a momentary act of awareness. We will return to Broad's analysis shortly to see the perplexities involved with the specious present if acts of awareness really do have duration. Precisely such perplexities lead to the rejection of the specious present doctrine by Boring (1936) and Mabbott (1951). They argue that the fact that acts of consciousness do have duration makes nonsense out of the specious present.

Whether one accepts the specious present, as do James and Broad, or rejects it, as do Boring and Mabbott, it is always conceived in this Jamesian tradition as a sensed or "perceived" duration (Boring 1936, 521) that purportedly operates as a solution to what we have called "the problem of objective synthesis." That is, it addresses the problem of explaining how we can perceive objects as either changing or persisting over time, despite the fact that the past seems not to persist or have actuality. It also contributes to an explanation of a number of other philosophical and phenomenological problems—providing the empiricist, for example, with "a way of giving ostensive definitions of temporal concepts" (Mundle 1954, 22), or accounting for our immediate and direct experience of the past or of time itself (James and Broad). To those who accept the doctrine, it clearly appears to be a solution rather than a problem.

The details of the doctrine can be made clear by inspecting the various diagrams used to represent time-consciousness. First, we need to construct the diagram that James describes in his discussion of several other psychologists. Then we'll turn to the diagram proposed by Broad.

James agrees wholeheartedly with Volkmann, who expresses a Lockean insight, that "the successive ideas are not yet the idea of succession, because succession *in* thought is not the thought *of* succession" (cited in James 1890, 629). On the basis of this remark James suggests that one would be able to construct a diagram to represent the specious present.

> If we represent the actual time-stream of our thinking by an horizontal line, the thought *of* the stream or of any segment of its length, past, present, or to come, might be figured in a perpendicular raised upon the horizontal at a certain point. The length of this perpendicular stands for a certain object or content, which in this case is the time thought of, and all of which is thought of together at the actual moment of the stream upon which the perpendicular is raised. (1890, 629)

Although James aims for a "clear understanding" here, this is all he actually says of the diagram which he does not draw. Figure 2.1 is a rendition of his described diagram.[1]

Figure 2.1: James's Diagram

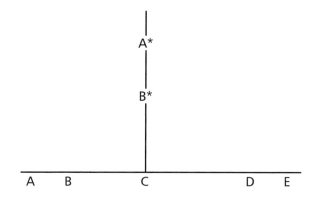

The perpendicular measures the specious present sensed in any one instant of consciousness. In the figure, A–E represents the stream of consciousness; C represents the present instant of that stream, so that A lies in the past and E lies in the future. At point C we are aware not of an instantaneous moment, but of a specious present represented by the perpendicular. A* and B*, embedded in the perpendicular, represent the past "time thought of." The length of the perpendicular, James says, represents the length of the specious present. Of course, simply the length of the perpendicular does not tell us enough about how much of the just past or how much of the immediate future is included in the specious present—in James's terms, how much of the specious present is in the rear of C and how much forward of C. It might be clearer if we turn the perpendicular 90 degrees to make it parallel to A–E. This is represented in figure 2.2 as the horizontal line A*–D*. Although this diagram allows us to specify how much of the past and how much of the future is included in the specious present, it goes beyond James's own description.

James enlists the aid of another psychologist, James Ward, in developing his explanation of the diagram. Ward, who had proposed a similar diagram, indicated that the perpendicular line is meant to represent our intuition of time. "In a succession of events, say of sense-impressions, ABCDE . . . the presence of B means the absence of A and C, but the presentation of this succession involves the simultaneous presence in some mode or other of two or more of the presentations ABCD. In reality, past, present, and future are differences in time, but in presentation all that corresponds to these differences is in consciousness simultaneously" (Ward 1878–89, cited in James 1890, 629–30). So, in terms of the diagram where C is represented as the present moment of consciousness, A*, B*

Figure 2.2: James's Diagram Modified

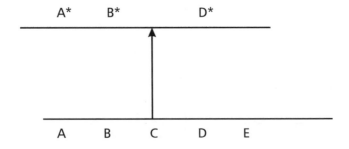

and D* are "in consciousness simultaneously," constituting the specious
present.

This is also Herbart's view. As James summarizes it, Herbart maintained that temporal ordering is established "when, with the last member
of a series present to our consciousness, we also think of the first; and
then the whole series revives in our thought at once, but with strength
diminishing in the *backward* direction" (1890, 632 n.). Volkmann too:
"if A and B are to be represented *as occurring in succession* they must be
simultaneously represented. . . . We must *think* of them both at once" (cited
in James 1890, 629).

Herbart, Volkmann, Ward and James are in general agreement
on these points. James also notes that Volkmann simply repeats what
Lotze had already said in his *Metaphysic* (1887). There Lotze explains
that in order to see A and B as successive it is necessary "that the two
presentations of A and B should be objects, throughout simultaneous,
of a relating knowledge, which itself completely indivisible, holds them
together in a single indivisible act" (§ 154). Lotze, however, recognizes
that this situation involves what we have termed the "cognitive paradox,"
namely, that to be aware of *successive* objects consciousness needs to
compare the earlier and later objects in an operation that makes the
earlier and later *simultaneous*. Seemingly, sensed content would, in some
fashion, need to be at once both successive and simultaneous, both past
and present. As a way of avoiding what he acknowledges to be a disturbing
paradox, Lotze proposes a theory of temporal signs according to which
sensed content contains markers derived from an objective time-order. In
contrast, James simply ignores the paradox, even after citing Volkmann's
characterization of it as an "antithesis," that is, an apparent opposition
between succession and simultaneity. Rather than recognizing this as a
paradox, James characterizes it as the solution to the problem of objective
synthesis. It is just the way that the mind combines its contents into a unity.
As he puts it in regard to Herbart's explanation, it is a "simple description
of time-perception" (1890, 632 n.).

In effect, James incorporates the cognitive paradox as a seemingly
unproblematic part of his description of the specious present. We find
James's confirmation of this in a later work. In an essay written several years after the *Principles*, James continues to ignore the paradox
qua paradox, and to treat it as a clarifying description: "earlier and
later are present to each other in an experience that feels either only
on condition of feeling both together" (1894, 77). The simultaneous
presence of earlier and later moments "is just like what we find in any
other case of an experience whose parts are many," even though "most
of these experiences are of objects perceived to be simultaneous and

not to be immediately successive as in the heretofore considered case" (1894, 78).

James's acquiescence with the paradox is predicated on his acceptance of two connected propositions that we shall call "Lotzean assumptions" because of Lotze's clear statement of them. They are built into the James-Volkmann-Ward diagram, and taken together, they form a clear statement of the cognitive paradox. We will label the first Lotzean assumption LA1.

> *LA1:* *The perception of succession requires a momentary and indivisible, and therefore durationless act of consciousness.*

LA1 is perfectly consistent with James's doctrine of the specious present and his diagram. What he calls the law of time's discrete flow depends on a succession of momentary and discrete acts of consciousness summarized in phrases such as "now, now, now." This discreteness, he explains, is "merely due to the fact that our successive acts of *recognition* or *apperception* of *what* it is are discrete" (James 1890, 622). Discrete and momentary acts are represented in James's diagram by points such as C.

The second Lotzean assumption, LA2, is this:

> *LA2:* *A sequence or succession is represented in the momentary act of consciousness by persisting sensations or memory-images.*

James prefers to explain this persistence in terms of brain activity. The specious present, which is this grouping of persisting sensations, operates "by virtue of some fairly constant feature in the brain-process to which the consciousness is tied" (1890, 630). James cites a number of psychologists who agree on this fundamental fact, namely, "that the brain-processes of various [successive] events must be active simultaneously, and in varying strength, for a time-perception to be possible" (1890, 633 n.). He summarizes his view in the following terms.

> The phenomena of "summation of stimuli" in the nervous system prove that each stimulus leaves some latent activity behind it which only gradually passes away. . . . With the feeling of the present thing there must at all times mingle the fading echo of all those other things which the previous few seconds have supplied. Or, to state it in neural terms, *there is at every moment a cumulation of brain-processes overlapping each other, of which the fainter ones are the dying phases of processes which but shortly previous were active in a maximal degree.* (1890, 634–35)

Due to the effects of such neural processes, events do not pass out of consciousness absolutely, despite the discreteness of conscious acts.

After a perceptual (or more generally, cognitive) event there remain "processes which are present. To those processes, however caused, the mind would still respond by feeling a specious present, with one part of it just vanishing or vanished into the past" (1890, 641). James also indicates that just as there are "fading brain-processes," so also there must be "dawning processes" that supply the sense of future within the specious present (1890, 638 n.). Today one might easily think of Libet's (1992) experiments which show anticipatory neural activity prior to conscious awareness. For James, such neural activity could operate as the basis for a vague sense of the future.

The two Lotzean assumptions, taken together, clearly state the cognitive paradox. In one momentary now of consciousness the present coalesces with both the past and the future. The past is both past and present. The future is both present and future. Lotze had recognized this as a problem and sought to resolve it by appealing to objective temporal signs that come to be embedded in experience. The past event, for instance, continues to appear in present consciousness, but it is clearly marked as past in its objective characteristics. In contrast, James, by endorsing the Lotzean assumptions, allows the paradox to stand. His appeal to brain processes in no way dissipates the problem. Even if scientifically credible, it would at best indicate the mechanism for the paradoxical experience of succession as simultaneous. In James, the concept of the specious present remains, at bottom, a paradoxical explanation; in some sense, an unexplained explanation.

Broad's Difficulties in Getting Clear of LA1

Broad's account of the specious present also depends on the two Lotzean assumptions. However, while he admits that the definition of the specious present requires the assumption of a momentary act of awareness (LA1), he nonetheless wants to drop this assumption and still retain the specious present doctrine. His attempt to do so results in the diagram shown in figure 2.3,[2] and a host of objections from J. D. Mabbott.

Although Plumer (1985) claims that Broad's diagram is more or less the same as the one described by James, it differs in several important ways. The top line A–C represents acts of consciousness; the bottom line V–Z represents the sensible field of consciousness. Point A represents a momentary act of sensing which senses a specious present V–X. In Broad's diagram, in contrast to James's, nothing depends upon the length of A–X, whereas everything depends on the triangle AVX.[3] We note also that

Figure 2.3: Broad's Diagram

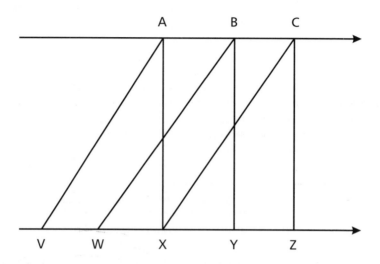

Broad does not include a piece of the immediate future in the specious present, but only the just past: "what can be sensed at any moment stretches a little way back behind that moment" (Broad 1923, 348). B is a second act of consciousness; it senses the specious present W–Y which overlaps with the specious present V–X. In this overlap there is an interval W–X which is common to the two specious presents and which is sensed by both acts of consciousness. V–W, however, is not sensed by act B, and X–Y is not sensed by act A.

LA2 operates as an assumption throughout Broad's analysis. He expresses it precisely in terms of sense-data that, taken together, constitute a sensory field. Within a sensible field temporal change takes place, but "the qualitative differences between its earlier and its later sections will be sensed *together;* i.e., the observer will actually sense the changing and will not merely notice that something *has* changed" (1923, 352). In effect, actual, past sense-data persist into present consciousness. This may be why Broad limits the specious present to past and present; past and present sense-data have some existential status—they are really there, actualized or actual—whereas there are as yet (that is, in the present) no future sense-data to be included in the sensory field.

Having defined the specious present in this way, on the basis of both LA1 and LA2, he then relaxes LA1, the assumption of the momentariness of the conscious act, and he lets the line segment A–B represent an enduring act of consciousness. Although this view of the conscious act is more realistic, Broad fails to clarify what happens to the specious present in this case. On a quick reading there are three possibilities. The first one, which, however, must be ruled out by LA2, is that the specious present of A–B consists of V–Y, that is, the summation of the specious presents previously defined for the momentary acts A and B. This is ruled out by LA2 because LA2 requires the earlier and the later parts of the specious present to be present simultaneously, to be "sensed throughout the whole of a finite process of sensing." The specious present means that "I sense this finite field as a whole, I actually sense the way in which its earlier half joins up with its later half to make up the whole" (Broad 1923, 352, 353). V–Y, however, is never present as a whole to the enduring act of consciousness A–B, for at point A, when the act of consciousness begins, the part of the sensible field represented by segment X–Y is not yet present. More importantly (for Broad if not for James), at point B, when the act of consciousness is completed, the part of the sensible field represented by segment V–W has faded out of present consciousness.

This leaves two other possibilities. One is taken up by Mabbott, who demonstrates its absurdity. The other is defended by Mundle and is probably what Broad intended, but is also problematic.

Mabbott interprets Broad's diagram to mean that the specious present of the enduring act A–B consists of the overlap of the two originally defined specious presents. In other words, the specious present of A–B is W–X. But this leads to the absurdity that "the specious present of an act of awareness varies inversely with the duration of the act" (Mabbott 1951, 158–59). Mabbott reasons as follows: assume that the specious present of the originally defined momentary act of consciousness A is six seconds long. That would make the specious present of A–B, the overlap W–X, three seconds long. Even though A–B is itself longer than the momentary act A by three seconds, its specious present seems to have shrunk. If the act of consciousness lasts six seconds (e.g., A–C) the specious present shrinks to momentariness (0), since there is no overlap at X. Thus, conscious acts of six seconds or longer would have no specious present. This absurdity leads Mabbott to conclude "that the doctrine of the specious present is untenable and sheds no light on our normal apprehension of temporal events" (1951, 159).

Mundle defends Broad from this charge and shows that what Broad really meant, but did not clearly state, was that the duration of the specious present remains constant no matter how long the duration of the act is. Mabbott apparently confused the specious present with the possible overlap between abstractly defined specious presents. Mundle suggests that a good analogy for Broad's specious present is one proposed by Mabbott himself—that of "a searchlight which moves along the upper line and illuminates a constant span of the lower line" (Mundel 1954, 30, 28). This would be the most consistent interpretation of Broad's text, and would avoid any logical absurdity. Still, there are problems of an empirical nature with this solution. The studies cited by James, and then again by Mabbott, indicate that the specious present does not remain constant, but varies, not only from one individual to another but even within a single individual. Broad's assumption that the specious present remains constant is unrealistic.

Still, one could defend Broad on this count by pointing out the inadequacy of the diagram and the analogy of a searchlight for capturing a nonspatial process. But there is a more serious inadequacy involved in the accounts given by both Broad and James. Their accounts are not really accounts *of* the specious present, they are accounts *by* the specious present. They take the specious present as a solution to the problem of time perception but do not view the specious present itself as problematic. In effect, they fail to explain how the specious present itself is possible. In this regard Mundle asks the right question of Broad. Given that the act of consciousness is spread out in its own duration and therefore contains temporal "phases" of its own, "the question as to how these phases are combined to yield awareness of a gestalt would surely be just as relevant (or irrelevant) as [Broad's] original question as to how sense-contents are combined" (Mundle 1954, 32). The problem lurking behind Broad's silence about what happens to the specious present when acts of consciousness are more than momentary is linked to a lack of clarity about LA2, i.e., how memory-images, or just-past sensa, in some way persist so that a comparison or synthesis might be accomplished in the present act of consciousness. In effect, the question is, how does one explain the constitution of the specious present when the synthesizing act is involved in its own expiring duration, and when the specious present, rather than being a stable gestalt, turns out to be involved in its own overlapping succession?

Perplexities Involved in the Specious Present Doctrine

We are now in a position to examine some of the more specific objections raised against the concept of the specious present by various commentators. These objections take shape as a set of perplexities.

Terminological perplexity

Numerous commentators have mentioned the problem involved in call-ing the sensed duration "specious." Clay calls it "specious" because as a duration it includes not only the strict (immediate) present but also part of the past. The specious present, then, is not, strictly speaking, all present and it is "delusively given as being a time that intervenes between the past and the future" (Clay 1882, 167). James, although he retains Clay's term, suggests that the strict present, which Clay calls the "real present," is genuinely "an altogether ideal abstraction" (James 1890, 608). E. G. Boring, who had accepted the concept in agreement with James, and had asserted that the nonextended, present instant was the "specious" one (Boring 1933, 134), later came to reject James's doctrine and to suggest that what is specious in the specious present is its duration (Boring 1942). Gerald Myers, however, defends James on this point: "his whole point was that its duration is *real,* the 'instantaneous present' being the specious concept" (Myers 1971, 355). Broad, by admitting that the concept of a "momentary sense field" can only be defined by "extensive abstraction" from the specious present, also agrees with James (Broad 1923, 350).

The philosophical, and specifically ontological, question lurking behind the terminological perplexity is whether the specious present or the instantaneous present is real or not. Mundle, who argues for a real and objective specious present, and Plumer, who argues for the reality of the instantaneous present, both recommend dropping the term "specious" and adopting either "conscious present" or "sensory present" (Mundle 1954, 47; Plumer 1985, 20). In current psychological studies the concept still survives under the title of "psychological present" (Block 1990). A resolution to the terminological issue, of course, would still not solve the ontological question that continues to lurk in the background.

Measuring the specious present

James had rehearsed a multitude of psychological experiments that seemed to deliver differing objective measurements of the maximum and minimum durations of the specious present. Mabbott points out several problems involved in such psychological experiments. (1) The cited experiments had not been properly designed to measure the unit of temporal experience; rather, they measured "the maximum duration of a set of sounds which could be recognized without error." In effect, the experiments discovered that the set could be identified without error, and "inferred that it was therefore remembered as a whole and must accordingly have been heard as a whole." (2) The unit of experience cannot be properly defined since the maximum duration varies between individuals, and within one individual varies with practice and with fatigue, and even across different sense modalities. (3) The maximum duration of a set of sounds that can be recognized without error will vary depending on the content attended to—for example, merely rhythmic tones may involve a relatively short duration; a familiar melody may involve a relatively longer duration (Mabbott 1951, 162–65). Mabbott indicates that any precise measurement of the specious present would also depend on a measurement of the corresponding duration of the act of awareness, and that this is problematic, for (at least on his reading of Broad's account) there is no way to measure the duration of an act of attention without running into contradictions. Mabbott cites Boring on this point: the act of attention (or observation) "in a way begins with the [sensed] duration in question and it ends a little way after it, when the integration has fulfilled itself observationally. . . . It is just as true to say the observation is the end phase of the integration and therefore comes after it" (Boring 1933, 137). Mabbott concludes that any attempt to discover the duration of the specious present "is doomed to failure" (1951, 166). Furthermore, because such attempts were made to play the role of empirical, psychological evidence for the specious present doctrine, Mabbott concludes that the assured failure of such attempts is good reason to reject the doctrine.

Immediate experience

As we have already noted, Mundle shows how Mabbott's main objection against Broad's account of the specious present was based on a misreading. Mabbott, however, offers a more "tentative" conclusion that Mundle does not directly address. Mabbott questions the notion of an "immediate experience" of time implied by the doctrine of the specious present. The doctrine of the specious present, as it is found in James and Broad, seems to involve a structureless immediate intuition of duration. But if the specious present is construed as a process of integration of parts, this, according to Boring and Mabbott, is not an immediate experience. Direct or immediate experience, for Mabbott, means "absence of organization, of structure, of intelligible relations" (1951, 167). So the specious present doctrine promises something that it does not deliver—an account of immediate experience. This objection is closely related to what I take to be a major problem in James and Broad, namely, that they use the specious present to explain experience, but fail to explain how the specious present is possible.

An argument inspired by McTaggart

McTaggart puts forward a curious argument in favor of the specious present. It is curious only in the sense that, taken out of context, it looks like an argument against the specious present. McTaggart's argument is this:

> Now the "specious present" varies in length according to circumstances, and may be different for two people at the same period. The event M may be simultaneous both with X's perception Q and Y's perception R. At a certain moment Q may have ceased to be part of X's specious present. M, therefore, will at that moment be past. But at the same moment R may still be in Y's specious present. And, therefore, M will be present, at the same moment at which it is past. (1908, 472)

The fact that a particular event M could be both past and present at the same time seems impossible only if we consider time to be objectively real and absolute.[4] But McTaggart rejects the view that time is real and he cites the concept of the specious present as consistent with his rejection. Accordingly, there is no difficulty with M being both past and present as long as we consider time to be subjective; simply put, M would be past for X while present for Y. There seems to be a contradiction only if we presume time to be real. In effect, temporal relations are always *observed* in a specious present, but there is no *real* time in which events (even observations themselves) endure. On this assumption, McTaggart's argument supports the specious present doctrine.

In contrast, Plumer takes the objectivist's view, namely, that time is real. In that case he can, and does, treat McTaggart's argument as good reason to reject the very concept of the specious present. Plumer suggests the following example. Two runners, X and Y, are at the starting point of a footrace waiting to hear the starting gun fire. If X's experience conforms to McTaggart's theoretical description of it, then, on the supposition that the specious present extends into the near future, X would hear the gun before it actually fired. "Suppose the gun will go off at time F, a full 30 seconds in the objective future. It follows that [X] will start running immediately after *now* (E), because that is when [X] will first *hear* the gunshot; it is something of which [X is] '*sensible*,' however indistinctly" (Plumer 1985, 22). E is, of course, just shy of thirty seconds before the gun actually fires. Assuming that the specious present varies in length for each runner, Y might not hear the gun until fifteen seconds before it goes off. X would have the jump on Y and there would be all sorts of objections raised by observers of the race (assuming that their specious presents were closer to Y's!). The fact that observers would object suggests to Plumer that there is something wrong with the specious present concept. Intersubjective agreement about such things as when a race really starts shows us that the specious present cannot be "the slippery interval that James describes."

Intersensory differences in the specious present

The results of empirical research suggest (and the Jamesian view seems to be) that the specious present may vary across different sense modalities (sight, touch, hearing) even within the same individual.[5] Mabbott (1951) found this disconcerting. If in some instances we use two senses at once we could supposedly experience a serious incongruence of sound and sight. For example, I watch my daughter perform her ballet. If my auditory specious present is not identical with my visual specious present, then the music would appear to be out of sync with her movements. She would always be a little behind or ahead of where I think she ought to be.

Plumer also objects to the idea of intersensory differences. He proposes the following example, involving seeing, hearing, and touching. "Suppose one is holding a duck which produces a quack. If the [specious] 'presents' of those three senses were out of whack, one would first hear the quack, then feel the duck's diaphragm move, then see its beak open (or whatever). This is wild" (1985, 25). Quite obviously, since this does not appear to represent our actual experience, either intersensory differences are resolved in some fashion, or the specious present doctrine is wrong.

Some other perplexities associated with Lotzean assumptions

Plumer's arguments concerning footraces and ducks depend on a model of the specious present based on LA2, the Lotzean assumption of the persistence of memory-images. This is also the case with Plumer's argument about sentence comprehension. He maintains that if the specious present is extended over some short duration, then we would simultaneously *hear* the beginning and the end of a similarly enduring uttered sentence, and therefore we would be hearing a confused chorus of words rather than an organized sentence (1985, 25–26). Since our experience is not like this, the specious present doctrine, and LA2, must be wrong.

In a further argument Plumer discusses an issue raised by both Broad and Mundle, namely the fact that we do not perceive a movement that happens too fast or too slow. Plumer maintains that this depends on how long we look. A rapid glance at a clock's second hand will not allow me to see that it is moving. Plumer argues, on this basis, that "sensation at an instant . . . encompasses objects as they are at an instant . . . not as they are over some 'fraction of a second' . . . as Broad would have it" (1985, 27). In this case, like Broad's definition of the specious present, Plumer's own argument toward the concept of an instantaneous sensory present depends on LA1, the Lotzean assumption of the momentariness of the act of consciousness ("sensation at an instant").

I want to suggest that the objections and perplexities just invento-ried are valid and real only so long as the specious present is conceived on the James-Broad model. More specifically, any analysis that maintains the two Lotzean assumptions, LA1 and LA2, will be open to these or similar objections. Does this mean that we have to conclude with Mabbott that the concept of the specious present is untenable, or with Plumer that "sensation at an instant encompasses objects as they are at an instant"? The answer I suggest, in the next chapter, is *no*. I want to show that all of the perplexities that infect the concept of the specious present as it is developed in the Jamesian tradition can be resolved by getting rid of the two Lotzean assumptions and avoiding the cognitive paradox.

3

Husserl and the Specious Present

The majority of theorists who provide an account of the specious present doctrine, whether to defend it or to reject it, take their point of departure from the tradition that began with E. R. Clay, and whose most famous representative is William James. For reasons that are both historical and terminological, various commentators have associated Edmund Husserl with this tradition. In contrast to this usual interpretation, however, it is clear that Husserl took his starting point not from Clay or James, but from a tradition begun by the psychologist William Stern and his notion of *Präsenzzeit* (a term that has been mistranslated and often misinterpreted as "specious present"). Moreover, Husserl's analysis of time-consciousness is significantly different from the one developed in the Jamesian tradition. What I want to show is that Husserl's account provides for a possible explanation of the specious present that disarms the traditional arguments directed against this concept and escapes all of the perplexities outlined in the previous chapter.

Although Husserl neither uses the term "specious present" nor provides an analysis that takes this concept as its explicit theme, it is clear that some concept of the specious present is operative in Husserl's phenomenology. It is not, however, equivalent to the Jamesian notion. In contrast to James and Broad, for example, Husserl does not take the specious present to be the explanatory solution to the problem of our experience of time, but views it as precisely that which requires explanation. The concept of the *Präsenzzeit*, as it is developed by Husserl, rather than being the equivalent to the specious present, shows how the specious present is possible and provides a more adequate account of temporal experience than the concept of the specious present alone. The fundamental differences between James and Husserl, in their analyses of time-consciousness, are due to the acceptance (by James) and rejection (by Husserl) of the two Lotzean assumptions identified in the previous chapter.

Husserl and the Jamesian Tradition: A Critique of the Existing Scholarship

There are historical and philosophical connections between James and Husserl that have been well summarized in the scholarly literature (e.g., Spiegelberg 1976; Stevens 1974; Wilshire 1968). The influence is clearly one-sided and not extensive: Husserl studied James, but not vice versa. A brief glance at James's *Principles of Psychology* demonstrates James's extensive familiarity with the German philosophers and psychologists a generation prior to Husserl. So James knew the work of Herbart, whose students included Brentano, Lotze, Wundt, and Volkmann. James met and corresponded with Brentano's student, Karl Stumpf, who had also studied with Lotze. After Brentano sent Husserl to study psychology with Stumpf, the latter advised Husserl to read James's *Principles*. Husserl's marked-up copy of the *Principles* is still in the Husserl Archives in Louvain. As Herbert Spiegelberg points out, Husserl made "intensive markings" on the text of James's chapters on "The Stream of Thought," "Attention," and "Conception." Husserl also marked up the chapter entitled "The Perception of Time," which includes James's famous discussion of the specious present.[1] Despite Husserl's study of James, he seems to have learned more about time-consciousness from another student of Stumpf, namely, William Stern.

Perhaps the fact that Husserl read and was impressed by James's *Psychology* has motivated the misunderstanding that is clearly operative in many scholarly interpretations of the relation between Husserl's account of time-consciousness and the notion of the specious present as it is developed in the Jamesian tradition. Several commentators, for example, have equated or have claimed a strong similarity between the analyses of Husserl and James. Aron Gurwitsch (1943) clearly equates James's analysis of the specious present with Husserl's description of the retentional-protentional structure of consciousness. Gurwitsch further notes that the "time-diagram which Husserl gives in *Vorlesungen zur Phänomenologie des inneren Zeitbewusstseins*, [section] 10, agrees perfectly with that proposed by James in *Principles*, I, p. 629" (1966, 304 n. 9).[2] Stevens follows suit: "On this level of the primordial givenness of temporality, [Husserl's] analysis follows the same general lines as that of James. . . . This seems to be precisely what James meant by his theory of the specious present" (1974, 66). More recently, Errol Harris (1988), although careful to note that Husserl did not use the term "specious present," nonetheless associates Husserl and James on the basis of this concept. Gurwitsch, Stevens, and Harris are not alone, however; Broekman (1963), Brough (1970), Evans (1990), and Wälde (1985) make similar associations.[3]

James Churchill's translation of Stern's term *"Präsenzzeit"* as "specious present" no doubt contributes to these associations (Husserl 1964, 41).[4] Perhaps the mistranslation is what leads Izchak Miller (1984, 163–64) into making the claim that Stern espoused a version of the specious present which is similar to James's doctrine. But other commentators have also equated the concept of *Präsenzzeit* with the specious present concept. John Brough (1970, 202 n.), for example, calls the two notions "quite similar"; J. N. Findlay (1975, 7–8) equates the two concepts; David Wood (1989, 68) associates Stern on this point with James and Clay.

The association between Husserl and James has also been extended to include C. D. Broad's contribution to the Jamesian tradition. Findlay writes:

> Husserl sums up his account of the mechanics of retention in a remarkable two-dimensional diagram, which lends exactness to the vivid poetry of William James's account of the same machinery, and also agrees very largely with a diagram worked out by C. D. Broad in his account of the phenomenology of time in his commentary on McTaggart. The convergence of the accounts of Broad and Husserl is certainly very remarkable. (1975, 7–8)

Miller, noting a number of differences between Husserl and Broad, still asserts that precisely to the extent that Husserl embraces the doctrine of the specious present there exists a "basic similarity between Broad's and Husserl's accounts of temporal awareness" (1984, 171–72).

Plumer has recently provided in three propositions a concise summary of the ways that Husserl has been associated with the specious present doctrine. Plumer maintains:

> (1) That James' position and Husserl's position are (or *"might* be") similar;
>
> (2) That Broad's diagram of the specious present "has some affinity with" Husserl's diagram of time-consciousness;
>
> (3) That according to Husserl the specious present "is an *instant* flanked by intervals of 'retention' and 'protention.'" (1985, 21 n. 3)

But the differences that can *easily* be found between the approaches taken by Clay, James, and Broad, on the one hand, and Stern and Husserl, on the other hand, speak against the assertions and associations made by Plumer and all of the above named commentators.

In agreement with Clay, James and Broad describe the specious present as the temporal structure of the sensed or appearing contents of a conscious experience. It is an intuited duration; *"the short duration of which we are immediately and incessantly sensible"* (James 1890, 631). Furthermore, this concept of an immediately sensed duration does not imply, on the noetic side, an enduring act of awareness. Indeed, in the Jamesian tradition the specious present requires a *momentary* act of consciousness for its explanation. C. D. Broad clearly recognizes the problems involved in this limitation but, despite his attempt to introduce the concept of an enduring act of consciousness, he relies upon the conception of a momentary act of awareness in his definition of the specious present.

If the specious present is conceived in this Jamesian fashion, as an intuited duration that requires a momentary act of consciousness, then it cannot be equated with Stern's concept of *Präsenzzeit,* or with Husserl's account of the retentional-protentional structure of the conscious act. In his study of time perception and the perception of change Stern denies the concept of a momentary act of consciousness or a "single moment of perception." In fact, the *Präsenzzeit* is precisely the temporal extension of the psychical act, not the temporal extension of the sensed content that James calls the "specious present" (Stern 1898, 19). Stern, however, does not deny that the sensed content also is extended, so that it would not be wrong to say that Stern himself holds for a specious present as a temporally extended segment of content unified in and by consciousness. Indeed, what James calls the "specious present," Stern refers to as a *"Zeitstrecke"*—a short duration that stretches over no more than several seconds. But the *Zeitstrecke* is not the *Präsenzzeit;* rather, only because there is a *Präsenzzeit,* an extended presence of a conscious act (*"streckenhafte Gegenwärtigkeit eines Bewusstseinaktes"*), can there be something like a specious present, a temporally extended sensed content.[5] Stern understands the *Präsenzzeit* as that which accounts for the possibility of the specious present; there can be a specious present only because the *Präsenzzeit* holds it together. Elements that appear to consciousness one after the other are taken up "within one and the same act of apprehension, within one *Präsenzzeit"* (Stern 1897, 329, cited in Husserl 1966a, 21 n. 2). A melody, for example, can be sensed qua melody because its successive notes are held together by an act of consciousness that itself is stretched out in the structure of the *Präsenzzeit.* Stern believes that the concept of *Präsenzzeit* as a unitary, but not momentary, act of consciousness—he called it a "flowing, unitary, and continuous conscious act" (1898, 68)—explains not only how a sensed stretch of time is held together in experience, but also how it is possible to apprehend a temporal constancy.

Brentano's analysis of time-consciousness, like Herbart's and Volkmann's, and Meinong's, had relied on the notion of the momentariness of consciousness. Husserl, in his critique of Brentano and Meinong, cites

Stern's objection to this dogma. Stern "maintained that there are cases in which on the basis of a temporally extended content of consciousness a unitary apprehension takes place which is spread out over a temporal extension (the so-called '*Präsenzzeit*')" (Husserl 1964, 41; this is where Churchill mistranslates "*Präsenzzeit*" as "specious present"). Husserl, too, recognizes a *Zeitstrecke* or specious present, but acknowledges the importance of Stern's insight, which might be summarized in this way: the concept of the specious present does not solve the problem of time-consciousness. Rather, the specious present is precisely what needs to be explained. The concept of *Präsenzzeit* is a step in the right direction insofar as the specious present can only be explained by appealing to an *act* of consciousness that structures experience. An act of consciousness, moreover (and here Husserl agrees with Stern in opposition to Brentano and Meinong), is itself stretched out in time. "It is certainly evident that the perception of a temporal object itself has temporality, that the perception of duration itself presupposes the duration of perception, that the perception of any temporal form itself has its temporal form" (Husserl 1991, 24; see 1966a, 222, 225, 232).

But if Stern takes a step in the right direction, Husserl does not think he went far enough. One still needs to explain precisely how, in a temporally extended act of consciousness, experience gets structured and results in a specious present. Husserl develops the concept of the *Präsenzzeit* further than Stern by describing it as having a retentional-protentional structure that allows for both the perception of duration and the unity and connectedness of consciousness.

In contrast to James and Broad, Stern and Husserl understand the specious present not as a solution but as the problem, the thing that needs to be explained. If we say that James embraced the doctrine of the specious present, then we must say that Husserl did not. Rather, the specious present is one problem for which Husserl provides an account in his phenomenology of time-consciousness. In order to place Husserl within the Jamesian tradition, as the commentators have done, one must ignore the basic difference between the specious present, as the intuited (sensed) duration, and the *Präsenzzeit*, as the duration of the act of consciousness. Moreover, as we'll see in the following sections, one would also have to ignore fundamental differences that exist between the Jamesian tradition and the Stern-Husserl analysis concerning basic assumptions about how consciousness functions.

In the previous chapter we saw that James's analysis is based on two assumptions (LA1 and LA2). Both Stern and Husserl identify these assumptions as deriving from Herbart and Lotze, and explicitly reject them. LA1 states: the perception of succession requires a momentary and indivisible, and therefore durationless act of consciousness. According to Husserl, "it appears to be an evident and quite inescapable assumption of this conception that the intuition of an extent of time occurs in a now, in one time-point" (1991, 21). LA1, although perfectly consistent with James's doctrine of the specious present and his diagram, is precisely what Stern opposes with his concept of the *Präsenzzeit*. Siding with Stern on this point, Husserl maintains that the idea of a momentary act of consciousness is an idealized "fiction" (1991, 232), an "abstractum" (1991, 234), and that contrary to this assumption, the perception of a temporal object itself has temporal extension.

LA2 states: a succession of objects or temporal points must be represented simultaneously in the momentary act of consciousness by persisting memory-images or sensations. Again, this assumption is consistent with James's diagram. Stern, however, contends that there "is no need for the artificial assumption that the comparison always occurs because the memory image of the first tone exists side by side with the second tone" (cited by Husserl 1991, 23). The wording seems directed against *both Lotze*, who had described the perception of the succession of A and B in terms of a "comparison" of A and B within a momentary consciousness in which they appear simultaneously, *and Wundt* who had proposed the same doctrine in terms of "persistent images."[6] Husserl again sides with Stern on this point, and in the end he calls LA2 absurd and wrongheaded (1991, 36). We'll see, however, that despite his theoretical agreement with Stern in 1905, it took Husserl several years to work his way clear of this second Lotzean assumption.

While Wundt, Volkmann, and Ward could all line up on the side of the Jamesian conception of the specious present, Stern and Husserl rejected their fundamental assumptions. We can begin to see the far-reaching implications of this rejection by looking again at C. D. Broad's diagram of the specious present (see fig. 3.1). According to Findlay, Gurwitsch, Miller, and Plumer, Broad's diagram is more or less the same as James's and has some affinity with Husserl's diagram. Broad, however, while admitting that the *definition* of the specious present requires LA1, the assumption of a momentary act of awareness, nevertheless wanted to drop this assumption and still retain the specious present doctrine.

To remove the assumption of the momentariness of the conscious act Broad lets A–B represent an enduring act of consciousness. As we have noted, however, Broad fails to clarify what happens to the specious present. Although there are several possibilities, Mabbott's interpretation indicates precisely the inadequacy of Broad's diagram. The diagram does not really give an account of the specious present; it rather takes the

Figure 3.1: Broad's Diagram

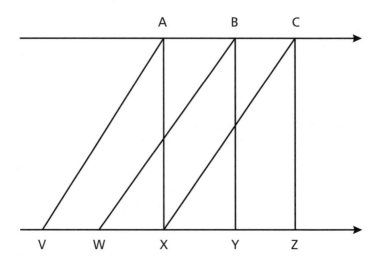

specious present for granted, as if it were the solution to a problem but
not problematic itself.

    We noted that Mundle posed the right question with respect to
Broad's analysis. If the act of consciousness is spread out in its own
duration and therefore contains temporal "phases" of its own, then
how are the phases of consciousness synthesized to allow for a consistent perceived duration? The problem lurking behind Broad's silence
about what happens to the specious present when acts of consciousness
are more than momentary is linked to a lack of clarity about LA2,
the Lotzean assumption that in some way memory-images, or just-past
sensa, must persist so that a comparison or synthesis might be accomplished in the present act of consciousness. The two Lotzean assumptions
are connected in such a way that it's impossible to get clear of one
of the assumptions without getting clear of both. In effect, the question is, how does one explain the constitution of the specious present
when the synthesizing conscious act is involved in its own expiring duration, and when the specious present, rather than being a stable *Gestalt,*
turns out to be involved in its own overlapping succession? Once this
question is asked, the difficulties seem to be doubled, since now explanations are required not only for the synthesis of perceived content
(Broad's line V–Z) but also for the synthesis of the perceiving act (Broad's
line A–C).

Although Mundle raises the right question, he backs away from the difficulties involved in describing what happens in an extended but synthesizing act of consciousness. He avoids answering it by rehearsing a number of metaphysical alternatives that would be consistent with the specious present doctrine. He was apparently unaware that fifty years before he asked the question, Husserl was working his way toward an answer.

Husserl had raised a question against Stern similar to the one Mundle raises against Broad. Stern's concept of the simple *Präsenzzeit* accomplishes nothing more than Broad's claim that the act of consciousness is not momentary but has extended duration. We might say that both Broad and Stern take a step in the right direction but they only go far enough to motivate the basic question that Husserl tries to answer. If both the act of perceptual consciousness and the perceived event are involved in expiring duration, how does perception make sense out of experience?

Time-Consciousness and Intentionality

Although Husserl, in 1905, both agreed with Stern's rejection of LA1 and LA2, and yet criticized Stern for not providing the complete and detailed phenomenological description of the *Präsenzzeit*, we have noted that it took Husserl several more years to work his way clear of LA2 and thereby reach his mature account of time-consciousness. His analysis in 1905, and even as late as 1908, depended implicitly on the Lotzean assumption that sense-data of past events were in some way synthesized in present consciousness.

Time-consciousness: circa 1905

To understand Husserl's later solution we need an explication, in broad strokes, of Husserl's notion of time-consciousness, as he conceived it in his lectures of 1905.[7] Although he recognizes and struggles with the cognitive paradox of succession represented in simultaneity, we'll see shortly that he is forced to revise this early account to free it from this paradox. In 1905, however, Husserl takes his point of departure in a critique of Brentano, Meinong, and the Lotzean assumptions that, following Stern, he wants to reject.

Brentano argued that duration or succession is represented in consciousness thanks to an amalgamation, an "original association" of representations. In each moment of perceptual consciousness we are not only perceptually aware of the present sensation but also, through memory, we are aware of past sensations that, although no longer persisting in consciousness, are re-presented in acts of memory. A representation of the future, produced by an act of expectation, is also associated with the present moment. So Brentano's theory might be diagrammed as shown in figure 3.2.

Husserl's criticism of Brentano is threefold. First, focusing on the notion of representation in the original association, he asks, how is the act of memory within the original association that gives us our intuition of time, different from an act of memory that provides us with a recollection of the remote past? Husserl objects to the idea that an intuitive presentation of a succession already includes, on Brentano's analysis, a re-presentation (*Vergegenwärtigung*) in an act of memory, and that a subsequent act of memory would have to be a re-presentation of a re-presentation. "Re-presentation is the opposite of the act that gives something originally" (Husserl 1991, 47), so re-presentation, as an act of memory, cannot be involved in the original intuition of time.

Second, on Brentano's account it would be impossible to really *perceive* a temporal (enduring or successive) object, such as a melody. Rather, at any moment of consciousness, we perceive only one now-moment of the object and combine it with a remembered (therefore, not perceived) moment and an expected (not perceived) moment. On this view, "I do not hear the melody but only the single present tone. That

Figure 3.2: Brentano's Theory

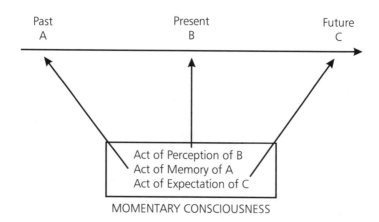

the elapsed part of the melody is something objective for me, I owe—or some will be inclined to say—to memory" (Husserl 1991, 25). Husserl doesn't think this is right since it seems phenomenologically apparent that we do hear (perceive) melodies.

Third, a point we will come back to, Brentano fails to make certain essential distinctions in his theory of intentionality, with the result that his characterization of time-consciousness falls victim to some form of the cognitive paradox. In other words, Husserl claims, it is not clear why a past content represented in the present moment of consciousness will be taken as past rather than as present. If the content A* is represented in present consciousness, why would it appear to us to be past?

> The being-present of an A in consciousness through the annexation of a new moment, even if we call that new moment the moment of the past, is incapable of explaining the transcending consciousness: A is past. It is not able to furnish the slightest representation of the fact that what I now have in consciousness as A with its new character [A*] is identical with something that is not in consciousness now but that did exist. (Husserl 1991, 19)

Brentano's theory fails to address this issue because it started with the Lotzean assumptions, LA1 and LA2.

Husserl attempts to circumvent these problems in his own analysis. Thus, he refuses to posit an original association of re-presentation in the form of recollective acts of memory with perception. Rather, he conceives perception itself as structured in a way that automatically retains the past, without the need for a full-blown act of recollection. So rather than having two or more separate acts of consciousness synthesizing content by simultaneous association, as Brentano had maintained, Husserl builds into the very structure of perception, or in general any act of consciousness, a retentioning function that he calls "primary memory" or "retention." Perception, itself extended in time, not only includes an impression ("primal impression") of the now-phase of the object, but also includes a retention of the just-past phases. Moreover, a primal expectation or protentional function allows perception to stretch a bit toward the future.

Husserl is careful to distinguish the "strong phenomenological differences" between the retentional function of an act of consciousness and recollection or memory proper (1991, 47). Recollection, as a re-presentational act, delivers over its content not as something perceptually given, but as not given. The now, before, and after of the recollected object are re-presented as not present, but as remotely past. Perception, in contrast, "is the act that places something before our eyes as the thing itself" in a presence that is extended into the near past and near future. Retentioning, as part of the structure of perception, and thus, in contrast to recollection, enables us "to *see* [i.e., perceive] what is past; only in it does the past become constituted—and constituted presentatively, not re-presentatively" (1991, 43).

These are the broad strokes that Husserl began to paint even prior to his 1905 lectures. He wrestles with the "aporia" of what we have called the cognitive paradox, with Brentano's theory of original association, and with the distinction between retention and recollection even in texts dating from 1900–1901 (see 1991, 163–64, 169ff., 176ff.). But in the details of the theory he works out between 1900 and 1908 it is not clear that he escapes the cognitive paradox entailed by LA1 and LA2, or how his analysis is that much different from James's notion of the specious present. To understand the details of these problems and their ultimate solution in Husserl's phenomenology, we need to become familiar with the notion of intentionality that he develops, again, under the influence of and in contrast to Brentano.

Intentionality

The notion of intentionality has a long history that is still not finished. One could start with Empedocles's doctrine: "like is known by like," and trace the concept through Aristotle and the Scholastics to Brentano, Husserl, and contemporary discussions. An abbreviated history of this concept can help to throw some light on Husserl's use of it.

Intentionality is first of all a relation. For Aristotle, perception is viewed as a purely formal relation. To sense something means to relate to the sensible form, but not to the matter (*hyle*) of the thing. Perception is a process similar to impressing a shape (*morphe*) onto wax where the wax (like the mind) doesn't record the material which does the impressing, but only the shape (*De Anima*, 424a17–20). In this process the intellect becomes what is other than itself while still remaining itself. This is also what Aquinas means when he claims that knowledge is nonmaterial. "Whatever is received exists in the recipient in accord with the recipient's mode of being" (Aquinas 1951, I, 84, 1c). Since the knower's soul is immaterial then what is apprehended by the soul or intellect must also be immaterial. The exclusion of the material element from the intentional means, for Aquinas, that intentionality is a relation to something that is always beyond the knower, something that is never completely under the knower's control, something that is never completely reducible to the knower.

Intentionality is neither a "transitive act," which, in Aquinas's view, passes over into the external thing, nor an "immanent act," which remains within and perfects the knower (1951, I, 54, 2). Nor is it a mere "relation of reason," existing only in the mind. Aquinas identifies it as a "mixed real" relation. A *real* relation is one that exists in the very nature of the things related (1951, I, 28, 1). A real relation is *mixed,* rather than mutual, when one relatum is affected by the other relatum, but not vice versa. So, if the intentional relation is a mixed real relation, it is real because both the knower and the known have their own existence, but it is mixed, or one-sided because intentionality exists only in the knower and not in the known. In other words, the known has an effect on the knower, but not vice versa.

Brentano objected to this view. For him, the intentional relation is not real because it does not require a real, transobjective known; rather, the known can just as easily be an imaginary sense. Moreover, Brentano tends to think of real mutual relations as the only kind of relations, so, in his view, intentionality is hardly a relation at all. "One may well ask, therefore, whether we are dealing with something which is in a certain respect similar to a relation, and which therefore, we might describe as being something that is 'relation-like' [*etwas 'relativliches'*]."[8]

Husserl's general formula for intentionality reads: "All consciousness is consciousness of something." Although his phenomenological method allows him to ignore questions about the metaphysical reality of the "something," that is, the known object, he still finds himself wrestling with the traditional question of real relation. With respect to this issue he insists on the simple phrase "intentional relation" and cautions against language that would lead to two misunderstandings:

> first, that we are dealing with a real [*realen*] event or a real relationship, taking place between "consciousness" . . . on the one hand, and the thing of which there is consciousness, on the other; second, that we are dealing with a relation between two things, both present in equally real fashion in consciousness, an act and an intentional object, or with a sort of box-within-box structure of mental contents. If talk of a relation is here inescapable, we must avoid expressions which tempt us to regard such a relation as having psychological reality. (1970a, 557–58; also see 1962, § 36)

For Husserl, a real relation could only attain between two nonconscious entities or "things." One of these entities could be a person, but only considered as an object or thing, not as conscious being. For example, there is a real relation between my shoe and my foot, but there is no real relation between my shoe and my perception of it. The relation that consciousness has to other things is the special kind of relation Husserl calls "intentional relation."

To explain how intentionality actually works, Husserl relies on a structure that he calls the schema of apprehension–content of apprehension (*Auffasung-Auffasungsinhalt*). The content in this noetic schema consists of sensations or sensible materials, which Husserl terms "hyle" or "hyletic data," and which he defines as real (*reell*), that is, nonintentional, contents. The distinction between real and intentional is central to Husserl's concept of intentionality and to his solution to the problems of time-consciousness. Husserl uses the term *"reell"* to signify something that is *actually* immanent in consciousness, in contrast to something that is *intentionally* present. An act of perception, for example, is a real event that takes place in consciousness; but in the intentional relation of perception the object perceived is not really (*reell*) in consciousness; in itself, it has reality as a (*real*) thing located in the external environment; in relation to consciousness it has intentional status. Intentional content is "irreal," perceived by consciousness but not actually immanent in consciousness. Hyletic content, on the other hand, is *reell* content, actually present in consciousness. Hyletic content, however, does enter into a larger intentional process, and this is explained in terms of the noetic schema.

The perceptual process gets its intentional character from the apprehension which "bestows" sense (*Sinn*) upon the *reell*, present sensation. In the schema "we find these sensuous moments overlaid by an 'animating,' sense-bestowing stratum. . . . Sensuous data present themselves as material for intentional formings or sense-bestowals at different levels" (Husserl 1962, §85; see Husserl 1973a, 46; and Gallagher 1986). Apprehension, however, does not objectify the hyletic content or bring it to thematic presence. Apprehension does not make us aware of sensations. Rather, the noetic schema subtends a full-blown intentional act. A conscious act like perception is based on this prereflective performance of the schema, but neither the apprehensions, nor the hyletic data, nor the animating processes appear as the object of consciousness. Still, whatever does appear as the object of consciousness is based on the prereflective performances of the schema. The noetic schema, then, is what Aquinas had called the "that by which" the intentional relation to an object is set up. The noetic schema allows for there to be—is "that by which" there is—an appearance; it constitutes the intentional act that brings an object to thematic presence within consciousness.

In perception, the appearance of an intentional object is not a reduplication of the real, external thing. Brentano had corrected himself on this point. In his early theory of intentionality he spoke of an immanent objectivity. On this view mental phenomena would include within themselves an intentional object (Chisholm 1960, 51). The perception of X, where X is some real spatial object, would thus involve the existence of a mental representation X, an intentional object in the sense of a real image, that is an *ens rationis,* the scholastic *esse intentionale* that borrows its existence from the perceiving consciousness. In 1905, however, Brentano revised his theory: "what we think about is *the object* or *thing* and not the 'object of thought' [*vorgestelltes Objekt*]," i.e., not an *ens rationis* or immanent object (Brentano 1966, 77). The perception of a particular X does not involve the production of an extra object really (*reell*) existing in consciousness. Intentionality goes directly to the thing.

Husserl himself had already made this correction. He rejected Brentano's earlier notion of a real immanent object existing in consciousness. There is only one object present to consciousness, not two. In intentional experience "the intentional 'relation' to an object is achieved, and an object is 'intentionally present'; these two phrases mean precisely the same" (Husserl 1970a, 558). The perceptual object is not a mental phenomenon or immanent object; it is nothing other than the object that we intend. The object is not represented by an image in consciousness; there is no reduplication. "I perceive the thing, the object of nature, the tree there in the garden; that and nothing else is the real object of the perceiving 'intention.' A second immanent tree, or even an 'inner image' of the real tree that stands out there before me, is nowise given, and to suppose such a thing by way of assumption lead only to absurdity" (Husserl 1962, § 90; see Husserl 1970a, 594).

The only question that we are left with, one that is still the theme of an ongoing dispute, concerns the status of what Husserl calls the "noema." The concept of noema involves meaning (*Sinn*). The function of the noetic schema of apprehension-content allows consciousness to grasp the meaning of the intended object. Apprehension informs hyletic content, an act takes on a particular character, and as a result, I not only perceive an object, but I perceive an object that means something. A certain intentional, meaningful content (noema) is made to appear. "Perception, for instance, has its noema, and at the base its perceptual meaning, that is the *perceived as such*" (1962, § 88). The noema is the intentional meaning (*Sinn*), which, in the case of perception, is the perceived *as such,* the perceived *as* it is intended. It is an intentional (but not real) immanence in perceptual experience.

Consider the following example. I open my eyes and I see a tree, just where it is, at the side of the road. The noematic content is "that which appears as such"—in this case, "a particular tree at the side of the road." This is a meaning that may also include the further significance that the tree offers shade on a hot day, or fruit, or the task of trimming it, and so forth. It may also be the case that I am hallucinating. Perhaps there is no real tree there, or actual road. For Husserl, as phenomenologist, the existence or nonexistence of the tree or road does not affect the fact that it appears as it appears. The noema is the same whether the tree really exists or not. The *"tree plain and simple,"* if it exists, can burn; the *perceived tree as such* as the meaning of the particular perception cannot burn. Of course, if the tree actually burns, and I see this (or if I am hallucinating about a burning tree) then the noema changes to "perceived burning tree as such," although the noema or meaning does not itself burn.

The noema, thus, has a semantic status. It is a meaning. It does not necessarily involve an image; it is an *esse intentionale* only in the sense of being the meaning of a perceived object. For our present purposes we need not explore this notion any further, although we will return to consider some aspects of an ongoing conflict of interpretations concerning Husserl's concept of noema (in chapter 8).

Time-consciousness revisited

In his 1905 lectures, and up until 1908, Husserl's explanation of time-consciousness relies on the noetic schema in which an apprehension interprets a hyletic content. In other words, retention, primal impression, and protention have an intentional structure involving the schematic form: apprehension–hyletic content. The question, then, is whether the apprehension or the content is the temporally significant element. On Husserl's reading, Brentano attributes temporal change to change in content. This leads him directly into the cognitive paradox (see Husserl 1991, 17–18, 178). Husserl takes a different view: the temporal character of experience belongs to apprehension rather than to the hyletic contents. The hyletic contents flow in a temporal fashion only because they are caught up within the noetic schema (see, e.g., 1991, 179).

> Briefly stated: The temporal form is neither a temporal content itself nor a complex of new contents that somehow attach themselves to the temporal content. Now even if Brentano did not fall into the error of reducing, after the fashion of sensualism, all experiences to mere primary contents, and even if he was the first to recognize the radical separation between primary contents and act-characters, his theory of time nonetheless shows that he has just not taken into consideration the theoretically decisive act-characters. The question of how time-consciousness is possible and how it is to be understood remains unanswered [in Brentano]. (1991, 20)

Husserl's answer is that "an act claiming to give a temporal object itself must contain in itself 'apprehensions of the now,' 'apprehensions of the past,' and so on; specifically, as originally constituting apprehensions"

(1991, 41). In the noetic schema hyletic data remain generally neutral with respect to intentional meaning, awaiting interpretation by the apprehension. So, Husserl suggests, in the context of time-consciousness hyletic contents remain temporally neutral and require the bestowal of temporality by apprehension.[9]

Only in 1908 does Husserl start to see that this conception is not viable and is just as prone to the cognitive paradox. According to his schema theory of time-consciousness, the sense (hyletic) contents must remain simultaneous with one another in the now-phase of consciousness while the noetic apprehension bestows upon them their successive order.[10] This, however, as Husserl finally came to see, is not essentially different from LA2, the paradoxical Lotzean assumption of having simultaneously present sense-contents function to represent succession.

> *Do we have a continuum of primary contents simultaneously in the now-point and, in addition to this and simultaneous with it, a continuum of "apprehensions"?* . . . [C]ertainly everything that "really" [*reell*] belongs to this consciousness exists in it simultaneously—that is to say, exists in it "now." . . . The primary contents that spread out in the now, *are not able to switch their temporal function:* the now cannot stand before me as not-now, the not-now cannot stand before me as now. Indeed, if it were otherwise, the whole continuum of contents could be viewed as now and consequently as coexistent, and then again as successive. That is evidently impossible. (1991, 334–35)

Husserl recognizes, then, that his original explanation of time-consciousness in terms of the noetic schema, requiring sense-contents to be both now (simultaneous) and not-now (successive), involves an absurdity (see 1991, 35–36, 335).

Husserl resolves this absurdity and escapes the cognitive paradox by employing his concept of intentional relation and the distinction between *intentional* contents and real (*reell*) contents of consciousness. In terms of his new analysis of time-consciousness Husserl contends that that which is not-now, e.g., a just-past musical tone, is still in consciousness but not as a sensation that is really (*reell*) present; not as real hyletic content (1991, 336). He thus jettisons the schema and distinguishes the sound-sensation and its possible sensible reverberation from the intentionally *retained* sound. What Husserl calls "retention" is still not an individual act of consciousness like perception or memory. An act of consciousness is precisely "an immanent duration-unity constituted in a series of retentional phases" (1991, 122). Even this statement is somewhat misleading, because retention is not fully a phase of the conscious act. Rather, it is part of the structure of an act of consciousness, or more precisely, part of the structure of a phase of the act of consciousness. As part of this phase-structure retention functions to keep or retain the just-past phase "in view." Actually it would be better to say that the word "retention" signifies a function or a performance of consciousness rather than a phase, part, or structure of consciousness (see Gallagher 1979).

To avoid LA2 Husserl emphasizes the special *intentional* nature of the retentional performance. He points out that the retained sound "is not a present tone but precisely a tone 'primarily remembered' in the now: it is not really [*reell*] on hand in the retentional consciousness" (1991, 33). Retentioning performs as a direct intentional intuition of the past, rather than as an apprehension of a real sensation or memory-image of the past. Thus, retentioning "is not a modification in which impressional data are really [*reell*] preserved, only in modified form: on the contrary, it is an intentionality—indeed, an intentionality with a specific character of its own" (1991, 122). The retentional performance of consciousness allows it to carry within itself an intentional sense or meaning of the past, but not a real sensation of it. Retention takes the just-past as a semantic referent. It "transcends itself and *posits* something as being—namely, as being past—that does not really [*reell*] inhere in it" (1991, 355–56).

Husserl's Diagram: Double Intentionality

Retentioning involves a kind of intentionality that does not thematize its object, as a full-blown intentional act does. Rather, its intentionality "keeps hold of" (*im Griff behalten*) the just-past (Husserl 1966a, 118). "Retention itself is not an act of looking back that makes the elapsed phase into an object" (1964, 161 / 1991, 122). Indeed, I can be thematically conscious of something only because I already "keep hold of" the elapsed phase of consciousness. This actually involves a double intentionality. Husserl offers a diagram (fig. 3.3) in explanation.[11]

No matter how you turn this diagram it cannot be made to look like either James's or Broad's diagram. Moreover Husserl's diagram could not be interpreted in the same way as James's diagram because Husserl, like Stern, was moving beyond the two Lotzean assumptions that are implicated in James's account. Furthermore, its meaning is different from Broad's diagram because Husserl, moving beyond both Broad and Stern, was attempting to diagram the answer to a question that neither Broad

Figure 3.3: Husserl's Diagram

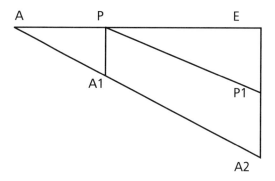

nor Stern had asked, namely, how precisely an enduring perception can make sense out of temporal objects.

The horizontal line of the diagram represents a segment of sensed duration. Consider the line A–P to represent one segment of a duration and the full line A–E to represent the complete duration. For example, A–P may be a musical note which itself has duration. A–E would then represent a sensed succession of notes. The hypotenuse represents an enduring act of consciousness which perceives (senses) the melody. The vertical lines represent a growing "thickness" of consciousness, the product of its retentional structure.

Husserl's diagram is oversimplified in two ways, however. First, it assumes that the act of consciousness (represented by the hypotenuse of the triangle) begins precisely when the note or melody begins at A. Second, it assumes that there is no protentioning of the just-future. Since these are assumptions that do not operate in Husserl's analysis, his own diagram inadequately represents his theory of time-consciousness. Moreover, it is poorly designed to serve its purpose. It is a diagram that, instead of helping to explain his theory, requires the theory to explain it. It will be better to turn our attention to a diagram that more adequately represents Husserl's theory in order to clarify the differences between it and the diagrams of James and Broad. Figure 3.4 is an adaptation of a diagram proposed by Brough (1970) to represent Husserl's concept of time-consciousness.

This diagram and Husserl's theory not only explain how the specious present is possible given an enduring act of consciousness, they also explain how consciousness unites itself (qua *Präsenzzeit*) through time.

Figure 3.4:   Husserl's Diagram Modified

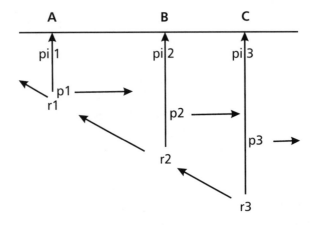

The horizontal line ABC represents a temporal object such as a melody of several notes. The vertical lines represent abstract momentary phases of an enduring act of consciousness. Each phase is structured by three functions: primal impression (pi), retention (r), and protention (p).

Primal impression allows for the consciousness of an object (a musical note, for example) that is simultaneous with the actual phase of consciousness. Let phase 3 represent the actual now-phase of an enduring act of consciousness. In phase 3 there is a primal-impression (pi_3) of the now sounding note C. In the just-past phase 2 there is a just-past primal impression (pi_2) of B, which has now stopped sounding; and in phase 1, a just-just-past primal impression of A.

In phase 3 there is also a retentioning (r_3) of the previous phase of consciousness 2. Of course phase 2 had its own retentioning of the prior phase 1. This means that there is a retentional continuum—$r_3(r_2[r_1])$, and so forth—that stretches back over prior experience. Husserl characterizes this retentioning of retentioning as the horizontal or longitudinal intentionality (*Längsintentionalität*) of retention (1991, 85). But the retentioning function not only retains a retentional continuum, it retains the whole previous phase, and therefore it retains the previous primal impression which had been a consciousness of the previously sounded note. So indirectly, in what Husserl calls the "transverse intentionality" (*Querintentionalität*) of retention, each phase of consciousness retains, in an intentional manner, the previously intuited objects (notes).

Since retentioning functions in an *intentional* way, what remains present in consciousness, i.e., what remains present as part of the specious present, is not the just-past note itself, or the memory-image, or the sensation of the just-past note (these alternatives would represent different versions of LA2). Rather, the only thing that is really (*reell*) present in the specious present is delivered by the current primal impression; the just-past is retained as part of the specious present only as the perceptual meaning or significance of the previous note qua "just-past." It is *intentionally* retained and helps to constitute the intentionally intuited duration (the specious present). Thus the specious present does not consist of a set of simultaneous sense-data; rather, it has a semantic or intentional status. The transverse intentionality of the retentional function of consciousness explains how the "rearward" portion of the specious present is constituted.

It is important to remember the distinction between memory (which is itself an act of consciousness with its own retentional-protentional structure), and the retentional performance of consciousness. Retentioning is a constant feature of consciousness. For that reason Husserl maintained (against Brentano) that we perceive a melody rather than just one note at a time. On Brentano's theory, we would have to conjoin a momentary act of perception with a re-presentational act of memory in order to be conscious of a temporally extended object. In this sense Brentano would have to reject the concept of the specious present. For him we could only sense one instantaneous object at a time. In contrast, on Husserl's theory, one could maintain that perception, and all other acts of consciousness, involve a specious present—i.e., an intuited (intentionally constituted) duration. More than that, one can legitimately claim that, in contrast to the Jamesian school, which takes the specious present as a solution, Husserl actually provides an explanation of how the specious present is possible.

Husserl's analysis further shows how the specious present (understood as an intentional unity) is possible only through a structured *Präsenzzeit*, i.e., a temporally extended act of consciousness with a retentional-protentional structure. Transverse intentionality is dependent on horizontal intentionality, i.e., it is accomplished in an indirect manner through the retentional continuum. Horizontal intentionality thus accounts for the duration of the act of consciousness, i.e., what Stern calls the *Präsenzzeit*—the fact that consciousness is a unified act over a stretch of duration, rather than the punctiform or momentary act required by LA1. In effect, Husserl has shown how Broad could have been right, without appealing to any of the metaphysical alternatives listed by Mundle, and without depending on either of the Lotzean assumptions.

What has been said of retentioning can be predicated mutatis mutandis of protentioning. The latter adds the forward dimension to the specious present. In contrast to retentioning, however, protentioning is an unfulfilled intentioning of an immediate but indeterminate future. Since the intended about-to-be phase of consciousness has not yet taken place, there is nothing determinate for protentioning to protend and there can be no protentional continuum. Rather, there is at most a protentional horizon due to a continuous protentional functioning—James calls it a forward "fringe" (1890, 613). The protended future is pure possibility rather than something actual or actualized.

This analysis of the protentional functioning of consciousness suggests that the specious present is asymmetrical with regard to the past and future. The specious present is a semantic mix of the determinate, actualized just past and the indeterminate, possible just-to-come. Although James suggests that there is a forward dimension to the specious present, this suggestion is actually inconsistent with his maintenance of LA2. Either some vague sense of the indeterminacy of the future, or some definite sense of inconsistency kept Clay and Broad from including the just-about-to-be in the specious present. For any theory modeled on LA2 to include a protended future within the specious present would require the indeterminate future to be really and determinately present. In contrast, Husserl's analysis shows that the future appears, not really (reell) but only intentionally in the specious present. Protentioning is a present projection toward or an expectation of an indeterminate future; protentioning itself is actual, the just-about-to-be-future is not.

Husserl, in contrast to the Jamesian tradition, provided an explanation of the specious present without depending on either of the Lotzean assumptions. It should be clear from the above analysis that the various claims made by the commentators concerning Husserl's relation to the Jamesian tradition are problematic. The positions of James and Husserl are not similar, since James accepted and Husserl rejected LA1 and LA2. Broad never gave up LA2, and while attempting to escape LA1, still depended on it to define the specious present. In this sense there can be no affinity between the respective analyses or diagrams provided by Broad and Husserl. Finally, since the retentional-protentional structure of the act of consciousness belongs to the description of what Stern called the Präsenzzeit, it would not be correct to describe the specious present, as Plumer does, as "an instant flanked by intervals of 'retention' and 'protention'" (1985, 21 n. 3). Retention and protention describe functions of the act of consciousness. The specious present, as the intuited duration, contains no retentions or protentions; rather it is made possible by the retentional-protentional performance of the acts of consciousness.

4

Reinterpreting Time-Consciousness

usserl's analysis of time-consciousness, which describes the flow
of consciousness as a rational structure, perfects the Lockean,
phenomenological paradigm. By providing an account of the flow
that is not dependent on the Lotzean assumptions, LA1 and LA2, Husserl
avoids the cognitive paradox that would make experienced succession reducible to experienced simultaneity. To further demonstrate the strength
of the Husserlian account of time-consciousness, I want to show how
this account resolves the various objections and perplexities associated
with the Jamesian concept of the specious present. Then, to clarify the
theoretical intricacies of the analysis, I offer a critical examination of
the principle of simultaneous awareness as interpreted by Izchak Miller
(1984). Finally, however, we need to understand the internal limitations
involved in Husserl's theory. These internal limitations help to define
some of the continuing aporias discussed in the following chapters.

Perplexities Resolved

In the light of Husserl's analysis of time-consciousness we can now reexamine the various objections and perplexities raised in connection with
the specious present doctrine.

The speciousness or the reality of the specious present

Is the specious present real or not? Since Husserl never uses the term
"specious present," or a German equivalent,[1] we might be tempted to say
that he avoids the problem concerning its reality or nonreality implied
by the term "specious." He could easily agree with Mundle, Plumer, and

others who have suggested the alternative terms "conscious," "sensory," "lived," or "experienced" present. One might suggest the term "intentional present" as most appropriate. Husserl sometimes uses the word "temporal field" (*Zeitfeld*) to signify the phenomenon of the intentional present (see, e.g., 1991, 32, 90).

The problem, of course, goes beyond terminology. Still, outside of terminological issues, one might claim that Husserl is able to skirt even the metaphysical issue. Husserl's phenomenological method requires the phenomenologist to "bracket" the whole question of whether what we experience in consciousness is objectively *real* or *not real*. He begins his analysis of time-consciousness with his famous phenomenological reduction, that is, he excludes "every assumption, stipulation, or conviction with respect to objective time" (1991, 22). Perhaps he is careful to avoid the term "specious" for this reason, that is, in order to refrain from explicit metaphysical judgment about the status of its reality.

Within the reduced phenomenological realm—in effect, within transcendental consciousness—Husserl is faced with the question of the phenomenological status of the past, present, and future. His insight here, insofar as he is able to reject LA2 without rejecting the specious present, distinguishes him from Herbart, Brentano, Lotze, and Meinong, as well as Wundt, Volkmann, Ward, James, Broad, Mundle, and most others who follow in the Jamesian tradition. He distinguishes between real (*reell*) and intentional contents, and in this sense, the specious present is not a real present. The specious present is not a present composed of real elements of the past, or real elements of the future, as if the past was still actual and the future was more than just a possibility. The specious present has an intentional status; it is a sense of time but not an actually sensed time. A past experience or object is "in the present" not with the status of a real sensation, but with the status of intended meaning. Consciousness intends the past as past, not as present. A possible future does not appear in present consciousness as an actual future; it appears as an expected future, as one that is not yet actual. Precisely this insight concerning the intentional status of the experienced present provides solutions to the remaining perplexities.

Measuring the specious present

Psychological experiments deliver differing objective measurements of the maximum and minimum durations of the specious present. Mabbott concludes that the assured failure of these attempts is good reason to reject the very notion of the specious present. Husserl's methodological exclusion of objective time from the phenomenological field helps to resolve this long-standing problem concerning the measurement of the specious present. His analysis suggests a way of accepting Mabbott's judgment that any attempt to measure the duration of the specious present and the act of consciousness is "doomed to failure," without, however, necessitating the rejection of the notion of the specious present.

The psychological experiments designed to measure the specious present attempt to apply objective, clock time to a phenomenon that cannot be correlated precisely to *objective* duration. The lived or experienced duration of a specious present cannot be measured in objective time.[2] The specious present is exactly as long as retention's reach into earlier experience and protention's projection into the indeterminate future. The retentional reach and the protentional projection, however, are never objectively exact. Retentioning involves a *fading* of past experience, and in the fading process there is never an absolute or discrete point of objective conclusion. Moreover, from one experience to the next retentional reach and protentional projection are variable and are modified by experiential and empirical factors. On Husserl's account we should expect precisely what the psychologists find in their experiments—a wide range of variations. These results, then, do not speak against the concept of the specious present, but are consistent with Husserl's account of temporal experience.

Immediate experience

Do we have, in the phenomenon of the specious present, an immediate experience of time? Does immediate experience imply the absence of organization, structure, and intelligible relations, as Mabbott (1951) suggests? If the specious present itself remains unexplained in James and Broad, this does not mean that it is unexplainable or that it consists of unintelligible relations. The virtue of Husserl's account is that it shows both that we have an immediate, direct experience of temporal duration, and that this experience is not without organization or structure but consists of intelligible relations of retention and protention. Precisely this rational and predictable structure of consciousness accounts for the possibility of the specious present as an immediate experience of duration.

The argument from McTaggart

Turning to McTaggart's argument concerning the specious present, Plumer is able to make sense of temporal experience only by reducing the specious present to an instant. Husserl provides a way to redeem the specious present without reducing it to an instant. This does not mean that he would lead us back to McTaggart's psychologism, or that he would necessarily reject some version of an objectivist theory of time.

One might first be tempted to say that Husserl would not accept Plumer's assumptions about the reality of time, that is, that there is an objective and measurable time-series that can be characterized in relations of past-present-future. It is true that for his phenomenological considerations Husserl excludes all assumptions and convictions concerning objective time. This exclusion, however, does not entail the denial of objective time. Indeed, Husserl makes it clear that the ultimate aim of his analysis is to "put objective time and subjective time-consciousness into the right relation" and to see how objective temporality comes to be constituted for consciousness. He does not deny that from the objective viewpoint "every experience, just as every real being and moment of being, may have its place in the single objective time," or that there are a number of interesting questions to be investigated in this area (1991, 4–5). Notwithstanding his bracketing of objective time, Husserl even takes up the question of the objective simultaneity of objective events and perception (1991, 114–15). Here Husserl notes that there is no strict simultaneity of perception and perceived event because of the temporal lags connected with the "external conditions" of the speed of light and the physiological (or hyletic) processes that underpin perception.

We do not need to define Husserl's position with respect to the reality of time, however, to learn from him how to address Plumer's argument. Let's reconsider Plumer's example of the footrace. Let's say that sometime in 1908 Husserl and McTaggart are at the starting point of a footrace waiting to hear the starting gun fire. If McTaggart's experience conformed to his own theoretical description of it, then, on the supposition that the specious present extends into the near future, McTaggart, the runner, would actually hear the gun before it fired. Suppose that the gun will go off at time t, which is still some number of seconds in the objective future. If McTaggart's specious present includes a real element of the future, McTaggart will start running before t (let's say t_{-12}, twelve seconds prior to t) because, according to Plumer, "that is when he will first *hear* the gunshot; it is something of which [he is] '*sensible*,' however indistinctly" (1985, 22). Assuming that the specious present varies in length for each runner, Husserl might not hear the gun until t_{-5}, five seconds before it goes off. McTaggart would have the jump on Husserl and we would expect all sorts of hoots and objections raised by phenomenology fans observing the race, assuming their specious presents corresponded somewhat with Husserl's.

Both McTaggart and Plumer conceive of the specious present on the Jamesian model defined by LA2; that's why Plumer thinks that, according to the specious present doctrine, McTaggart would actually and paradoxically *hear* the future sound. On Husserl's theory, however, things would not work this way. The runners' protentional projections of the gun's firing would not cause them to *hear* the gunshot at t_{-12} or t_{-5}, respectively, but simply to anticipate or expect the firing of the gun at some point in the immediate future. On Husserl's model both McTaggart and Husserl, the runners, would only *hear* the gunshot on the basis of a primal impression that occurs almost immediately upon t when the gun objectively fires. The specious present is not constituted so as to confuse our perception of time, making our future appear to be present. Rather, the protentional structure of consciousness allows for a *present anticipation* of the future. The future has only an intentional presence within the specious present, and precisely a presence *as something about to happen*. The protentional function tells us not that point t is occurring at point t_{-n}, but that point t *will* happen sometime to the future of t_{-n}.

As Plumer indicates, McTaggart's argument would also suggest the following. If there were a third runner, let's name him Broad, whose protentional consciousness was for some reason not functioning, and he only caught the sound of the gun through the retentional performance of consciousness, he might begin running at t_{+12}, twelve seconds after the gun fires, "still able to claim that he *hears* it" (Plumer 1985, 23). Again, on Husserl's model, and in reality, this is not what actually happens. It is not the case that Broad would continue to *hear* the sound of the gun after it had stopped firing. Rather what the retentional structure of consciousness intends should not be confused with either an after-image (reverberation), or a "memory-image" that remains present. This would be to return to the Lotzean assumption, LA2, rejected by Husserl. Rather, retentioning retains in the specious present what is just-past qua just-past, not qua present. The retentioning function will tell each runner at t_{+n}, not that the gun is still firing, but that the gun has already been fired.

Plumer's objection can hold only on the model of the specious present that maintains the Lotzean assumption of the persistence of memory-images, LA2. Husserl provides a model of the specious present that does not reduce the past or future to an objective present. Husserlian runners, like all normal runners, would anticipate the firing of the gun; would actually hear the gun almost immediately upon its being fired; and, as they started running, would be aware of the gunshot as receding into the past in a way analogous to the spatial receding of the starting line, which also would be faster for some than for others. It may well be that for some runners the gunshot may cease to be part of their specious present objectively sooner or later than for other runners, depending on the retentional reaches of the runners, but that would not make the event objectively or even subjectively past and present at the same time, as McTaggart had suggested.

Intermodal differences in the specious present

Plumer's example of hearing the duck's quack before feeling the duck's diaphragm move, and this before seeing it open its bill, certainly would be wild, as he suggests, but it would only take place on a model of the specious present that depended on LA2. On Husserl's model the following situation would be perfectly consistent with a non-Lotzean specious present. It may have been the case that I anticipated (by means of the protentional function) the duck to quack, but failed to anticipate the movement of the diaphragm (because, for example, I was ignorant of duck anatomy). This would not mean, however, that I *hear* the quack before I *feel* the diaphragm. Or again, the retentional reach of my sense of sight might be more finely tuned—my visual retentioning may reach further back, in contrast to a shorter auditory retentional reach. This does not mean that I perceive the duck as keeping its bill open longer than required for the quack to come out. The open bill and the quack are sensed in a complex of primal impressions at the same time as the movement of the diaphragm. The difference in retentional reach means that, having seen the opening and closing of the bill and having heard the quack more or less simultaneously, the visual sense of the opening and closing of the bill stays with me, as a just-past event, slightly longer than the auditory sense of the quack. In other words, the sound is simply not retained as long as the vision. This is not an unusual occurrence even on the more complex level of an act of memory. I often remember faces but fail to remember the names that go along with them, even if I had originally seen the face and heard the name together. On Husserl's model, we might say, Plumer's duck is really a red herring.

Some other perplexities associated with Lotzean assumptions

Plumer is right to object to the idea that in the specious present we *hear* the beginning and the end of an enduring uttered sentence simultaneously. If this were the case we would indeed end up with a confused chorus of words rather than an organized sentence. But this would be the case only if the view proposed by the Jamesian tradition were correct. Plumer's objection does not touch an account of the specious present that rejects LA2. The "fading" that occurs in retentioning does not mean that the sound still lingers around, really present in consciousness but with less and less intensity, getting less and less loud. Rather, "fading" means that the sound takes its place in a just-past moment or duration that continues to recede. We retain the sound not as present but with the temporal modification of just-past. The sound is "present" only intentionally, not as actually sounding. The "fading" that occurs is a formal, temporal fading, not one that can be described in terms of Humean "force and vivacity" (cf. Plumer 1985, 27, 33). It is not that the sound persists, only with less force; it is rather that the sound gradually distances itself from our current experience.

Plumer argues that "sensation at an instant . . . encompasses objects as they are at an instant" (1985, 27). His concept of an instantaneous sensible present depends on LA1, the Lotzean assumption of the momentariness of the act of consciousness ("sensation at an instant"). Husserl and Broad give up this assumption as unrealistic. Even a quick glance takes time. But even if we equate the quick glance (in the case of glancing at the clock, for example) with one phase of consciousness, the length of the specious present does not depend upon the duration or lack of duration of some sensed movement or non-movement. If, in a quick glance, I see the second hand stationary, this is simply one momentary objectivity or event that falls within a succession of objectivities or events encompassed by the specious present. Since my sensing intends an interval of duration, thanks to the retentional-protentional performances of consciousness, the sensed stationary second hand can take its place within a context of a wider sensed duration, just as a sensed note of a melody will take its place within the sensed melody. In no case does the sensed content of one event have to fill up the entire interval of the specious present in order for there to be a specious present.

By embracing the two Lotzean assumptions, LA1 and LA2, Plumer actually returns to Brentano's (and ultimately, an Augustinian) theory of time-consciousness. Not only does his theory share with Brentano's the two Lotzean assumptions, but also, in arguing that sensation at an instant encompasses objects as they are at an instant, he embraces precisely the conclusion that Husserl had found so troubling in Brentano, namely, that on such an account we do not really experience (sense or perceive) melodies or any temporally extended objects. We sense only momentary instances and then must add "phantasy presentations" (Brentano) or memory (Plumer). So, as Plumer puts it, "in the clock example, no matter what hand you are looking at, at an instant you are *seeing* the hand where it is at an instant and *remembering* it where it has been" (1985, 28).

Husserl indicates a number of unresolvable difficulties associated with this kind of theory (1991, 16ff.). One such difficulty is apparent in

Plumer's argument against Mundle. Mundle had made the experiment of moving a white piece of paper across his field of vision at a fast rate of speed. He reported seeing a "white streak" even after the paper had stopped its movement. Mundle claimed that this indicates that "visual sensations linger and fade for an appreciable period," and he wanted to equate this period with the specious present (1953, 38). Whether Mundle is right to claim that the white streak that we see is really an aspect of the external physical event, or Plumer is right to claim that the white streak is an after-image, Plumer is still forced to admit that we *see* the white streak. Even if what we are seeing is the result of an after-image, the white streak is a temporally extended object that we *see*.[3] It is not the case that we see only one moment of the white streak and then associate a memory or a series of memories with that momentary seeing in order to construct the image. Regardless of the metaphysical and epistemological claims one can make about the status of the white streak, the phenomenological evidence that Mundle cites is convincing.

In conclusion, we can say that Husserl's theory, which accounts for the possibility of the specious present, disarms the standard arguments that have been directed against the specious present concept. Husserl's theory is capable of explaining, not only the structured nature of immediate experience, and our lack of ability to measure the specious present, but also the less abstract phenomena of footraces, quacking ducks, clocks, sentences, and white streaks. Husserl's theory should not be equated with James's, Broad's, or Mundle's theories of the specious present, nor is it equivalent to the theory that is criticized by the arguments of Mabbott and Plumer.

The Principle of Simultaneous Awareness

In the previous chapter I reviewed a number of interpretations of Husserl that failed to see the difference between his account of the specious present and that of the Jamesian tradition. One of the more influential of these interpretations is made by Izchak Miller. His reading of Husserl fits into a larger project to develop a reinterpretation of Husserl in light of his possible contribution to cognitive science (Miller 1982, 1984).

Miller bases his interpretation of Husserl on what he calls "The Principle of Simultaneous Awareness" (PSA). Although he declines to give a general formulation of this principle, he bases it on Husserl's summary of LA1 and LA2, the assumptions that, Husserl says, derive from Herbart and Lotze, and that continue to operate in Brentano's analysis of time-consciousness. Husserl paraphrases Lotze's assumptions in the following way: "In order to grasp a succession of representations (a and b, for example), it is necessary that the representations be the absolutely simultaneous objects of a knowing that puts them in relation [= LA2] and that embraces them quite indivisibly in a single and indivisible act [= LA1]." (1991, 21). Husserl goes on to explain that for Brentano LA2 requires LA1: "It appears to be an evident and quite inescapable assumption of this conception that the intuition of an extent of time occurs in a now, in one time-point" (1991, 21). But LA1 appears self-evident only if LA2 guides the interpretation. Husserl, however, as we have seen, critiques Brentano and rejects both LA1 and LA2.

In referring to PSA, Miller confuses the positions of Brentano and Husserl. After citing Husserl's text on Brentano's Lotzean assumptions, he correctly formulates the following statements to explain Husserl's point about the Lotzean conception at work in Brentano: "An awareness of succession derives from simultaneous features of the structure of that awareness. . . . A *continuous* awareness of a tone as enduring must involve an awareness of (at least) some temporally extended part of the tone at any given *instant* of that awareness" (Miller 1984, 109). These statements, which define PSA, do construe Husserl's position correctly, but, in contrast to what Miller implies, they are not really elaborations or extensions of the Lotzean conception. In the Herbart-Lotze-Brentano conception, as Husserl characterizes it, a succession of representations are made simultaneous objects. Husserl's own position does not require a simultaneity of objects or contents, but does require, as Miller rightly puts it, "simultaneous features" of the act of continuous awareness (that is, the retentional-protentional structure of consciousness) so that in any instantaneous phase or cross section of that continuous awareness I am aware of the object as enduring. There is a clear difference between Brentano's position, which depends on both LA1 and LA2, and Husserl's position, which depends on a rejection of LA1 and LA2.

Despite this difference Miller claims that "Like Brentano, Husserl regards PSA as a necessary condition for temporal awareness" (1984, 120). In this regard he again cites Husserl, a text from 1909: "But it surely does belong to the essence of the intuition of time that in each point of its duration . . . it is consciousness *of what has just been* and not merely consciousness of the now-point of the object that appears as enduring" (Husserl 1991, 33–34). Husserl's statement, however, does not imply LA2, and more to the point, since the intuition of time has its own duration, it denies LA1. To say that at any instant (that is, in any momentary phase) of an enduring act my awareness must simultaneously involve "earlier and later temporal perspectives" does not require either of Brentano's Lotzean assumptions.

Miller continues to confuse the difference between Husserl and Brentano by suggesting that PSA is actually equivalent to the Lotzean assumptions. More specifically he states that "the dogma of the momentariness of a whole of consciousness," by which Stern means "the necessary isochronism of its members," or in other words, LA2 with LA1 implied, all of which Stern rejects, is "a rough formulation of, what I called earlier, *The Principle of Simultaneous Awareness,* or PSA" (1984, 165).

According to Miller, "Stern was convinced that the requirements of PSA" could only be satisfied by what we have been calling LA2, which Stern clearly rejected as "artificial." So, on Miller's reading, Stern rejects PSA. But, Miller continues, "Stern was mistaken in assuming that the requirements of PSA can be satisfied only through [LA2]." In fact, Miller claims, Husserl maintained PSA although he rejected LA2. But Miller would still have Husserl maintaining LA1. "Stern's main reason for rejecting PSA is that the latter involves the postulation of *instantaneous states of awareness* ('the dogma of the momentariness of consciousness') [LA1], and he maintained, it seems, that there are no such states of awareness. This objection, if sound, is as much an objection to Husserl's theory as it is to Brentano's" (1984, 165).

I think that Miller misinterprets both Husserl and Stern on this point. It is possible to formulate PSA (and Miller comes close to doing so) without equating it to, or requiring, LA1 or LA2. If, as Miller puts it, "an awareness of succession derives from simultaneous features of the structure of that awareness," that does not mean that the awareness is instantaneous, as LA1 would have it. If, as Husserl indicates, every point of the duration of the intuition of time involves a consciousness of what has just been, this means, first of all, that the act of intuition is an enduring one rather than a momentary point. Husserl explicitly rejects the momentariness of consciousness. For example, in trying to sort out the question of whether the temporality (duration) of the act of consciousness objectively corresponds or does not correspond to the perceived duration (1991, 74, 114f.), Husserl always maintains that the perceptual act is itself a duration and that it always appears that way to phenomenological reflection (1991, 53, 116). Thus, Husserl characterizes an act of consciousness as "an immanent duration-unity constituted in a series of retentional phases" (1991, 122).

Notwithstanding his claims in this regard, Miller himself seems to acknowledge that for Husserl the act of temporal awareness has its own duration. Immediately upon claiming that Husserl maintains PSA, Miller cites a text in which Husserl speaks of the intuition of time having its own duration (Miller 1984, 120; Husserl 1964, 53–54; Husserl 1991, 33). In his analysis of Husserl's position Miller frequently remarks on "the past and future of the *act* itself," the "concurrency" of the temporal object and the act of perception, the progression of an act through an extension of time, the "temporal 'passage' of our very acts of consciousness," and the act of consciousness as "temporally extended" (1984, 123, 126, 142, 149, 150). He writes, for example, that "my continuous awareness of the temporal continuity of the act requires, at any given *instant* of the duration of that act, an awareness of a *temporally extended* part of the act" (1984, 151).

Despite his recognition of Stern's rejection of LA1 and LA2, Miller goes on to associate Stern with the Jamesian tradition of the specious present. He assumes that "what [Stern] meant by 'apprehension' is similar to, if not identical with, Wundt's use of the term to designate an act of *judgment*" (1984, 166ff.). But Wundt, like Lotze, and in contrast to Stern, treats the temporal synthesizing judgment as a momentary act that makes successive contents simultaneous, implying LA1 and LA2. In fact, Stern clearly distances himself from Wundt's conception of *die Auffassung der Empfindung* and claims that his own "collective concept" of apprehension (*Auffassung*) has a wider and more complex sense than Wundt's concept, since it includes sensorial or perceptual processes in which we become aware of temporal change (Stern 1898, 12–13, 122–23).

In his analysis of Broad's doctrine of the specious present Miller adopts Mabbott's analogy of the searchlight and asserts that it works equally well for Husserl's account. "According to that analogy, our act of sensing is like a searchlight, with a constant span of illumination (representing the span of the specious present), which is continuously moving parallel to, and along, its 'target'—the sense datum—as it 'illuminates' it" (Miller 1984, 171). Miller, however, rejects Mabbott's criticism of the analogy, that "it makes the source of illumination punctiform" (Mabbott 1951, 161). Mabbott, like Stern, rejects LA1, the possibility of "a momentary act of apprehension." Miller, however, reasserts LA1 and attributes it to Husserl and to Broad. He ignores the fact that both Husserl and Broad drop the abstract assumption of the momentariness of consciousness. Only at the very end of his analysis of Husserl's account of time-consciousness does Miller seem to suggest something different.

> Husserl, indeed, acknowledges that all the acts which we reflectively observe have some positive duration. It might even be a *necessary* fact that all our acts extend over a greater than zero interval of time. However, if it is a necessary fact, then the principle governing it *must be compatible* with PSA. . . . That is, it must be compatible with the details of Husserl's account. (1984, 174)

It would seem, then, that either Husserl is inconsistent in maintaining *both* PSA, which, on Miller's interpretation, includes at least LA1, the assumption of momentary consciousness, *and* that perception itself has its own duration, or Miller is inconsistent in his interpretation. It seems clear to me that in his final analysis Husserl was consistent, and that his consistent rejection of both Lotzean assumptions enabled him to give an adequate account of time-consciousness in the relation between an extended *Präsenzzeit* and a specious present. It also seems clear that PSA can be made consistent with Husserl's account only if it is not equated with LA1. The "simultaneous features" of awareness do not entail the momentariness of awareness, but actually account for the intentional unity of an extended act of consciousness.

However, even if we go this far to allow PSA a consistency with Husserl's theory, I would maintain that it wins this consistency at the cost of abstraction. Simultaneous awareness, in spite of the fact that it can only be an aspect of a nonmomentary act of awareness, nonetheless remains an abstract aspect, explainable in terms of abstract phases that then require an artificial conception of integration. These are issues to which we now turn.

Some Internal Limitations of Husserl's Analysis

Distortion and reification in phenomenological reflection

Husserl's description of time-consciousness is based on the concept of a *phase* of consciousness. In contrast to the unrealistic assumption LA1, an act of consciousness is said to have duration. Yet, the functions of primal impression, retentioning, and protentioning are pictured as structures within an abstract, momentary phase of the enduring act. Husserl calls this phase a "cross section" (*Querschnitt*) of the conscious act. Consider the following description of the perception of a melody according to Husserl's analysis. If a melody is sounded and perceived, our perception of the melody as a whole must have phases corresponding to each note so that the notes are perceived in the proper temporal order of earlier and later. Each phase of the perceptual act, therefore, although it corresponds to a particular present note in the melody, must (if it is to intend in the proper order) intend several successive points of the temporal object (melody) in various temporal modes, and not simply the present note to which it corresponds. So, in order to intuit the temporal position of the present note in relation to the other (past and potentially future) notes of the melody, there must be a perceptual phase for each note which includes a primal impression of that note, a retentioning of the previous note, and a protentioning of that which is to follow.

In this account the impression, retentioning, and protentioning are not individual phases of perception; rather, each phase is triadically structured by these intentional functions. The phase is a cross section of the act. Husserl writes, "Thus every perception breaks down into cross-sections [*Querschnitte*]" (1991, 239; see 1966b, 316). He describes a cross section of perception as "thick," in the sense that it has a certain "depth" to it, or that it is the perception of more than simply the present note of the melody.

The idea that the phase is momentary, without duration, seems to lead us back to LA1, or to the old notion, rejected by Hume, among others, that the parts of a duration are themselves without duration. Some clarification of the status of the phase or cross section of consciousness is required. I want to suggest that what Husserl called a *Querschnitt* or *phase* is really a *Querschnittansicht,* a cross-sectional *view* of the perceptual process. A *Querschnitt* can only be a descriptive abstraction from the enduring process or flow of consciousness, an ideal limit useful for the clarification of the structure of consciousness, but not itself a momentary act. In the actual process of perception, or any other cognitive act, there is no such thing as a phase, because, as Husserl notes (1991, 55), a phase has no possibility of being an enduring extension, and an act of consciousness is precisely that, an enduring extension. Indeed, if an act of consciousness were momentary it would not be necessary for Husserl to appeal to the notion of a phase at all.

The use of this descriptive abstraction in Husserl's account is the only way in which his analysis is similar to Broad's explanation of the specious present. Broad first abstractly posits a momentary perception, just as Husserl abstractly describes a momentary phase of perception. As both Broad and Husserl realize, however, perception never actually functions momentarily or as an abstract *Querschnitt*. Although Husserl maintains that it belongs to the essence of experience that it "must be extended in such a way, that a punctual phase can never exist by itself" (1991, 49), he tends to reify or hypostasize the phase and to treat it as something that is actually "for itself" in consciousness. He tends to localize the phase so that it would almost seem to occupy a measurable place within objective time. The result is that these phases are characterized as discrete even within their interdependency. Consider the following example: "Phases of experience and continuous series of phases exist in the flow. . . . To be sure, in a way it is also an objectivity. I can direct my regard towards a phase that stands out in the flow or towards an extended section of the flow, and I can identify it in repeated re-presentation, return to the same section again and again, and say: this section of the flow" (Husserl 1991, 118). The unity or continuity of consciousness is thus pictured as an interconnectedness of separable and identifiable phases (see Husserl 1962, § 78; 1966b, 315ff.; 1991, 211ff., 235, 243, 249, 282–83).

Closer to the truth, the phases of the continuous flow of consciousness are not distinct from the flow itself; they appear as such only in phenomenological reflection. They represent the form or structure that the flow of consciousness takes in reflection. The abstract phases are not *things* in the flow, but are the flow abstractly described (see Husserl 1991, 29). In reading Husserl, we need to take more seriously the following warning about reflection, which Husserl himself provided:

> We must therefore distinguish: the prephenomenal being of experiences, their being before we have turned towards them in reflection, and their being as phenomena. When we turn towards the experience attentively and grasp it, it takes on a new mode of being; it becomes "differentiated," "singled out." And this differentiating is precisely nothing other than the grasping [of the experience]; and the differentiatedness is nothing other than the being-grasped, being the object of our turning-towards. (1991, 132)

Reflection itself is an act of consciousness that does not escape the flow-structure. Reflection itself has its own impressional, retentional, and protentional functions that turn the reflected flow into a temporal object with earlier and later parts. But this is a distortion that Husserl recognizes and tries to work around. It would be absurd, Husserl says, "to doubt whether in the end, the *Erlebnisse,* which pass into the [reflective] glance, are not changed, precisely through that [glance] into something totally different" (1962, § 77).

Husserl's worry about the distortions that can be introduced even by the most careful phenomenological reflection extends to the structures that seem to characterize the flow of experience. Reflection has the tendency to freeze the incessant movement of experience. He suggests that impressional, retentional, and protentional performances, as well as phases, and acts *"are non-temporal; that is to say, nothing in immanent time"* (1991, 346; see 79). He thus cautions against reification. "One should not reify [*verdinglichen*] the structure of consciousness, one should not falsify the modifications of consciousness into modifications different in principle, etc." (1966a, 324 / 1991, 337, trans. revised). Reification not only takes the form of spatialization, which Lotze (1884) and Bergson (1965) warn against, but also temporalization. Reflection distorts the flux of consciousness by imposing upon it the form of objective time.

Does Husserl ever seriously consider that the concept of "the flow" itself might be the product of reflection, a metaphor used by reflection to structure experience? At one point he suggests that the flux itself is "quasitemporal," so the functioning of the flux cannot be "in time" (1977, 200; also see 477; 1966b, 316; 1991, 88, 205, 382, 393). Reflection, perhaps, distorts the quasitemporal status of the flux of consciousness.

What precisely does "quasitemporal" mean? Husserl's famous qualification here is that "for all of this, names are lacking" (1964, 100). This appears as an aporia in Husserl's theory unless one is willing to accept the interpretation that the quasitemporal is in some way nontemporal, something with a Kantian, transcendental status. Husserl seems to take this route. In the following chapters I want to explore other possible routes that take seriously the idea that "names are lacking." For now, however, we suggest that this aporia indicates one of the limitations of phenomenological reflection.

Integration, protentioning, and content

What Husserl says of the phase he also says of primal impression: it is "only an ideal limit, something abstract, which can be nothing by itself" (1991, 42). This must also apply to retention and protention to the extent that we may be tempted to define them as discrete parts of phases. In fact, however, they are neither things nor ideal limits; they are functions or performances. Moreover, a primal impression is nothing *in abstracto* but is always integrated with retentioning and protentioning. The integration of performances counts as everything in this analysis. Miller rightly notes that the intentionality of the retentional-protentional structure depends on the integration of that structure. Retentioning is not a discrete intentionality that can function independently of its place within the flow of consciousness (Husserl 1984, 142, 159). The concept of integration, however, is left undeveloped in Husserl. I think the reason for this lack of development is the underdevelopment of another concept: protention. Husserl says everything there is to be said about retentioning, but very little about protentioning.

Husserl does identify protention as a primal expectation.[4] Similar to the retentional performance, protentioning is not a conscious act of expectation; it does not thematize or make what it intends into an object. It is a tacit intentional performance of consciousness whereby the immediately intended horizon of consciousness yet to come is integrated into the specious present. In several texts Husserl hints that protentioning is simply the reverse or inverse of retentioning, that is, a turned-around, forward-directed retentioning (see 1991, 57f.; 1962,

§§ 77, 81). This cannot be the case, however. First, retentioning is always a fulfilled intentioning of previous functionings of consciousness that are actualized and determinate. In contrast, protentioning is necessarily, as it functions, an unfulfilled intentioning directed toward an immediate but indeterminate about-to-become. That which is protended is pure possibility rather than something actual or actualized. There is nothing determinate for protentioning to protend since the intended about-to-be functioning of consciousness (i.e., the just-future phase) has not yet taken place. Thus, while retentioning is intentionally fulfilled, protentioning is intentionally unfulfilled (Husserl 1966b, 323ff.).

It follows, secondly, that whereas retentioning always involves a retentional continuum, a retentioning of previous retentioning, protentioning cannot be a continuum, a protentioning of protentioning, since the would-be intended protentional functionings of consciousness have not yet occurred. At one point Husserl speaks of a "horizon of protentions" (1991, 118). This is preferable to what he refers to in *Ideas* as a "protentional continuum" (1962, § 81). Protentioning cannot be a gradual and orderly fading into obscurity; it must be an unregulated, relatively indeterminate, and temporally ambiguous sense of what is to come.

The asymmetry of retentioning and protentioning is implied by Husserl himself when he indicates that the "style" of actual protentioning is modified by the ongoing retentional functioning in a way that protentioning could not modify retentioning. Just as what we have already experienced often constrains what we expect to happen next, so the intentional content that is retained would seem to influence the protentional process. In a completely different way, actual protentioning will affect retentioning that has not yet occurred, in the sense that retentioning will always be a retentioning of just-having-been protentioning, but not vice versa. Husserl also indicates a relation between protentioning and primal impression: the primal impression of a later phase of consciousness will define the fulfillment or the "disappointment" of the just-having-been protentioning (see Husserl 1966b, 323–24). We would also expect this sense of fulfillment or disappointment to affect the "style" of the retentioning that follows. All of these relations, if better specified, could help to define the necessary integration of these functions.

The nature of this integration, then, needs to be further explored. Husserl suggests that this integration is purely formal, depending not on the content of consciousness, but on the purely structural or functional aspects of consciousness. The idea that there has to be a formal integration among impressional, retentional, and protentional functions, however, may indicate another instance of reflective reification. Are these concepts best construed as separate functions within a phase of consciousness, or is it possible to conceive of these three functions as simply different aspects of an already unified performance? Alternatively, in the concepts of "style," "fulfillment," and "disappointment," one may start to recognize the possibility that the *content* of experience may be responsible for shaping what Husserl takes to be purely formal (content-independent) structures. Perhaps reflection, directed at this microcognitive, quantum-experiential level, falls subject to a phenomenological uncertainty principle. This constitutes a further aporia that results from the internal limitations of phenomenological reflection.

PART 2

THREE STUDIES OF
PRENOETIC EFFECTS

5

The Theater of Personal Identity

It is no accident that Hume's thought fascinated Husserl more and more.

—*Jacques Derrida*

The philosophical problem of personal identity has been traditionally defined on the basis of Locke's conception of time-consciousness. Briefly stated, the problem involves determining whether I, who consciously experience myself in the present moment, am the same person who had been experiencing in the just-past moment, or in even more remotely past moments. There are a variety of approaches that attempt to resolve this first-person identity problem. James (1890), for example, took the view that a continuous, marginal awareness of one's own body, an experience that is constantly in the background or horizon of one's consciousness, sufficed to unify personal experience. On this account, however, as on many others, the problem is simply pushed back. It involves what Anthony Quinton (1975) calls a regressive criterion. How do I know, with any degree of certainty, that the body I experience at this moment is the same body that I experienced in the past? Furthermore, how do I know that I am the same person who experienced this body in the past? The proposal that the unity of consciousness is guaranteed by the experiential unity of the personal body is regressive because the unity of the experience of the personal body, as a conscious experience, depends on the unity of consciousness.

As a solution to the regressive nature of bodily identity, James had posited a comparative judgment that synthesizes the past and the present and thus forms the basis for ascertaining identity. This solution, however, depends entirely on the possibility of time-consciousness bringing the past and the present, successive states, into the simultaneous synthesis of a single cognitive act. As we have already seen, James's conception of this synthesis involves the cognitive paradox; thus his account of personal identity remains problematic.

Husserl, on the other hand, escapes the cognitive paradox and so, it might be proposed, offers a solution to the problem of personal identity on the fundamental level of time-consciousness. I want to explore this proposal in a wider context that relates Husserl's phenomenology both to the traditional problem of personal identity and to more recent poststructuralist decenterings of subjectivity. Although there are various poststructuralist approaches to the question of subjectivity, I focus my considerations on Jacques Derrida's reading of Husserl's account of time-consciousness. More specifically, I will examine the issue of personal identity within a historical context, placing Derrida at the most recent point of a philosophical conversation that includes Hume and Husserl.

Hume-Husserl-Derrida: this is no arbitrary grouping, for Derrida places himself directly into this conversation by deconstructing Husserl's attempt to answer Hume's challenge to identity in general and personal identity in particular. To the extent that Derrida contests Husserl's answer to Hume, he not only begins to uncover the metaphysical underpinnings of Husserl's phenomenology, but introduces an uncertainty into the very certainty Husserl's account seemed to offer. Derrida not only forces us to confront the question of the adequacy of Husserl's account of time-consciousness to the problem of personal identity, he does so in a way that throws the phenomenological paradigm itself into doubt.

Husserl's Reading of Hume

In order to address these questions we take our point of departure and orientation from Hume's famous text on personal identity in his *Treatise*. Hume's text contains both a critique of personal identity and an affirmation concerning the nature of consciousness.

> For my part, when I enter most intimately into what I call *myself,* I always stumble on some particular perception or other, of heat or cold, light or shade, love or hatred, pain or pleasure. I never can catch *myself* at any time without a perception, and never can observe any thing but the perception. . . . [We] are nothing but a bundle or collection of different perceptions, which succeed each other with an inconceivable rapidity, and are in a perpetual flux and movement. . . . The mind is a kind of theatre, where several perceptions successively make their appearance; pass, re-pass, glide away, and mingle in an infinite variety of postures and situations. There is properly no *simplicity* in it at one time, nor *identity*

in different; whatever natural propension we may have to imagine that simplicity and identity. (1739, 252–53)

The fundamental reality of consciousness is temporality—a temporal flow or succession of perceptions (impressions and ideas) that perpetually and spontaneously glide away. This flow is characterized by immanent disconnection. It is a *system of differences:* "the true idea of the human mind, is to consider it as a system of different perceptions or different existences, which . . . mutually produce, destroy, influence, and modify each other" (Hume 1739, 261). That one perception is different from another means, in Hume's mind, not only that each is distinct from every other—"is a distinct existence, and is different, and distinguishable, and separable from each other perception" (1975, 259; see 233)—but that consciousness is composed of *unconnected* perceptions and is therefore not a unitary phenomenon.[1] Difference takes priority over system; cinematic succession takes priority over theatrical structure—and precisely for this reason identity is put into doubt. Identity "is nothing really belonging to these different perceptions, and uniting them together; but is merely a quality, which we attribute to them, because of the union of their ideas in the imagination, when we reflect on them" (1975, 260). This line of thought radically opposes the metaphysical concept of identity and, seemingly, undermines Locke's solution to the problem of personal identity, that is, that memory guarantees the unity of consciousness over time. If, as Voltaire had maintained, Locke gave us the *history* of the soul, Hume gave us the soul as a romantic *fiction* written by the imagination.[2]

This was Husserl's reading of Hume, and for Husserl there was much to be admired here, but also much that required correction. We find Husserl's evaluation of Hume throughout his texts, from the *Logical Investigations* to the *Crisis*.[3] Aron Gurwitsch rightly noted that Husserl "repeatedly expressed a preference, even a marked one, for Hume rather than for Kant. According to Husserl, Kant did not fully see the problems which Hume had already posed in all radicality" (1966, 172–73). As Husserl himself stated: "Hume, as he is understood by Kant, is not the real Hume" (1970b, 95). Kant did not rightly see the "enigma" of the constitutional problem in transcendental subjectivity. In this respect, Hume "was much more radical than Kant" (1970b, 262). The term "constitution" for Husserl signified the result of a combination of conscious flow and its built-in unifying function (see 1962, §§ 230–33). To the extent that Hume brought us close to this concept in his analysis of the flow of consciousness, Husserl maintained, "he outlined for the first time what we call 'constitutional' problems" (1969, 256). But to the extent that he missed the intentional nature of the flow, he "completely *overlooked the fundamentally essential property of mental life* as a life of consciousness, the very property to which those [constitutional] problems relate" (1969, 257). In effect, the preference that Husserl had for Hume over Kant was tied to their different conceptions of the mind. For Hume the mind was a stream of consciousness, a flux of perceptions. For Kant, the mind was characterized by activities, functions, or operations autonomous and external to the flux.

Husserl, embracing Hume's radicality, viewed the mind as, at bottom, a flow of consciousness, but without the need for a special faculty, external to the flow, to account for its unity—without either an imagination that, according to Hume, habitually but mistakenly construes consciousness as a unified identity, or a formally independent transcendental function that, by Kantian accounts, imposes phenomenal unity on empirical consciousness. For Husserl, as we have seen, there is a unifying function built into the very structure of the flow that accounts for the intentional unity of consciousness. And this forms the necessary basis for a genuine (i.e., nonfictitious) personal identity. In effect, Husserl set out to defend identity from Humean difference while still maintaining a Humean flux.

For Husserl, in contrast to Hume, there is continuity rather than discontinuity in the flow of consciousness; a unity of process rather than difference. Husserl accounts for the unity of consciousness as well as the identity of the perceived object in the double intentionality of the retentional structure of consciousness.

In reference to the problem of objective synthesis, Husserl argues, in immediate opposition to Brentano, that we actually perceive a temporally extended object, such as a melody, in a temporally extended act of consciousness. The temporally extended object hangs together as a unity through any number of specious presents because the temporally extended act of consciousness is able to maintain its own continuity through its own retentional structure.

As we have seen, each momentary phase of an enduring act of consciousness is structured by three functions: primal impression, retentioning, and protentioning. For our purposes here, we focus on the retentional functioning. Again we may refer to the Husserlian diagram of time-consciousness (fig. 5.1). Consciousness functions in its primal impression so that it is consciousness of a simultaneously present object (e.g., a musical note as it is sounded). In its retentional function consciousness has an *intentional* awareness of the just-past phase of consciousness that contains its own (now elapsed) primal impression, and its own retentioning of the "just-just-past" phase of the act. This means that there is a retentional continuum that stretches back over prior experience—a retentioning of retentioning. The double intentionality of retentioning accounts for (1) the fact that retentioning intends, in the retentional continuum, the previous phases of consciousness as they elapse and move back into the short-term past; and (2) the fact that retentioning also intends, indirectly (in "transverse" intentionality), the previously intuited objects (e.g., the notes of a melody).

Thus, on the basis of this double intentionality Husserl explains how it is possible for consciousness to perceive a temporally changing or unchanging object as one identical object, without relying on the notion of the simultaneity of sense-data, LA2. Transverse intentionality ties together (constitutes) the appearing object; it allows consciousness to perceive the object in its continuity. A melody appears as a melody rather than as a succession of unconnected notes, because consciousness ties the succession into a sequence with continuity. Transverse intentionality, however, is only possible on the basis of horizontal intentionality, i.e., it is indirectly accomplished through the retentional continuum. Horizontal intentionality, for its part, unifies consciousness. The succession of phases of the act of consciousness are tied together, not externally, as if they were a *bundle* of disconnected and momentary perceptions, but internally, in their very structure.[4] Here one does not require an "external," extraperceptual act, such as memory (Locke), or imagination (Hume), or a form of intuition (Kant), to artificially unite perceptual consciousness—consciousness synthesizes itself in a passive, automatic self-constitution.

Fig. 5.1: Husserl's Diagram Modified

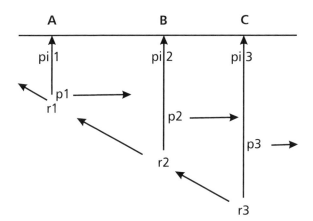

Precisely on the basis of this auto-affective self-unification Husserl predicates the continuity and identity of consciousness. "The stream of lived experience with its phases and intervals is itself a unity which is identifiable," not as a fictitious creation of the imagination, but in an act of memory or reflection that captures what is actually there and already constituted. "I who now perceive and perform this perception am identically the same one who find[s] myself in recollection as the I who has perceived the past. I recognize the absolute identity in reflection" (Husserl 1977, 159). I recognize identity in reflection only because the unity of consciousness has already been constituted within the flux itself. "The stream of experience with its phases and extents is itself a unity identifiable through memory together with the directing of one's regard towards what flows. . . . This unity becomes constituted originally through the fact of the flow itself; that is to say, it is the flow's proper essence not only simply to exist but to be a unity of experience and to be given in internal consciousness" (Husserl 1991, 121). Indeed, according to Husserl, the retentional continuum accounts for the very possibility of reflective self-consciousness. If reflection can grasp only what is just-past in consciousness (and this Husserl maintained—see 1991, 122) then for Hume to be able to see the bundle of perceptions that form his consciousness, retentioning must already be functioning to provide him with that which he sees in reflection, i.e., the just-past perceptions. If there were no retentional continuum Hume could not have reflectively examined his experience; his perceptions would not have appeared to him, in reflection, as bundled or as successive—indeed, reflection itself would be impossible since there would be nothing there to look at.

Husserl refers to the self-constituting, self-appearing flow of consciousness as an "absolute subjectivity" that maintains an identity in its continuous being (1991, 79). In this respect, Husserl acknowledges, the transcendental and self-identical ego is not ultimate; the self-identity of the ego is itself constituted on the basis of the self-constituting flow (see 1962, § 216). If the ego remains formally and "absolutely self-identical in all real and possible changes of experience," it does so only because the stream of consciousness binds itself together into "*one* single stream of experience, that, namely, which is mine" (1962, § 156). The transcendental ego, in this regard, is simply the formal, intentional but not real (*reell*) identity of the individual stream of consciousness. Indeed, Husserl contends that no real (*reell*) moment of the flux can be identical.[5] This is precisely where Hume's phenomenologically astute insight took him in the wrong direction. He looked for a *real* identity; unable to find one he concluded that identity must be fictional, a false image created by the imagination. For Husserl the identity of consciousness is intentional; not fictional, but not real (*reell*) in the sense of being an actual part or piece of the flow.

Husserl's analysis, from the ground up, depends upon the structure of the now-phase of consciousness with its intentional inclusion of the just-past and just-future. This is what Husserl calls the "living present." It makes reflection possible, and indeed, it makes possible the phenomenological "principle of all principles," i.e., the immediate intuition that brings to self-evident presence the phenomenon to be described. The structure and operations of the living present thus account for the possibility of phenomenology as a first-person science of consciousness. Husserl's science, as Derrida puts it, depends on "the purity of ideality, that is, openness for the infinite repeatability of the same" in a reflection that is determined by the living present as its source (Derrida 1973, 53). Because, for Husserl, there is a source-point that can be re-presented in reflection, then the pure ideality that phenomenology reaches in reflective intuition is not fictitious. As Derrida rightly notes, "this theme appears very early, and it will continually serve to feed the polemic against Hume" (1973, 55).

Derrida's Reading of Husserl

For Husserl the unity and identity of consciousness in self-presence is not broken up by differences or by disrupting forces that would be alien to the pure intentional immediacy of self-consciousness. In this regard, pure immediacy excludes extra-intentional elements, such as linguistic signs. Derrida characterizes Husserl's position as the traditional one. "Language and its representation is [*sic*] added on to a consciousness that is simple and simply present to itself, or in any event to an experience which could reflect its own presence in silence. . . . Signs would be foreign to this self-presence, which is the ground of presence in general" (1973, 58).[6]

To show how Husserl himself undermines the immediacy and non-difference on which depend self-presence and identity, Derrida goes directly to the "fundamental" level of time-consciousness. According to Derrida's reading, which sets out to show how Husserl goes against his own expressed intention, the immediacy of self-presence is always already disrupted by the mediation of retentioning that is built into the very structure of the now-phase of consciousness. "One then sees quickly that the presence of the perceived present can appear as such only inasmuch as it is *continuously compounded* with a nonpresence and nonperception, with primary memory and expectation (retention and protention)" (1973, 64). Retentioning introduces something other than the present, something disruptive into presence, i.e., something absent, the past, a trace of the past, a *sign* of the past. "This alterity is in fact the condition for presence, presentation, and thus for *Vorstellung* in general" (1973, 65). This difference, which Derrida calls a *différance,* a deferral of presence, is not introduced into presence from the outside. It is, as Husserl took pains to show, essentially built into the structure of presence, and thereby, according to Derrida, "destroys any possibility of a simple self-identity" (1973, 66). The living present depends upon the possibility of a retentional trace, and indeed has its origin in its nonidentity with itself. Derrida thus invokes the transcendental pluperfect: the present is "always already a trace" (1973, 85). The system of presence that guaranteed for Husserl the possibility of the self-identity of consciousness and the identity of self, is at bottom a system of differences. The "identity" of consciousness is "rooted in the finitude" of the retentional continuum, which is a continuum of nonpresence. If there is a continuity of consciousness, it is one based on a noncoincidence that is part of the very structure of consciousness. The difference of temporality thus undermines the identity of presence.

We can take this analysis slightly further along the lines of Derrida's reading, by pointing out that in spite of all of Husserl's good intentions, his account of the self-identity of consciousness demonstrates the impossibility of a literal self-presence for the most basic now-phase of consciousness. The structure of the living present, as Husserl describes it, is entirely ek-static. Each of the three structural functions of the now-phase is intentionally directed away from itself, and none of them is directed toward either of the others. Retention is directed toward a past phase; protention toward a future phase; and primal impression not toward a phase of consciousness at all, but toward the present object. Husserl neither finds nor provides for a self-reflective function built into the now-phase itself. So even if the retentional structure of the now-phase explains how consciousness can be reflectively aware of itself, the self-awareness happens only after the fact, and thus, at the cost of a lack of self-presence in the present moment of consciousness. The now-phase is absolutely absent to itself at the very heart of the process. There is nothing to capture the "living present" *in the act.* The living present turns out to be a living absence-to-itself that can only be made self-"*present*" when it is just-past, and therefore "*self*"-present, not to itself but to a new and different phase of consciousness.

Derrida does not argue against Husserl; he does not set out to show that Husserl's analysis is wrong; rather, he attempts to show that it holds within itself conclusions that Husserl failed to draw—conclusions that contradict the primordial nature of pure self-presence and identity.[7] Husserl demonstrates, even better than Hume, Hume's conclusions about personal identity. In this sense, Husserl convinces Derrida. "In the originary temporalization and the movement of relationships with the outside, as Husserl actually describes them, nonpresentation or depresentation is as 'originary' as presentation. *That is why a thought of the trace can no more break with a transcendental phenomenology than be reduced to it*" (Derrida 1976, 62).

What happens, then, to the conception of self-identity? Derrida maintains that the flux of *différance* is not something that happens to an already constituted transcendental subject; rather, "it produces a subject" (1973, 82). In Husserlian terms, the subject is not self-constituting, an absolute origin for itself; it is produced in a process that is more than what can be contained in its own intentional system. Thus, Derrida concludes, "the concept of *subjectivity* belongs *a priori and in general* to the order of the *constituted*. . . . There is no constituting subjectivity. The very concept of constitution itself must be deconstructed" (1973, 84–85 n. 9).

Subjectivity is not a self-constituting, closed sphere, but an opening to otherness, to differences already embedded in experience. It is openness to otherness and difference precisely because it is nothing *in itself* and requires as "compensation" a "supplement" "to *make up for* a deficiency . . . to compensate for a primordial nonself-presence" (1973, 87). Personal or self-identity has the same structure as a sign. It "arises in the role of supplement as primordial substitution, in the form 'in the place of' (*für etwas*)"—it stands in for something missing (1973, 88–89). The retentional trace *indicates* and thereby *signifies* something other than living presence, and as such it is an interweaving, a "text," an archewriting, a linguistic system in the most basic sense. Such linguisticality, as a system of differences, is not produced by the subject; the subject is produced in the system.

> Nothing—no present and in-*different* being—thus precedes *différance* and spacing. There is no subject which is agent, author, and master of *différance,* who eventually and empirically would be overtaken by *différance.* Subjectivity—like objectivity—is an effect of *différance,* an effect inscribed in a system of *différance.* . . . [T]he subject is not present nor above all present to itself before *différance,* [rather] the subject is constituted only in being divided from itself." (Derrida 1981a, 28–29)

Return to Hume?

From the purview of a poststructuralist reading of the inadequacy of Husserlian time-consciousness, we are motivated to reexamine the radicality of the Humean position. Does Derrida send us back to the radical thought of Hume? The answer will not be a simple "yes" or "no," but a compound "yes and no." First, we note that Hume, Husserl, and Derrida agree on a radical conception of consciousness as flux, in contrast to the Kantian model of cognitive faculties and operations. Indeed, this is the most radical and challenging aspect of Hume's thought for Husserl. Faced with the radical abyss of this nonrelational flux, however, Husserl cowers, and then bravely attempts to save the modern Cartesian *cogito* with its identity and certitude. In contrast one can find in Hume a certain postmodern-like courage in his willingness to let the Cartesian subject vanish into the discontinuous flow of experience. The displacement of Cartesian certitude in a self-identical *cogito* is certainly the common mark of all poststructuralist decenterings of subjectivity. But here we must start to qualify what might count as Hume's poststructuralism.

There still remain a number of Cartesian elements in Hume's analysis of personal identity, and in contrast to them we might see where Derrida is heading.

1. Hume's stated project, to provide an "accurate anatomy of human nature" (1975, 263), where human nature is placed in "the capital or cen-tre" of knowledge (1975, xvi), indicates a Cartesian-like foundationalism that centers rather than decenters subjectivity. The science of man, Hume notes, "is the only solid foundation for the other sciences, so the only solid foundation we can give to this science must be laid on experience and observation" (1975, xvi). To the extent that Hume would be consistent with his displacement of subjectivity, then his radical skepticism would have to undermine his stated project of defining human nature. In place of a "science of man" one could attain, at best, a science-fiction of man.

2. Hume's reliance on sense experience and observation is ex-pressed in terms of an appeal to evidence. This latter concept is, in Hume, no less than in Descartes and Husserl, understood to be an appeal to what is *present* in consciousness to a phenomenologically clear and distinct reflective grasp. In this regard, Husserl remarks that Hume "was the first to *treat* seriously the Cartesian focusing purely on what lies inside" (1969, 256). Derrida characterizes modern thought as this search for evidence; the privilege of conscious self-presence—the living present— "defines the very element of philosophical thought, it is *evidence* itself, conscious thought itself, it governs every possible concept of truth and sense" (1973, 62). To the extent that Hume would be consistent with his displacement of subjectivity, then, as we learn from Husserl, his access to *evidence* would be made impossible, i.e., his denial of the retentional continuum would amount to a foreclosure on the possibility of veridical reflection.

3. A third aspect of Hume's analysis reveals that his "displacement" of subjectivity was only half-hearted. We could say that in Hume only one-half of subjectivity was displaced; the other half was doing the displacing. The *imagination,* and along with it, memory, seem able to escape the flux. The status of these faculties would require a longer analysis. It is clear, however, that rather than vanish with the Cartesian ego, they continue to operate behind the scene, so to speak, to create the scene, the theater of subjectivity. Gilles Deleuze has pointed out that for Hume the imagination operates like a location: "the imagination is not a factor, an agent, or a determinate determination; it is a place which it is necessary to localize, that is, to fix in a determinable way. Nothing is done *by* the imagination, everything is done *in* the imagination" (Deleuze 1953, 3). If the *cogito* vanishes in the flux, the *excogito,* a simulacrum of the *cogito,* maintains itself slightly offstage. In the end, human nature is constituted as the constant or fixed imagination that, in turn, dependably constitutes the fiction of identity. Given this re-placement (rather than displacement) of the *cogito,* we should not, then, be surprised that Hume expresses a Cartesian concern to divide the subject and, indeed, personal identity, into distinct categories. "We must distinguish betwixt personal identity, as it regards our thought or imagination, and as it regards our passions or the concern we take in ourselves" (1739, 253).[8] In the realm of passions, temporality and the play of differences are moderated and mediated by the appearance of identity, so that in a less radical interpretation, Hume reiterates the solution put forward by Locke: "memory alone aquaints us with the continuance and extent of this succession of perceptions, 'tis to be consider'd, upon that account chiefly, as the source of personal identity" (1739, 261).

Hume's text seems to retreat from a poststructuralist interpretation. And yet, two remnants of Hume's analysis are retained, with certain modifications, in Derrida's analysis: the concepts of fiction and theater.

The poststructuralist decentering of subjectivity is won by Derrida in part through his struggle with Husserl's correction of Hume. Neither ego, nor *cogito,* nor *excogito* escape the play of *différance* that is the flux of con-sciousness. The subject is neither Hume's identity-producing imagination nor Husserl's *cogito,* a self-presence based on a self-constituting, unifying retentional structure, but a constituted product of this textualizing reten-tional interweaving. The personal subject is itself a text, a "fiction" of self-presence, produced by a prepersonal, infrastructural, extra-intentional textualizing that, Derrida says, "is not a *primum movens* [but] . . . imprints upon the whole a movement of fiction" (1981b, 57; see 1978, 226).

Yet, this fiction, unlike Hume's, is not written by the faculty of the imagination or traced out by memory. Unlike Husserl's retentioning we cannot even say that the text of subjectivity writes itself. In this respect Derrida denies "auto-affection" because that would imply a true subject behind the false one (1973, 78ff.). He denies that the living text of consciousness is an "auto-bio-graphy." Rather, the subject is written by writing, language, arche-trace. "The subject of writing is a *system* of relations between strata: the [Freudian] Mystic Pad, the psyche, society, the world. Within that scene, on that stage, the punctual simplicity [self-presence, self-identity] of the classical subject is not to be found" (1978, 227). Like any text, in Derrida's view, it has no intentional identity or unity of meaning. It is open to multiple readings. Personal identity is displaced by a polysemic flux that is anterior to personal and intentional existence (see 1976, 65). "Constituting and dislocating it at the same time, writing [trace, *différance*] is other than the subject, in whatever sense the latter is understood. Writing can never be thought under the category of the subject . . . the substantiality of a presence unperturbed by accidents or . . . the identity of the selfsame [*le propre*] in the presence of self-relationship" (1976, 68–69).

Like the concept of fiction, Hume's metaphor of the theater operates in a modified fashion in Derrida's analysis. More precisely, the poststructuralist moment pertains to the caution expressed about the metaphor, a caution that Hume had stated clearly: "The comparison of the theatre must not mislead us. They are the successive perceptions only, that constitute the mind; nor have we the most distant notion of the place, where these scenes are represented, or of the materials, of which it is compos'd" (1739, 253). Derrida also warns us about the "naive metaphorics of place" (1978, 212), which imply "the limpidity of an immobile, pre-given space" (1978, 213). This applies to Husserl's analyses, or at least those analyses that favor the static over the genetic: "the space of description," the "descriptive space" of phenomenology, "the phenomenological space," the "space of psychical [or transcendental] writing" (1978, 156, 157, 159, 212), the realm opened up by the phenomenological reduction which is, Derrida says, "*a theater stage*" (1973, 86).

In place of this pregiven space Derrida proposes an extra-intentional "spacing"; we could say that in place of the theater stage Derrida suggests a "theatering," a staging that is not under the control of intentional consciousness. The mind is not a space where meaning is produced; but meaning and space are equally produced in a play of difference that involves a process of "spacing" (1978, 123). Spacing, as "a certain spatiality inseparable from the very idea of system, is irreducible" (1978, 215). Conscious experience is etched in this system of *différance*/spacing, a system that "within that scene, on that stage," involves a continual disruption of "the punctual simplicity of the classical subject" (1978, 227).

Unlike Hume, however, Derrida does not leave a backstage intact; spacing displaces the "location" of the imagination and memory, as much as of the perceptual *cogito*. The entire theater of cognitive operations, what James too had called "the theatre of consciousness" (1890, 603) is, in this way, deconstructed. "The old theatrical organization has become unjustifiable," the subject has no fixed place, "except in the representation" it makes of itself to itself (see Derrida 1981b, 296).

The rejection of the theater metaphor challenges the Lockean-Husserlian paradigm which is that of a stream through a place. Lotze had pointed out the spatial nature of this paradigm very clearly:

> We cannot speak of a stream without thinking of a bed of the stream: and in fact, whenever we speak of the stream of Time, there always hovers before us the image of a plain which the stream traverses, but which admits of no further definition. . . . Nor is it this alone that disturbs us in the use of the image. Even the movement of the stream cannot be presented to the mind's eye except as having a definite celerity, which would compel us to suppose a second Time, in which the former (imaged as a stream) might traverse longer or shorter distances of that unintelligible background. (Lotze 1884, 239)[9]

In rejecting this metaphor Derrida displaces (de-spaces) the received image of consciousness and substitutes *différance*, spacing (which is neither space nor spatial). To deconstruct the space of consciousness, a present that is specious in more than one sense, he suggests a different metaphor, one that he finds in Mallarmé. Spacing is like "a hymen (out of which flows Dream), tainted with vice yet sacred, between desire and fulfillment, perpetration and remembrance: here anticipating, there recalling, in the future, in the past, under the false appearance of a present" (1981b, 294).

Someplace between Hume and Derrida, Husserl's project to make personal identity secure by solving the cognitive paradox goes astray. Husserl's account, even if it perfects the phenomenological paradigm, cannot account for the effects of certain extra-intentional, prenoetic factors, like the linguisticality and the alterity that Derrida finds embedded in the metaphorical stream of experience. We explore these extra-intentional factors further in the following chapters.

6

Disrupting Seriality: The Idea of a Post-Husserlian Temporality

B y identifying time-consciousness as the fundamental level of constitution, the very flux of human subjectivity, Husserl would make it the condition of possibility for all experience. Accordingly, every human experience would fall under this order, this law of constitution, this time principle. Experience necessarily would accord with the temporal structure explicated in the retentional-impressional-protentional performance of consciousness. On the one hand, an experience that would violate this law, understood as the eidetic norm of temporal structure, could only be classified as pathological. Psychopathology provides an account of abnormal experience as breaking the law, as exception, as variation.[1] On the other hand, however, if one could identify experiences that were not exceptional (at least not in the sense of the pathological), then one would have the basis for a different law, and, in effect, a critique of Husserl's account. Much of this critique is developed, in different ways, by Maurice Merleau-Ponty and Jean-François Lyotard. In part, their arguments are designed to undermine traditional conceptions of temporal succession. To see this clearly, and to best understand the concept of succession at stake in both Husserl's phenomenology and the criticisms of it, we briefly consider the concept of seriality as it is expressed in McTaggart's famous account.

Standard Concepts of Seriality

In his 1908 article on "The Unreality of Time," McTaggart introduced the important and clarifying distinction between what he called the A-Series and the B-Series. In defining the A- and the B-series McTaggart explicates both terminological and conceptual distinctions. The A-series is signified by the terms "past," "present," and "future"; the B-series by the terms "earlier" and "later." McTaggart explains that these two different vocabularies indicate an essential distinction in our concept of time. The meaning of the term "earlier" is not equivalent to the meaning of "past," nor is "later" the same as "future." Rather, one event can be earlier than another, and both events can be in the past, or both in the future.[2]

Conceptually McTaggart defines the A-series as involving change, movement, becoming. An event starts out in the remote future, is then in the near future, moves into the present, quickly becomes past, and continues to undergo temporal change in the sense that it becomes more and more removed from the present as it fades into the remote past. Thus events involve temporal change from future to present to past. The B-series, on the other hand, does not involve change. Once an event is earlier than another it remains that way. Events do not change their temporal position from earlier-than to later-than. The B-series expresses the *permanent order* of events. Caesar's conquest of Gaul happens earlier than Napoleon's defeat at Waterloo, and that order will never change. The B-series, then, signifies what we usually regard as the objective, chronological order of irreversible temporal succession: one thing comes after another, or as Whitehead famously put it, it's "one damn thing after another."

It is clear that Husserl, although unfamiliar with McTaggart's distinction, conceived of time as involving both an A-series and a B-series. The flux of consciousness undergoes continual change, constantly expiring in the retentional continuum, the present becoming past, and ever more past. Within the flow of the A-series, the retentioning process also maintains a certain temporal order among the phases of the flux, defining one phase as earlier than another in a series of expiring phases. Once a phase of consciousness expires, it never returns; it "runs off" in an orderly way according to the law of retentional fading. The *just*-just-past is earlier than the *just*-past, and it will continue to recede into the past in just this order. The operation of retention, even as it allows for the smooth and even A-series flow of experience, can nonetheless account for the permanent, serial order of temporal relations—the B-series.

The flow of consciousness, then, is an orderly flow organized by the retentional-protentional structure. It reflects the objective order of time and constitutes our access to it. Under normal circumstances an event will first enter into the intentional dimension of protention; it will then be impressed upon the present phase of consciousness, and as this phase flows into the past it will be retained in an orderly B-series, retaining its place earlier than some phases and later than others. The intentionality is straightforward and clear-cut; it does not twist the flow; it keeps the flux straight. The flux does not fold over upon itself making the earlier phase the object of a later protention, or the future phase already just-past. We avoid accidents in this way. I drive down the street and see a yellow traffic signal in front of me. I expect the signal to turn red. It does. I stop. I then expect the light to turn green. It does. I drive on. The red and the green are not simultaneously present in consciousness. There is no surprise; there are no ambiguous traffic lights. This describes our ordinary temporal experience of "one damn thing after another."

These concepts of seriality are pervasive, not only in the folk psychology of common experience, or in continental phenomenology, but in empiricist philosophy (Locke, Hume), traditional psychology (James), and recent philosophy of mind. Even in the cognitive sciences—where the connectionist idea of massively distributed parallel processing operates as the model for neural functioning, or where complexity and chaos theories are employed to describe how the brain works—when experience hits the level of consciousness, so to speak, it is inevitably characterized as a linear order that in some mysterious way emerges out of nonlinear, nonserial disorder. Dennett, for example, maintains that the "virtual machine" of consciousness, which emerges from the software of linguistic and cultural "memes," and which runs on a brain architecture that is parallel and that functions in a "pandemonius" way, is nonetheless a *serial* von Neumann-like machine. Dennett prefers to call consciousness a "Joycean machine" because it is still a stream, a serial phenomenon.[3]

I want to suggest that, to the extent that Merleau-Ponty and Lyotard develop a critique of Husserlian time-consciousness, specifically with respect to the issue of the seriality of conscious experience, this will also be a critique of these various other traditions, from British empiricism to the contemporary cognitive sciences.

Merleau-Ponty and the Reversibility of Temporality

Derrida's explication of *différance* in the very heart of Husserl's flux of consciousness is not without precedent. Merleau-Ponty finds in Saussure's structural linguistics the concept of diacritical difference, and, not unlike Derrida, he uses that concept to develop a critique of Husserl's account of time-consciousness.[4] He also recognizes the possibility of finding within conscious experience "a movement toward what could not in any event be present to us in the original and whose irremediable absence would thus count among our originating experiences" (1968, 159). In a way that suggests the inadequacy of traditional conceptions of succession and seriality, he identifies a certain disruption of time-consciousness that Husserl's analysis fails to account for.

Merleau-Ponty begins to develop his critique of the traditional view of time in his *Phenomenology of Perception* (1962). We note four aspects of this analysis. First according to Merleau-Ponty our experience of the A-series is tied, not as McTaggart would have it, to cognitive functions, but to our embodied perspectives. Change, he writes, "presupposes a certain position which I take up and from which I see things in procession before me: there are no events [temporal occurrences] without someone to whom they happen and whose finite perspective is the basis of their individuality. Time presupposes a view of time" (1962, 411–12).[5] Accordingly, time is not a process independent from or merely recorded by the experiencing subject. It arises from an embodied relation to the world. Second, he views the B-series as a form of measurement, not essential to time: "constituted time, the series of possible relations in terms of before and after, is not time itself, but the ultimate recording of time" (1962, 415). He learns this from both Bergson and Heidegger (1962, 420).

Third, Merleau-Ponty learns from Husserl to reject LA2. He maintains that "no preservation, no physiological or psychic 'trace' of the past can make consciousness of the past understandable. . . . A preserved perception is a perception, it continues to exist, it persists in the present, and it does not open behind us that dimension of escape and absence that we call the past" (1962, 413). In this same regard, Merleau-Ponty rejects the notion of an "intellectual synthesis" or synthesizing judgment that would combine past and present into an indistinguishable present. In this he recognizes the advantages of Husserl's account of retention (see 1962, 416–17), and, without mentioning James, he rejects the type of psychological explanation that James had embraced.[6]

Finally, Merleau-Ponty anticipates his own later analysis in *The Visible and the Invisible*, with concepts like *ecoulement* (lapse), *ekstase*, dehiscence, and transcendence. Still, it is clear that in his *Phenomenology of Perception* Merleau-Ponty remains very much under the influence of Husserl and Heidegger. Specifically, he identifies time with subjectivity: "we must understand time as the subject and the subject as time" (1962, 422). This is a position that he modifies in his later work, to which we now turn.

Limitations of reflection

We have already noted Husserl's caution about the distortion and reification involved in reflection (chapter 4). Merleau-Ponty makes this his starting point. Reflection, including phenomenological reflection, reads into experience, retrospectively, the origins of experience that it discovers only *post factum*. Reflection never coincides with the constitutive flow, nor does it simply retrace in a reverse direction the path taken by a constituting act of consciousness (see Merleau-Ponty 1968, 44–45; 1962, 243). Husserl had seen the temporal limitations involved in reflection which is both *in* the flow and *above* the flow. But had he taken them seriously? For Husserl, reflection is not installed within the flux; reflection is posterior to the flux and, as Merleau-Ponty points out, it finds, from that position, "a massive presence to self, the Retention's *Noch im Griff*, and through it the *Urimpression,* and the absolute flux which animates them" (1968, 49 n.).

> This is what Husserl brought frankly into the open. . . . To reflect is not to coincide with the flux from its source onto its last ramification; it is to disengage from the things, perceptions, world, and the perception of the world, by submitting them to a systematic variation, the intelligible nuclei that resist, and to proceed from one intelligible nucleus to the next in a way that is not belied by experience but gives us only its universal contours. (1968, 45–46)

Even here Merleau-Ponty is perhaps too polite. The point to be made is not that Husserl discovered a systematic method of reflective variation—the eidetic reduction—but that the variation brought on by reflective consciousness is systemic.[7] Not a discoverable method that delivers the essence of phenomena, but an unavoidable fact that introduces instability. Reflection does not capture the past in a way that is reliable enough for the precision needed for phenomenology. Perhaps it is this very instability that drives Husserl to eidetic abstraction. The universal contours of the *eidos,* however, smooth over the rough edges of particular differences in the temporal structure of consciousness. Thus we end up with abstract phases that have invariable, but essential functions, a frozen flux retrospectively constructed and laid out in a serial order, one phase after another.

Merleau-Ponty is motivated to ask whether a phenomenon that is essentially variation, change, flux, can be eidetically reduced to its invariable, unchanging, contours. Is it possible for every aspect of experience to be expressed in terms of essential invariants? Is it not the case that "certain beings—for example, the being of time—do not in principle elude this fixation?" (1968, 46). The fixation in the case of time, the linearity, the resulting seriality, helps the phenomenologist, as we have seen in the analysis of the specious present, avoid problems, perplexities, paradoxes, and reversals. But reflection requires that I forget or repress the "non-knowing of the beginning which is not nothing, and which is not the reflective truth either, and which also must be accounted for" (1968, 49). There is here a past that escapes the limits of reflective intentionality, a past, however, that is not nothing since it still has an effect on present experience.

Eidetic reflection is similar to the high-altitude thinking Merleau-Ponty calls the *Kosmotheoros*—a "sovereign gaze from elsewhere" that orders everything in its own temporal position and its own place. Like reflection, however, it is insufficient for an analysis of time, since even if I could attain the neutral sovereignty of a detached gaze I would still be embedded in a temporality that remains outside the theme of the gaze (see 1968, 113, 184). In effect, I would have to do the impossible, I would have to detach myself from the flow, i.e., from myself. I would have to "soar over my field," suspend "all the sedimented thoughts with which it is surrounded, first of all my time, my body—which is not only impossible for me to do in fact but would deprive me of that very cohesion in depth [*en épaisseur*] of the world and of Being without which the essence is subjective folly and arrogance" (1968, 112). In such a contemplative position our view is caught up within a timeless present that blocks our access to certain dimensions of temporality that we are directly involved in. Time is flattened out, smoothed over, reduced to the logical (and that means timeless) order of seriality.

Reflection makes this second order emerge from a first one that it is itself submerged in. As Johnson-Laird puts it, introspective reports "tend to force intrinsically parallel notions into a serial straitjacket" (1983, 470). Merleau-Ponty tries to think beyond seriality; he attempts to articulate time as diacritical difference. The now is not something *in itself*, a full presence that sequentially displaces other nows. Rather the now, like a sign in the system of language, is what it is only as a difference from every other now. Time, he suggests, is not the summation of temporal individual nows, "but the presence and latency behind each of all the others, and behind those of still others" (1968, 117). The interdependence of nows implies a "figurative" simultaneity, we might say a *specious* present, a virtual presence which Merleau-Ponty calls an "intertwining" (*entrelacs*), a chiasm, a reversibility. In this diacritical intertwining there are no simple, positive nows, no living presents fully in themselves, but only nows defined by what they are not, nows inscribed in a system of difference. The now is never immediate, but always mediated by a horizon of other nows that are not-nows, mediated by its lateral relations with these others.

This is not the straightforward intentionality suggested by Husserl. This is not the linear ordering of seriality without folds. Merleau-Ponty

suggests a latent twist in intentionality that disrupts seriality. What reflective phenomenology discerns as diachronous individual nows, and
retained presents, are what they are only by reason of an extensive
latent content of the past and the multiple possibilities of the future
that they both announce and conceal. We are so inextricably immersed
within temporal experience that in the prereflective order of things our
thoughts "do not hold under their gaze a serial space and time nor the
pure idea of series, but have about themselves a time and a space that
exist by piling up, by proliferation, by encroachment, by promiscuity"
(1968, 115).

"The serial time . . . is overcome"

Can we make sense out of this description (1968, 168) on a more experiential level? If in our "natural attitude" we tend to think of time
as constituting an orderly series of events; if, as Bergson suggested, we
ordinarily distort *durée* by spatializing it; and if something like that natural
distortion is still at work in phenomenological reflection, then Merleau-
Ponty's description would seem to be a description of pathological experience. Can we find examples of nonpathological experience that escapes
or undermines seriality.[8]

Let me begin by focusing on the nature of reflection, since that's
where Husserl hesitates and where Merleau-Ponty begins to shape his
criticism. An instance of pathology can show some surprising implications for the nonpathological. The pathology in question is known as
blindsight. In blindsight, the mechanisms of the eye and retina are intact,
but damage in the visual (striate) cortex region of the brain prevents the
subject from seeing. Much of the visual cortex can actually register visual
information coming in from the eyes, but due to neurological damage,
that information is never transformed into conscious experience. The
subject is blind. In experimental situations, however, if blindsight patients
are forced to guess about something (e.g., a flashing light or the position
or movement of some object) in their visual field, they do better than
chance in guessing the correct answer. The subject has some access to
the visual information in the brain, despite the blindness (Weiskrantz
1986). This sets the background for the following experiments.

Zihl and vonCramon (1980) asked three hemianopic blindsight
subjects to indicate when they "felt" that a light was present following
an auditory signal. They were asked to report their feeling in three
response genres: by blinking, by pressing a button, and by saying "yes."
Discriminative sensitivity turned out to be greater when the report was
in the form of a blink than in the form of a button press, and least in

the speech response. These results motivated Marcel (1993) to conduct further experiments.

1. In the first experiment, a similar blindsight patient, GY, was asked, when he *felt* a light come on, to respond in three ways (blink, button-press, verbal "yes") on each trial (an auditory click followed randomly on 50 percent of the trials by a light flash). Latencies were clearly not of a reflex type. On identical trials the subject's different detection reports dissociated. For example, the subject indicated a positive response with his eye, but not with his finger, or with his finger but not with his voice. The reverse pattern also occurred. Although he correctly remembered the instructions, he did not realize that there was a discrepancy in his reports.

2. In a second experiment GY was presented the same stimuli as in the first experiment, but each report genre was tested separately. Various constraints were introduced across several sets of trials concerning the timing of the report (immediate report, report after a two-second delay marked by an auditory click, report after an eight-second delay marked by an auditory click). In several sets of trials GY was instructed to guess when a light came on, irrespective of any conscious sensation. The results showed (a) that response delay on all response types had an effect; (b) that the genre of report still mattered—vocal responses, even at their best, were less accurate than other responses; and (c) that guessing performance was better than any corresponding sensing performance, and for guessing there was almost no difference between genres of report.

These are interesting results in a number of ways, and in at least one respect the interest extends beyond aspects of blindsight and goes directly to the issue of reflective access to one's own experience. We can see this more clearly in the following experiments.

3. A similar experiment to the second one was conducted on ten normally sighted subjects using a threshold luminance increment for the target. In response to a range of luminance increments subjects were asked to respond: "Definitely seen," "Guess yes," or "Not seen." The results of this experiment turned out to be almost exactly the same as for GY in the second experiment: separate effects of report genre and delay; greater accuracy in the guessing condition with almost no effect of report genre.

4. In a fourth experiment designed in a similar fashion to the first experiment with GY (all three report genres required on each trial, with the further condition that reports be made as fast as possible), normally sighted subjects again demonstrated similar results to GY.

How should we interpret this data? First, even for normal, non-pathological subjects, reflective access to perceptual experience is not the same across different genres of report. Subjects on the same trial are reporting with a button press that they see a light, and reporting orally that they do not see a light, or vice versa. If reports are indeed reports of experience then it appears that an experience is not independent of how it will be reported, but depends on both the genre and the timing of the report. This may mean that the nature of an intended report influences experience. Bisiach, Berti, and Vallar (1985) suggest that the nature of the response used to report a visual experience can alter the memory of the experience in as little as two seconds. But since in experiments 1 and 4 all three report genres were intended, this cannot be a complete explanation. An alternative hypothesis is that different ways of reporting have differential access to an experience. This would call into question the existence of a unitary reflective consciousness.[9] It would suggest not only a distinction between phenomenal experience (the sensed experience of the light) and reflective consciousness (the awareness that we are experiencing something which becomes the basis for the report), but divisions in the latter. The apparent contradictions revealed in the experiments (e.g., a subject's reports that he is both experiencing the light and not experiencing the light) are resolved only on the supposition that the experience is differentially available to divisions of reflective consciousness.[10]

If reflective access to the flow of experience is different after a delay on the order of seconds, or is different depending upon the mode of intended report, it would seem that there is no reason to trust that reflection, even of the phenomenological type, would be able to deliver a straightforward and reliable grasp of just-past experience. What should we say about the retentional structure of consciousness in such cases if it seems to work for subsequent reports that require button pushes, but fails to work for subsequent verbal reports? The seriality that retentioning is supposed to structure is open to the curious effect that a just-future experience (the report) can either enhance or cancel the just-past experience.

Consider the phenomenon of perceptual masking. Subjects are presented with a sequence of five letters in a fashion that masks two of them. When asked to indicate whether they saw a target letter, for example a *J*, the subjects respond in the negative with a "target absent" button push when it is one of the masked letters. Urged to report with a button push as fast as possible, however, subjects correctly indicate that the letter had been presented, but then go on to deny that it had been presented (Allport 1988, 174–75). It seems that the subject's phenomenal awareness of the letter was not only short-lived, but was then blocked, almost immediately, from both perception (the masking effect) and memory (at the time of report). The time frame (a matter of seconds) is such that only short-term memory is involved, or in Husserl's terms, retentions rather than recollection. In such cases the organization of intentional content causes a displacement or masking that reconfigures the retentional series. The retention of *J* seems to subsist for a moment and then disappear altogether, while the retentions of the other letters in the original sequence remain and are reinforced.

Merleau-Ponty points to different sets of experiences that disrupt seriality in a more esoteric manner. In cases of aesthetic experience, for example, we can find what he calls "a more occult time than natural time." Gary Madison (1981), pursuing this thought, suggests that in artistic expression there is a gathering together of the past in order to create a lateral universality. Art institutes a cultural/historical realm of meaning that is ordered differently than phenomenal seriality. The time of art and culture transcends mere succession. In cultural expression the past insists on remaining present; the earlier may in art be the later, the present may signify the future, the avant-garde.

What is at stake here is not a transcendent, universal, and therefore timeless realm of cultural or artistic truth, but a *different experience* of time. In the artist's experience one finds at work what Merleau-Ponty calls a "reversibility" of time. This must be like the experience Cézanne has with Mount St. Victoire. In his many experiences of painting that mountain, its sensuous nature and its history become one with his paints and his spirit, previous experiences blend into subsequent ones, and subsequent ones recreate the previous ones.[11] ("Nature is on the inside," Cézanne says.)[12] Experienced sensuality transcends the distinctions between past and present and aesthetically conflates, or nearly conflates, the one into the other. The aesthetic reversal that Merleau-Ponty describes is not something "real," measurable movement in objective time; rather it's a *specious* reversibility that manifests itself on the intentional level. It involves the present standing as the past, or the past posing as the present. "The 'world's instant' that Cézanne wanted to paint, an instant long since passed away, is still thrown at us by his paintings" (Merleau-Ponty 1964a, 169). But this is never a complete reversal; past and present never coincide; the reversal is always deferred. This experienced sensuality is like the experience of the body which Merleau-Ponty describes as "a reversibility always imminent and never realized in fact. My left hand is always on the verge of touching my right hand touching the things, but I never reach coincidence; the coincidence eclipses at the moment of realization" (1968, 147).

From the view of an objective observer Cézanne's experience of time must seem quite out of the ordinary. Yet this is something not exclusive to the painter's experience. Merleau-Ponty writes of the visible landscape holding within itself moments of the past, holding them "really *behind itself* in simultaneity, inside itself and not it and they side by side 'in' time" (1968, 267). Glenn Mazis (1992) finds an extremely appropriate example of this very communication between natural landscape and temporal experience expressed in Margaret Atwood's novel *Surfacing* (1976). In this work the narrator is fully caught up within a wilderness landscape that transforms her sense of time. "The temporal depths, still present within the layers of meaning of the landscape and within ancient and natural objects, are repressed by the sense of sequential time," but are opened up and confused with the narrator's own past experiences: in certain limit situations "time leaps, becomes lightening, past flares in over-whelming presentness and into other promiscuities" (Mazis 1992, 60–61).

Joyce's *Ulysses* (1914) presents a similar literary example. Molly Bloom, whose geographical and chronological location is Dublin in 1904, finds herself immersed in her childhood environs of Gibraltar: "the sea crimson sometimes like fire and the glorious sunsets and the figtrees in the Alameda gardens yes and all the queer little streets and the pink and blue and yellow houses and the rosegardens and the jessamine and geraniums and cactuses and Gibraltar as a girl where I was Flower of the mountain" (cited in Mazis 1992, 66). Objective Dublin time is fused and confused with childhood Gibraltar time, and again with a time in between, with Leopold Bloom on a hill. Merleau-Ponty's account of time allows for the possibility of such experience and, as Mazis indicates,

> allows us to understand how some phenomena might not be simply unfolding and gradually receding in the passage of time. Many aspects of the world so appear and take their place within the background of the world and our personal lives. However, there are also quantum leaps in time's passage: rendings, riftings, that are also radical shiftings, birthing transformations. They are not upsurges of creation *ex nihilo*. Time doesn't only "move ahead" in its flow. It circles back. (1992, 66–67)

Joycean consciousness is thus a "con-fusion," an intertwining of temporalities that escapes the order of Husserl's time-consciousness, and that will not be reduced to what Dennett identifies as the well-ordered seriality of the (mislabeled) "Joycean machine."

Science and art thus tell us of experiences in which time circumvents seriality: a particular now, a point of time can be transmitted to or confused with other not-nows, "without 'continuity' without 'conservation'" (Merleau-Ponty 1968, 267). Similar transmissions can happen in musical experience. Although Husserl's favorite example is the melody, it is not difficult to see how his completely formal and linear analysis of its temporality strips music of its genuine experiential nature. One almost begins to wonder whether Husserl ever listened to music. In his analysis it becomes simple succession in abstract air. Merleau-Ponty indicates the reason for this impoverishment: Husserl does not consider "the influence of the 'contents' on time which passes 'more quickly' or 'less quickly,' [the influence] of *Zeitmaterie* on *Zeitform*" (1968, 184). In listening to or in playing music one often finds oneself "carried away," not on a string of individually successive notes, but within a *Gestalt* that is composed not only of the tempo of the piece, but includes one's own temporality, irreducible to the present, involving ebb and flow, upheavals and turbulence. "Husserl's error is to have described the interlocking [of pasts by retention] starting from a *Präsensfeld* considered as without thickness, as immanent consciousness." This type of analysis, Merleau-Ponty tells us, ignores not only content, but embodiment—the "time of the body, taximeter time of the corporeal schema" (1968, 173; see 1964a, 161). The time of the body manifests itself, if anywhere, certainly in various forms of music and dance. The *Gestalt* of musical experience is, as Merleau-Ponty proposes, "a principle of distribution, the pivot of a system of equivalencies" (1968, 205). The musical note as I hear it or as I play it is "not a spatio-temporal individual, it is ready to integrate itself into a constellation that spans space and time—but it is not free in regard to space and time, it is not aspatial, atemporal, it only escapes the time and space conceived as a series of events in themselves" (1968, 205). Musical experience transcends seriality. It is irreducible to a collection of objectively successive points.

Screen memory

Memory ordinarily involves forgetting. Husserl's notion of retention helps to explain this, but does not go far enough. Retention fails to account for the discontinuity of forgetting. Forgetting does not happen in an orderly, systematically linear way in which, with the same force, the ever-new now pushes the old nows out of consciousness. Rather, Merleau-Ponty insists, "there are retentions that are not forgotten, even very remote ones" (1968, 195). Yet, other fragments of experience seem to drop out of consciousness totally and irrevocably. Forgetting, and so memory, is quite uneven. The process is not simply a passage of consciousness into nothingness; it involves something more positive, "a manner of being toward . . . in turning away from . . ." (1968, 196). We might say, forgetting allows for the possibility of intentionality; it is the necessary reverse side of intentionality. If intentionality is understood as a differentiation, an *écart*, forgetting is an undifferentiation; it involves no separation, no figure on ground, no articulation.

Thus, Merleau-Ponty suggests, Freud's notion of screen memory can provide another example of temporal disruption. Intentional acts have an uneven underside of forgetting and remembering that forms a filter through which pass the effects of a past that configures the present. The sense of the present is always overdetermined by the past. In screen memory the past is made inaccessible by a memory that conceals the genuine past experience. The memory that blocks out the past testifies that the past is still operative; a forgotten but not foregone past concealed in the present. This inaccessible past disrupts "the common idea of time as a 'series of *Erlebnisse*'" (Merleau-Ponty 1968, 243). It belongs to "a mythical time," to "the time before time," where this second mentioned time is well-ordered seriality (1968, 243, 168).

The effect of screen memory is something that goes beyond Husserl's noetic-noematic analysis. It is a "prenoetic" effect that involves, not a cognitive paradox, or a *reell* presence of the past, but a "figurative," *specious* simultaneity of past with present, a present that is a transcendence because it is reversibly intertwined with the past. There is, here, a reciprocal, reversible intentional reference that escapes Husserl's one-way (albeit double) intentionality. The overdetermining of the present, however, is not simply a matter of semantic content which, as Merleau-Ponty suggests, "contains the 'simultaneity'" (1968, 243). It is not so much a matter of contents as it is a matter of uncontained effects. Here, in screen memory, and in behavior motivated by what remains hidden behind the memory, the past insists on its rights, it forces itself onto the present scene, it dominates the present rather than the other way around. It is not that in the present I set out to remember something past—screen memory is invasive; the past imposes itself.

> The past is no longer here a "modification" or modalization of the *Bewusstsein von* . . . Conversely it is the *Bewusstsein von,* the having perceived that is borne by the past as massive Being. . . . The whole Husserlian analysis is blocked by the framework of *acts* which imposes upon it the philosophy of *consciousness.* (Merleau-Ponty 1968, 244)

The notion of *act* of consciousness misses the prenoetic dimensions of experience. The act of consciousness and its rule-governed expiration, as described by Husserl, is not the primary thing; rather, what is primary is "the vortex which this *Ablaufsphänomen* schematizes, the spatializing-temporalizing vortex (which is flesh and not consciousness facing a noema)" (Merleau-Ponty 1968, 244).

The concept of the intentional, specious reversibility of time is a difficult one to grasp, even if one has lived through experiences of screen memory or the kinds of aesthetic experiences described by Merleau-Ponty. Let me suggest two further ways that one might explain it. First, one could find an explanation of this reversibility effect in what seems to be a discordance between the temporality of brain processes and conscious experience. If, for example, one accepts Dennett's model of brain activity as a process of producing "multiple drafts" which are not ordered in a linear fashion—and there is good evidence from neuroscience in support of this model—then a specious reversibility of time on the intentional level is not surprising. Even if in much of normal experience the nonlinearity of brain processes is somehow translated into a serial order which we reflectively construe as a flow of consciousness, there is nothing to prevent this translation from being overrun or overwritten by the original nonlinear and piecemeal organization of subpersonal information. This possibility, which would certainly require a neurophysiological/neuropsychological account, but which I leave here as a suggestion phrased in metaphorical terms, could explain the experience of screen memory and reversibilities involved in aesthetic experiences, as well as the dissociative experiences of both blindsight and normal subjects in reflectively accessing just-past experience.

The other alternative, which is not inconsistent with Dennett's multiple drafts model, is to think of Merleau-Ponty's reversibility along the lines of William James's radical empiricism. What James, in his own critique of his earlier conceptions of consciousness, calls "pure experience," is, at bottom, not organized according to the serial rules of the stream of consciousness, but "is constituted as a room full of mirrors" (1912, 268). One part of experience is reflected or deflected into another part, not unlike the diacritical conception of a system of differences. This constitutes the material which is selectively translated into serial consciousness. This translation, just as we suggested in the multiple drafts model, can be disrupted so as to produce an experience describable as a specious reversal.

What this translation process is, in either case, is not certain. One might want to describe it in neurophysiological terms, or in terms that remain on the intentional level. It may happen in different ways. One suggestion that has been made with respect to the diacritical differential aspects of James's radical empiricism has been that pure experience is organized as a language (Cobb-Stevens 1982). One could also suggest that certain elements of linguistic experience might be responsible for both the common, linear arrangement of conscious experience, and for the disruption of that arrangement.

Lyotard: Phrasing and Forgetting

Lyotard shifts the analysis away from the phenomenological realm toward the linguistic practices that define our lives. Within these practices Lyotard finds much the same thing that Merleau-Ponty finds with respect to temporality. What Merleau-Ponty says of time and embodied subjectivity, Lyotard says of time and phrase: "There wouldn't be any space or time independent of a phrase" (1988, § 120). At first, however, seriality has a positive role to play in Lyotard's critique of phenomenology. There *are* temporally ordered series; phrases link on to one another in such fashion; there always is a succession of phrases, an "ordinal series of events" (1988, §§ 94–95). "Time takes place with the before/after implied in phrase universes, as the putting of instances into an ordered series. This serialization is immanent to them" (1988, 75). In Whitehead's turn of phrase, it's one damn phrase after another.

One can describe such a series in an approximately Augustinian-Husserlian fashion, still employing concepts like "originating now" and "retention," although in terms of phrases rather than consciousness. Parataxis, as Lyotard points out, the juxtaposition of phrases with the chronological connector "and" unstated but implied, "stresses the surprise that something begins when what is said is said. *And* is the conjunction that most allows the constitutive discontinuity (or oblivion) of time to threaten, while defying it through its equally constitutive continuity (or retention)" (1988, § 100). This temporal sequence is beyond doubt: *it,* rather than the *cogito* survives the test of universal doubt (1988, §§ 94, 101).

Lyotard carries this even further, however, eventually putting seriality to use against Husserl. Lyotard does not need Derrida to deconstruct the Husserlian account; he finds it already accomplished by Aristotle. For Aristotle, what McTaggart calls the B-series is simply number, expressed as before-now-after. For Lyotard, however, this B-series is not, as it is for Aristotle, in the soul or in consciousness, but in the phrase. Nonetheless, Aristotle, insofar as he does not give the *now* a primacy or privilege in the series, differs from Augustine and Husserl who embrace "the 'modern' version of temporalization . . . a constituting time, the 'living present,' in the charge of a transcendental subject, and a constituted diachronic time on the side of the object" (Lyotard 1988, 73). For Aristotle,

> The distinguishing limit between before and after, or the zone of contact between the anterior and the posterior, is itself affected by the before/after: the now is not now, it is not yet or already no longer, one cannot say now *now,* it's too early (before) or too late (after). . . . The

limit is not punctual or linear, the posterior incessantly encroaches upon the anterior. The now [*maintenant*] is precisely what is not maintained [*ce qui ne se maintient pas*]. We do not see how it can serve as the origin for distributing the positions of a moving body into before and after. (Lyotard 1988, 74)

Thus, to the extent that the before and after constitute the now, the B-series disqualifies "a constitution of time derived from the present" (1988, 74).

Just here, however, we can start to see something else: seriality itself gets deconstructed to the extent that the posterior "encroaches" upon the anterior. It is here that Lyotard links up again with Merleau-Ponty. Something extra-intentional, something that falls outside of the standard phenomenological account, haunts the extremes of that account. This pertains not only to the deconstructed *now*, Husserl's living present which is always deferred, which, like Beckett's Godot, "comes by not arriving" (Lyotard 1988, § 125), but to that which *exceeds* protention and that which *exceeds* retention: traces, silences, withdrawals, that cannot be brought under the control of a linear seriality. Here we find something similar to the Heideggerian notion of *Ereignis,* the "is it happening?" (*arrive-t-il?*): the present, in its presenting, happens, but cannot be grasped in its happening (Lyotard 1991a, 59). With respect to protention Lyotard calls it "the vertigo of the last phrase"—a "feeling that the impossible is possible. That the necessary is contingent. That linkage must be made, but that there won't be anything [any phrase] upon which to link. The 'and' with nothing to grab onto" (1988, 75).

Lyotard writes about that which cannot be accommodated, the past that cannot be retained, that which of necessity is forgotten, that which is not utterable in any language game, but which must fall within the realm of silence, closed out of sensation, *aisthesis,* art—although precisely art can bear witness to the fact of the forgetting, the nonretained exclusion. With a nod in the direction of Merleau-Ponty's discussion of Cézanne (Lyotard 1991a, 102), Lyotard finds Duchamp and Newman more revealing of a now that remains outside the control of the primal impression or the retentional-protentional structure (1991a, 78ff.).

Newman can certainly not have been thinking of the "present instant," the one that tries to hold itself between the future and the past, and gets devoured by them. This *now* is one of the temporal "ecstasies" that has been analyzed since Augustine's day and particularly since Edmund Husserl, according to a line of thought that has attempted to constitute time on the basis of consciousness. Newman's *now* which is no more than

now is a stranger to consciousness and cannot be constituted by it. Rather,
it is what dismantles consciousness, what deposes consciousness, it is what
consciousness cannot formulate, and even what consciousness forgets in
order to constitute itself. (1991a, 90)

Lyotard writes of the sublime, the holocaust, the Freudian unconscious
affect, the unsayable. These are aporias for art, for politics, for psychology,
and for philosophy, precisely because such disciplines and discourses
cannot accommodate unsayables. Such aporias lead him to the concept
of the *differend*—a conflict that cannot be resolved within the standard
order of seriality since it arises outside of its limits. Lyotard's project is
not to invent a discipline or discourse that could deal with differends,
but to acknowledge that there is no discipline, science, or discourse that
could provide accounts of what is unaccountable. Lyotard thus opposes
the conception of a theory or a consciousness "which figures and counts
(even if only approximately), [which] imposes its rule onto all objects,
even aesthetic ones." For such a consciousness would require "a time and
a space under control" (1990, 41).

Well-ordered seriality, however, the narrative of time-consciousness
that Husserl provides, "domesticates" the differend (Lyotard 1988, § 219).
For Husserl, the workings of retention help to explain not only remembering, but also forgetting. Of these two occurrences, forgetting, genuinely an essential part of the perceptual process, is even more natural
than, and has a primacy over, memory. The fading of the retentional
continuum leads quickly and ultimately to the forgetting of that which
is perceived. Forgetting is the long-term rule following up short-term
retentioning. Memory, as an act of consciousness, involves its own retentional performance, and depends on both the original perception
and the original forgetting. Memory follows its own rules in the representing (*Vergegenwärtigung*) of that which was forgotten. Moreover,
according to Husserl, the experiencing subject has conscious control over
the recollective process.

The total succession is originally given as presence. I can again have
a memory of this succession, and I can again have a memory of such
a memory, and so on *in infinitum*. By an eidetic law, every memory is
reiterable not only in the sense that an unrestricted number of levels is
possible but also in the sense that this is a sphere of the "I can." (Husserl
1991, 45–46)

Forgetting, for Husserl, is thus reversible. Memory, the reversibility of
forgetting (which is not the same reversibility that Merleau-Ponty speaks

of, or even the reverse of Merleau-Ponty's reversibility) takes place according to nonreversible rules that govern a nonreversible stream of consciousness.

In contrast to these well-ordered Husserlian laws, Lyotard shows that the mechanisms of time-consciousness fall prey to differends. For Lyotard, the flow of consciousness is more like the river Lethe (1988, § 124); the past is like a shadowy, vaporous, diaphanous Hades. He recognizes a different type of forgetting—a nonreversible forgetting (which, we might say, is a good reverse of Merleau-Ponty's reversibility). He aims "to establish clearly the difference between a representational, reversible forgetting and a forgetting that thwarts all representation" (1990, 5). A differend results from something forgotten, but not forgotten in a normal failure of memory—"nothing having been stored in memory"— something that "one can only remember as forgotten 'before' memory and forgetting, and by repeating it" (1990, 5).

So Lyotard, like Merleau-Ponty, introduces a heterogeneous temporality, in contrast to a temporality that is neatly spread out in well-ordered moments of past, present, and future. Heterogeneous temporality causes trouble for a theory of time-consciousness like Husserl's, a theory that cannot think the sense of "a past that is not past" but that "does not haunt the present, in the sense that its absence is felt," thus, an absence within presence that is not noted, "not the object of memory." The connotations of these phrases seem contradictory, but they are so only for a philosophy of consciousness that legislates eidetic laws for the phenomenological flow. Freudian metapsychology may be better equipped to deal with a past that is not past but always there; with a present, we might say, made specious by an unconscious past.

Lyotard thus investigates Freud's notion of an "unconscious affect" that can only be enframed within "a temporality that has nothing to do with what the phenomenology of consciousness (even that of St. Augustine) can thematize" (1990, 15). The notion of unconscious affect, like that of screen memory, disrupts the seriality of time-consciousness. It involves a reversal of before and after. The unconscious affect takes its effect, unmotivated, *after* that which has not happened; it is an affect that "informs consciousness *that* there is something [in the past] without being able to tell *what* it is. . . . that *there is* 'comes before' *what* there is" (1990, 16). The earlier comes after the later in a temporality that is not reducible to seriality.

> This time without diachrony where the present is the past and where the
> past is always presence (but these terms are obviously inappropriate),
> the time of the unconscious affect seems . . . a bit monstrous, unformed,

confusing, confounding. Ungraspable by consciousness, this time threatens it. It threatens it permanently. And permanence is the name for what happens in the lexicon of the consciousness of time. In truth, it is not even permanence." (1990, 17)

Such nonserial time is something that is in excess of even what Husserl called the quasitemporality of the flux, of which he said, "all names are lacking." It "exceeds every imaginative, conceptual, rational synthesis."[13] It eludes possible phrase-universes; it escapes the framework of the Kantian manifold that constitutes time; it disrupts the orderly flow of temporality; it cannot be represented on the mental stage; it falls outside of the theater of consciousness.

Prenoetic Effects: Form Disrupted by Content

When Merleau-Ponty said that Husserl failed to consider the influence of contents on the time-form, he indicated the common point of both his own and Lyotard's critiques. Even in nonpathological experience, semantic contents, in the sense of forgotten or displaced experiences, un-conscious affects, screen memories, and so forth, quite frequently invade the serial *form* of consciousness. The "Joycean machine" is constituted in a set of currents that flow virtually in every which way, its formal seriality disrupted by parallel and not so parallel contents, by the effects of pasts and futures. Post-Cartesian demons like language and historical effect, and mnemonic ghosts like Molly's childhood in Gibraltar and Leopold Bloom on a hill, bedevil and haunt Joycean consciousness. Breaking its formal seriality the content is not held to a lexical order. A semantic nonseriality disrupts, distorts, twists, confuses, or overflows the formal seriality of the stream. Husserl's concept of intentionality and its formal serial structure are inadequate to account for the frequent inordinance found in conscious experience.

Attempting to understand time-consciousness at the intersection of phenomenology, poststructuralism, and cognitive science, one tends to be pulled in different directions. Can one be satisfied with fruitful metaphors found along the poststructuralist road; or is it possible to cash in such metaphors by following the route of cognitive science? Is it possible to escape metaphors at all when one talks of the mind, consciousness, or intentionality? Whatever the answer to this, I want to give a brief indication, by way of an exploration of metaphors, of the direction that Merleau-Ponty and Lyotard indicate.

Husserl's analysis of the intentional process defines a beginning point and proceeds in a determinate direction on the space-time map of the mind. It can be represented in the following way:

Noetic Act ──── Noema ──➤ [Intended Object]
(Perception)

Abstracting from the serial flow, Husserl begins with a noëtic act of consciousness and outlines the intentional vector of this act in the direction of the noema. In his analysis of time-consciousness Husserl excavates the noetic depths in order to discover the retentional-protentional substructure of acts. On that level, abstracting from the flux once again, in a series of phases lined up one after another, the double intentionality of retention moves from the present to the past; it reaches from the present structure of noesis to the just-past cross section of consciousness that carries within it its just-past noematic phase. On every level and in every dimension the line of intentionality is drawn too straight. Everything happens "out front" in Husserlian intentionality. Everything starts from the present, as if that was the *Urpunkt* of origin and nothing, in terms of its constitution, came before. Intentionality is all too clear; it starts as a clean break from the past; it operates ex nihilo; it is pure spontaneity.

Sartre's analysis explicates the Husserlian notion of intentionality in this same way. Sartre rejects the metaphor of a "digestive" consciousness that would clutter the mind with contents. Rather, intentionality means the "bursting forward" of a consciousness that is "purified," that is clear as wind. "There is nothing in it but a movement of fleeing itself, a sliding beyond itself. If, impossible though it be, you could enter 'into' a consciousness you would be seized by a whirlwind and thrown back outside . . . for consciousness has no 'inside' " (Sartre 1970, 4–5).

This Husserlian-Sartrean conception of intentionality starts out too late in the process. It ignores the "from whence" of the act and the retention. What happens toward the rear of intentionality, backstage, in the aft of intentionality? If we look in that direction, instead of in the forward direction, we find complications, the kinds of complications that account for what Merleau-Ponty and Lyotard set out to describe. The intentionality involved in the retention-of-the-past itself involves a past that escapes retention and that affects consciousness in an anterior way. We not only retain the past, but *the past retains us,* has a prenoetic effect on us, operates in a way that is simultaneously "behind our back" and anterior to us. Retention is not a transparent intuition; it is loaded with baggage, saturated by past contents—not the past that it has in view, but the past that has an effect—a prenoetic effective history that makes a retention retain just in the way it does in any particular instance, and that makes the past appear in just the fashion that it does. It is further constrained by processes involved in unconscious affect and screen memory that, as Merleau-Ponty and Lyotard indicate, move us to represent the past so as to hide the past. The past, the unconscious, sedimented traditions, habits, the body, language—all of these influence, "con-found" intentionality on the levels of retention and act. The *content* that Husserl wants to reduce, the "not-knowing of the beginning which is not nothing" that, as Merleau-Ponty points out, is not accounted for by Husserl, twists intentionality and clouds the purity of its intuition.

In effect, we need to remodel the concept of intentionality to show that there is more than an explicitly noetic consciousness, more than the present, even the "thick present," operating in (and on) the scope of our experience; and more than a serial flow that originates in a living, experiential present. The phenomenal present is epiphenomenal; it only appears to maintain a structure, a specious one engineered by reflection, but genuinely produced from the material of prenoetic dimensions. One way to express this is to say that *intentionality is interpretive* even on the level of operative, retentional-protentional intentionality. Intentionality is not only being conscious *of* something but being conscious of something *as* something, where the *as* is hermeneutical, constrained by contents stored on the backstage of intentionality.

This starts to make the "backstage" of intentionality look more important. Perhaps Derrida deconstructs too much. Is his radicality too much like a radical surgery that kills the patient, the subject? Even if there is no faculty *excogito,* is there not a production process that Derrida himself wants to call the *mise en scène.* If so, where in the metaphor of the mind do we locate it, and what do we call it?

Merleau-Ponty warns us about the dangerous metaphor of the "*Erfüllung*" of the present. Husserl takes this as a concept of intentional fulfillment that would fit neatly into chronological succession. The other meaning of *Erfüllung* is performance—a metaphor that leads us back to the theater stage. Is there a metaphor that does not depend on a vocabulary drawn from the realm of the constituted, that could actually reach that for which all names are lacking (Husserl), that would therefore go beyond Husserl's flux, beyond intentionality, beyond the formal seriality of traditional faculties, beyond Jamesian streams, Kantian manifolds, and the mechanisms of Freudian metapsychology, and still not reduce us to the pandemonium of brain processes? Is there a single metaphor that would include all of these, and the prenoetic effects of body, language, and other persons? Or, perhaps, to approach that for which all names are lacking, we need a plurality of names and metaphors rather than one supermetaphor. Perhaps we could steal a phrase from Merleau-Ponty and suggest that there are no principal and subordinate metaphors: all metaphors are concentric (see 1962, 410), like the concentricity of flesh, a metaphor for which there are no names in traditional philosophy (see 1968, 138–39).

7

Time and Alterity

In the paradigm that governs from Locke through the Jamesian and Husserlian traditions, temporality is confined to the theater of subjectivity, acted out on the private stage of consciousness, presented in the lonely performance of solipsistic experience. Even objective time, to the extent that it is allowed to play its role, is something that is filtered through individual consciousness, something that appears at the end of the intentional process, a constituted noematic time. Excluded from these considerations, sometimes treated as a separate problem, intersubjective experience seems to have little relation to the problem of temporality. Reflection on time-consciousness and the philosophical concern for finding a unity and identity in consciousness leads to the suppression of alterity. This is the case, as Merleau-Ponty indicates, despite the fact that the flow of temporality involves futurity which opens subjectivity to that which is other, and a primordial present that is also a depresentation which "throws me outside myself" (1962, 363; 1968, 48 n.). The exclusion of alterity, and in particular, intersubjectivity, may count as a further limitation of the Husserlian account of time-consciousness.

This exclusion is not a simple inadequacy of the Husserlian analysis, however, as if one could make it more adequate by adding certain considerations about intersubjective experience to it. Rather, as I intend to show, the introduction of alterity completely overturns the Husserlian paradigm and leads us further into prenoetic dimensions. In the following sections, in order to consider a number of complications introduced by sociality and alterity, I enlist the help of several more thinkers. I begin closer to the Jamesian tradition and move gradually into post-Husserlian territory. First, George Herbert Mead's social psychology helps to show how sociality conditions the human sense of time. Second, Martin Heidegger's ontological analysis of human existence suggests how sociality can falsify temporality, and how a more authentic alterity (death) can operate as a condition of temporal experience. Finally, moving beyond both Husserl and Heidegger, Emmanuel Levinas radicalizes the question of time and alterity. As he asks it: "Is not sociality something more than the source of our representation of time: is it not time itself?" (1978, 93).

Before turning to these different theories, however, it may be helpful to first consider an important empirical example, and to set it as a reference point to which we will return several times in the following considerations. It is an example that involves intersubjective experience in a primary way, and that more obliquely suggests certain questions about the experience of time. I refer to the phenomenon of neonate imitation.

Studies of imitation in infants conducted by Meltzoff and Moore (1977, 1983) demonstrate that neonates less than an hour old can imitate facial gestures presented to them by others.[1] For example, an experimenter gains the attention of a newborn infant and presents a mouth-opening or tongue-protrusion gesture. The infant responds by imitating the target gesture. In terms of both the frequency and duration of the infants' response gestures, Meltzoff and Moore demonstrated with clear and statistically significant results that normal and alert newborn infants systematically imitate adult facial gestures. In the study, the youngest infant who showed a strong imitation effect was just forty-two minutes old at the time of the test. Infants as young as ten minutes are now known to be able to engage in similar imitative behavior. Meltzoff and Moore extended the range of gestures that young infants imitate to a wider set, showing that twelve- to twenty-one-day-old infants imitate three facial gestures (lip protrusion, mouth opening, and tongue protrusion) as well as sequential finger movement (opening and closing the hand by moving the fingers in a serial fashion).

In one experiment a pacifier is placed in the infant's mouth during the period of stimulus presentation, which prevents the infant from imitating while the gesture is being presented (Meltzoff and Moore 1977). In such circumstances, the infant actively sucks on its pacifier and shows no tendency to open its mouth and let the pacifier drop out during the mouth opening display, or to push out the pacifier with its tongue during the tongue protrusion display. The pacifier is removed only after the adult completes his gestural display and assumes a passive-face pose. Thus, imitative responses are delayed and only allowed when the gesture has vanished from the perceptual field; nonetheless, under these conditions, infants imitate after the delay.

This kind of imitation is not a matter of a "reflex" or release mechanism. First, unlike reflexes, which are highly specific, that is, narrowly circumscribed to limited stimuli, the range of behaviors displayed by infants would require one to postulate a distinct reflex for each kind of behavior: tongue protrusion, mouth openings, lip protrusion, head movement, finger movement, as well as smile, frown, etc. Second, the delaying effect of the pacifier suggests that the imitative behavior involves memory and representation, which are incompatible with a reflexive response. Finally, infants improve or correct the imitative response over time (Meltzoff and Moore 1994). They get better at the gesture after a few practices. Their first attempts at imitation do not necessarily replicate a gesture with a high degree of accuracy. When tongue protrusion is displayed, infants quickly activate the tongue; but they improve their motor accuracy over successive efforts. Again, this is incompatible with a simple reflex.

This experience, which involves a relation between an infant and another person's face, strikes me as a very basic and presuppositionless social experience. The infant seems capable of attending to the face of the other person, recognizing it as something similar to its own face, which it has never seen, and recognizing the gestural action as something that it can also accomplish. This is an activity that, from the infant's perspective, has no precedent; it comes without a past, and yet expresses everything about the possibility of a future self.

Sociality and Time

In the *Cartesian Meditations* Husserl explicates the "other" as the "alter ego" that is "evinced and verified" in the intentionality of the transcendental ego (1970c, 90). Other persons appear to consciousness as noematic content; their subjectivity is reduced, for the experiencing ego, to a noematic moment of an intentional objectivity. The sense of the other person is *given* to *my* intentional gaze; constituted within *my* constitutive synthesis, within, but as going beyond, "my monadic very-ownness" (1970c, 94). The primacy and a priori status of my intentional consciousness over the possibility of being influenced by the other is made clear in the methodological *epoché* employed by Husserl: "I obviously cannot have the 'alien' or 'other' as experience . . . without having this stratum [of what is peculiarly my own] in actual experience; whereas the reverse is not the case" (1970c, 96). In other words, it cannot be the case that what is peculiarly my own is somehow dependent on the other person. The sense of community that Husserl discovers by such an analysis is a "community of monads," externally related to each other, *really* separated, but constituted in an "intentional communion" (1970c, 129).

On this model we have no direct access to others—to their private subjective streams of consciousness; as such they are only indirectly presented in what Husserl calls "appresentation." In the case of the perception of another person, I perceive first the other's body. I perceive it as an animate living body, however, only by transferring that sense of animation from my own body, which is the only experiential access I have to the sense of animation. This "apperceptive transfer" is not a direct perception of the other person as an animate body, but depends on a process of analogy: that body over there is like my body. Thus, according to Husserl, the other is a "modification" of myself, a modification of my intentional life.

Appresentation does not involve an intellectual inference, but depends on a perceptual "pairing," an association of my body and the other body on the basis of similarity. In pairing, the other person and myself are intended *simultaneously*. Husserl's treatment of intersubjectivity presupposes but is also cut off from his analyses of time-consciousness. The noematic content "other" must, of course, be constituted within the flowing retentions of consciousness, but, like any other intentional content, it does not influence the temporal form of the flow, and, as Husserl notes, the analysis of the alter ego need not be a genetic (temporal) analysis, but only a static one (1970c, 106).

The sociologist Alfred Schutz, a student and colleague of Husserl, raises several critical questions that challenge the adequacy of Husserl's analysis of intersubjectivity. One of these questions concerns access to the other's temporality. According to Husserl this access depends on analogical appresentation. Schutz (1966) points out that this cannot be the case, since my experience of my own temporal flow is quite different from the experience I have of the other person's temporality. I can only grasp my own temporal flow in reflection, and therefore, as already *past*, whereas I grasp the alter ego in the *simultaneity* of a *present now*. The required analogy is disrupted by the difference between past and present. Schutz first made this observation, without, however, viewing it as a critique of Husserl, in his 1932 work entitled *Der sinnhafte Aufbau der sozialen Welt*. By the late 1930s, however, Schutz had read George Herbert Mead's work and subsequently recast his own thought using Mead's Jamesian notion of the specious present.[2] "What we grasp by the *reflective* act is never the present of our stream of thought and also not its specious present; it is always just past. . . . In other words, self-consciousness can only be experienced *modo praeterito*, in the past tense" (Schutz 1962, 173). In contrast, we apperceive the other's consciousness in its specious present—"not *modo praeterito;* that is, we catch it as a 'Now.' . . . We participate in the immediate present of the Other's thought" (1962, 173). Schutz makes this simultaneity with the other person the basis for the definition of the alter ego.

If Schutz here gives a nod to Mead's social psychology, it is clear that he still remains under the influence of Husserl's phenomenology which can only see the other person as alter ego, as another of the same. Schutz does not go so far as to adopt Mead's theory of the social origin of the self.[3]

In complete contrast to Husserl's analysis of self-other relations (and, of course, without reference to either Husserl or Schutz), Mead, not unlike Hegel in this regard, denies that an already constituted self simply projects itself into the other; rather, the self is *always already* "in the attitude of the other" (Mead 1938, 150). This means that the realm of transcendental consciousness, within which Husserl works, is already the product of a social process. Sociality predates the self and self-consciousness so that the individual becomes an object for herself only within a framework that is already social. The self is not initially present at birth; it arises within social experience; it develops as a result of social relations. We appear to ourselves *as selves* insofar as we take up the attitudes that others take toward us. I become who I am by acting out the role of others, for example in childhood play (see Mead 1972, 1980). In linguistic relations I find myself already tending to act toward myself as other people act toward me. Inner reflection is itself interiorized conversation with specific others, or with what Mead calls the "generalized other."[4]

The other person is not, first of all, a projection of self-experience. Individual experience is always mediated from the standpoints of other individuals or the generalized standpoint of the social group. There are no individual selves except in definite relationships with other selves. There is, Mead insists, no hard-and-fast line between our own selves and the selves of others, "since our own selves exist and enter as such into our experience only insofar as the selves of others exist and enter as such into our experience also" (1972, 227). Notwithstanding the lack of hard-and-fast lines, an individual does not lack individuality or uniqueness. Still, in contrast to the Husserlian primacy of the transcendental monad, Mead proposes an individuality that is possible only on the precondition of sociality, an individual self that reflects the social process "from its own particular and unique standpoint within that process" (1972, 234).

What Husserl reflectively takes as the flow of consciousness is, according to Mead, already penetrated with sociolinguistic form. Thinking, the mind, is constituted as an inner conversation, an inner flow of communication that is part of a larger social process within which the self has arisen. The stuff of the flow of consciousness is the result of an "importation of outer conversation" (Mead 1972, 42). The theater of conscious experience thus involves an inner dramatization of external communication.

In part, the issue, for Mead, is not self-identity in the flow of consciousness, but how the self is already constituted out of others, and how the self can consider itself as another. The inner flow of temporality does not have a primacy over our experience of other persons. Rather, since we are already a product of other-relations, our own experience of time is already conditioned by others. Because we are already in the attitude of others, we are able to put ourselves in another's place and time. We can establish a simultaneity with a distant other *which we would be,* and thereby establish our own possibilities, our own futures, within an expanded or specious present. "The establishment of simultaneity wrenches this future reality into a possible present. . . . We are acting toward the future realization of the act, as if it were present, because the organism is taking the role of the other" (Mead 1980, 172–73). Our present thus contains our possibilities to the extent that we are capable of putting ourselves "there" in the place of another, which means in the place of our own possible other self, in a possible future. In effect, we have a sense of the future only because we are capable of viewing ourselves as other than ourselves.

For Mead the past is also a source of possibility: "for all pasts are as essentially subject to revision as the futures, and are, therefore, only possibilities" (1980, 173). My own transformations effect transformations of the meaning of my own past. At every moment there is the possibility that I will become other than who I have been, and this possibility is actualized over time. The specious present holds together these dimensions of possibility (future and past) on the basis of our sociality.[5]

For Mead, within the specious present, we are constituted by others in our own possibilities, as a temporal becoming that is continually passing into the future. Other persons, and in most cases the generalized other, define our possibilities. For this reason, we appear as selves, as "social objects" within a temporality that is common to all. This is, in effect, the result that Husserl had been trying to establish (see Husserl 1970c, 128). He fails, however, because, as Schutz (1966) points out, starting from a transcendental realm of consciousness he cannot explain how we have access to the temporality of the other person. For Mead, in contrast, we have access to the temporality of others because it is already our own temporality, a temporality that has come from a society of others, as we ourselves have come.

The evidence from studies of neonate imitation both confirms and qualifies Mead's view in various respects. Before the newborn has anything like a sense of past or future, it has the capacity for entering into a temporality that is set by others. That the imitative act is not a momentary phenomenon can be seen in the fact that it must take its bearing from a temporally extended action of the imitated person. This fact, even as it suggests that from the very beginning of life there is a certain capacity for the perception of temporal objects, poses a challenge to Husserl's conception of intersubjective experience.

Husserl's theory depends on the experiencing subject making an "analogizing apprehension" between herself and the other person on the basis of the similarity between the subject's own body and the body of the other. Yet Husserl also holds a contrary view: I experience my body in a way that is very dissimilar to the way in which I perceive the other person's body. In contrast to the visual perception of the other's body, I visually experience my body with characteristic perspectival distortions—for example, I do not visually perceive my own face without the aid of mirrors. This kind of visual self-perception, and this kind of intersubjective analogy is not possible for the newborn. In truth, it is not precisely the image of the other's body in the sense of the other's objective appearance, or the way the other body looks, that forms the exteroceptive moment of this relation. The infant perceives and imitates the other person's *action* rather than the outward appearance of the other person. On this point, Merleau-Ponty is closer to the mark. "Thus it is in [the other's] conduct, in the manner in which the other deals with the world, that I will be able to discover his consciousness." The other presents me with "themes of possible activity for my own body" (1964, 117). The infant does not perceive the other as an object so much as it "recognizes," at the behavioral level, that the expression of another is one the infant itself can make.

The idea that the other's temporality transverses and is already at the origins of our own temporality finds verification not simply in the fact that the perceived action of the other person involves temporal extension, but in the fact that the infant must in some way internalize that temporality as its own possibility. That the human infant is already designed for temporal experience is clear. Neonates already have the capacity for the perception of temporal events such as actions. The retentional functioning of consciousness is already at work since it is only by retaining the sense of that action in the short term that the infant is capable of imitating it. As we have noted, the newborn is capable of remembering what it sees and imitating after a delay.

Advances in neuroscience have provided conclusive evidence that experience is an essential aspect of neuronal development. This suggests something similar for the formal structures of consciousness. In this context we want to say that *what* the infant experiences shapes or fine-tunes the formal structure of experience. This is certainly the case if consciousness in some way depends on neural activity. The shaping effect of experience is quite clearly shown in studies of vision. Both neuronal structure and phenomenological experience can be "misshaped" by raising animals in visually distorted environments (Barlow 1975; Hubel and Wiesel 1963; Shatz 1990; 1992; Sillito 1987; Wiesel and Hubel 1963). With respect to temporal structure, the metre and timing of the other's actions contribute to the shaping of the metre and timing of the infant's actions. Infants improve their imitative performance, making their gestures more precise, with practice, and this includes certain aspects of motor accuracy and of timing (Meltzoff and Moore 1994). Thus, at least in part, in the experience of alterity—perhaps, for human experience, something made most precise in the experience of another human— temporality is shaped as a structure of intentional experience.

The Retrieval of Authentic Time

Within certain polemical contexts, Jürgen Habermas tends to oversimplify matters that are in truth complex. In that vein he subordinates certain of Heidegger's analyses to those of Mead, he dismisses Heidegger's originality,[6] and he makes the following rather stark and simple judgment: "In *Being and Time*, Heidegger does not construct intersubjectivity any differently than Husserl does in the *Cartesian Meditations*" (1987, 149–50). The more complex story is that (1) certain concepts Heidegger developed in *Being and Time* (1927) were very much akin to the social psychology Mead was developing in the 1920s. One could easily compare Mead's notion of the generalized other with Heidegger's concept of *das Man* ("the they"). (2) Although concepts such as *das Man* were in some sense, as Habermas claims, "common currency" in Germany during the 1920s, Heidegger's analysis of this phenomenon does offer some original insights that clearly go beyond those offered by other theorists, including Mead. This is the case especially with respect to the temporality involved in sociality. (3) Finally, Heidegger's explication of intersubjectivity in *Being and Time* is completely different from Husserl's analysis in *Cartesian Meditations,* and this is easy to show.[7]

Heidegger, much like Mead, sets out to demonstrate, in complete contrast to the modern philosophical tradition from Descartes to Husserl, that individual human existence (*Dasein*) is from the very start social. The contrast to the philosophical tradition, however, is purchased by the qualification expressed in the following question: "who is it that Dasein is *in its everydayness*?" The contrast to Husserl is seemingly quite clear. Husserl makes his starting point the phenomenological *epoché;* Heidegger starts with what Husserl suspends: the natural attitude. In "everydayness" Dasein already finds itself immersed in sociality. The philosophical tradition, including Husserl, had always supplied the wrong answer to this question: Dasein is the "I" rather than the other; Dasein is the subject, the self which "maintains itself as something identical throughout changes in its Experiences and ways of behavior, and which relates itself to this changing multiplicity in so doing" (Heidegger 1962, 150). But to conceive of Dasein in this way is to make human existence into something it is not, something like an objective substance, something "present-at-hand." Heidegger suggests a different answer: "It could be that the 'who' of everyday Dasein just is *not* the 'I myself' " (1962, 150). Heidegger immediately rehearses what would be Husserl's objection to this suggestion, including the idea that everything other than the "I," including other "I"s, must be excluded. He then explicitly rejects the transcendental phenomenological approach that Husserl outlines in the *Cartesian Meditations,* suggesting that such an approach would lead us astray into a "pitfall" (1962, 151).

Heidegger starts with the fact that in everyday existence, in domestic and business arrangements for example, Dasein finds itself with other people. Dasein encounters a world that is already arranged for and by others. The others are not alter egos, however; they do not stand objectively in oppositional contrast to an "I." Rather, I come to discover myself only from out of a group to which I already belong. The others are "those from whom, for the most part, one does *not* distinguish oneself—those among whom one is too" (1962, 154). Heidegger refers to this as the "being-with" (*Mitsein*) of Dasein.

Heidegger's view here is not incommensurable with Mead's. Mead, for example, remarks that the human being is so essentially social that even in the situation of a Robinson Crusoe, the lone individual, in the absence of all others, is still a social being (1972, 39). Heidegger writes: "Being-with is an existential characteristic of Dasein even when factically no Other is present-at-hand or perceived. Even Dasein's Being-alone is Being-with" (1962, 156). Dasein understands the world and understands itself only from within the horizon of being-with-others. This existential characteristic of Dasein, however, tends to lead Dasein astray so that "a genuine 'understanding' gets suppressed" (1962, 163)—and even more than this. In Mead's terms, to the extent that we tend to understand ourselves through and in terms of the generalized other, not only is a certain distortion introduced into self-understanding, but we tend to lose ourselves in a self-alienation. This leads directly to an answer to the question with which Heidegger started: Who is Dasein in its everydayness?

The answer: *das Man,* "the they," the anonymous, generalized other. In its everydayness Dasein does not belong to itself: "its Being has been taken away by the Others" (1962, 164). Dasein is subjected to an incon-spicuous domination by the indefinite other through publicly established means of conformity that suppress originality and level Dasein down to everyday averageness. The result is that "we take pleasure and enjoy ourselves as *they* take pleasure; we read, see, and judge about literature and art as *they* see and judge; likewise we shrink back from the 'great mass' as *they* shrink back; we find shocking what *they* find shocking. The 'they,' which is nothing definite, and which all are, though not as the sum, prescribes the kind of Being of everydayness" (1962, 164).

This phenomenon has been described in various ways: Nietzsche had spoken about the dangers of the herd mentality, John Stuart Mill, in political terms, articulated the "tyranny of the majority," Gabriel Marcel decried "mass man." Heidegger speaks of the "dictatorship of the 'they,' " the control of publicness, the disburdening of individual responsibility. "Everyone is the other, and no one is himself. The 'they,' which supplies the answer to the question of the '*who*' of everyday Dasein, is the '*nobody*' to whom every Dasein has already surrendered itself in Being-among-one-another" (1962, 165–66).

We want to focus specifically on the question of the temporality of the they. Living as the they, Dasein lives inauthentically (*Uneigentlich*), that is, Dasein does not belong to itself. For Heidegger, this means that Dasein has failed to face up to its authentic finitude, a temporality that includes an awareness of the future in terms of possibilities, possibilities that (in contrast to Mead's view) have been hidden or leveled down by *das Man*. Primary among these possibilities is an authentic otherness: the possibility of my own death, an alterity as nonexistence. In its inauthentic everydayness *das Man* conceals the possibility of Dasein's own death. In the case of death, it's always somebody else—a neighbor or stranger—who dies; death is a common event that befalls others. With respect to my own death, it is not something close at hand; it is some event that will occur at the *end* of life, but not now: "right now it has nothing to do with us." Everybody else is going to die, but not us, or at least not now or in the close future. "This evasive concealment in the face of death dominates everydayness so stubbornly that, in Being with one another, the 'neighbours' often still keep talking the 'dying person' into the belief that he will escape death and soon return to the tranquilized everydayness of the world of his concern" (1962, 297). Some forms of religion, for example, tell us that death is the beginning of another life; a philosopher tells us that "where I am, death is not, and where death is, I am not." *Das Man* tells us, don't even think about it.

To be lost in "the they," to be robbed of our ownmost (*eigenst*) possibilities, to be protected from thinking of our own death, is to live the common temporality that belongs to the generalized other. This common temporality is, for Heidegger, a falsified time; a temporality of false consciousness that he wants to contrast with authentic temporality. Authentic temporality lies hidden within the inauthentic attitude. The fact that in everydayness Dasein flees the possibility of its own death attests that Dasein is already a "Being-towards-death" (1962, 298–99). To retrieve an authentic anticipation of death is to come back to myself from out of the they. Death, as Dasein's ownmost possibility, is a principle of individuation since "death *lays claim* to [Dasein] as an *individual* Dasein" (1962, 308). All of this is possible, Heidegger asserts, only because in its very being Dasein *is* or has the structure of temporality. Temporality, which can be lived authentically or inauthentically, is the very meaning of Dasein's way of being.

Heidegger's analysis of Dasein's existential structure reveals, first, that Dasein is always and essentially involved in a projection of meaning, which is a projection of its own possibilities toward the world. In temporal terms, Dasein anticipates, projects toward the future. This projection toward the future, when authentic, is Dasein's coming toward itself in its "ownmost possibility." Being-towards-death is worked out as something "futural" (1962, 373). Second, Dasein always finds itself "there," in the world, already attuned in some way, delivered over to a particular "mood" (*Stimmung*). Heidegger calls this existential characteristic "disposition" (*Befindlichkeit*). In temporal terms, Dasein finds itself always already thrown into the world in such a way that it *already was* or *has been*. Projection and disposition are not two separate qualities of Dasein; disposition always involves projection, and vice versa. On this basis Heidegger says that Dasein's future always involves its past, and its past always involves its future. Finally, precisely in being toward the future from out of its having been, Dasein "makes present" its surrounding world, so that Dasein is the "there" (*Da*) in which the present emerges.

Heidegger wants us to understand this temporal structure of Dasein, not in the ordinary sense of objective time. He is not saying that Dasein is earlier or later, or past, present, and future. Dasein is not something "present-at-hand," that is, some kind of objective substance running its course "in time." Its temporal structure is neither subjective nor objective, neither immanent nor transcendent. Rather, authentic time constitutes the existential structure of Dasein, and it can be retrieved from the common time of sociality, from the "they" that denies the possibility of Dasein's death, and which more generally conceals the freedom Dasein has to choose its own possibilities.

Heidegger, then, is not describing time-consciousness. If there is something like a time-consciousness as described by Husserl, it is only because Dasein, human existence, is already ontologically structured in a temporal fashion. Time cannot be reduced to processes of intentionality; human consciousness is intentional, finds itself in a meaningful world, only because in its being it is already temporalizing. The existential, onto-logical character of Heidegger's analysis displaces Husserl's phenomeno-logical focus on the intentional structure of consciousness. Dasein, as it lives its temporality, already does so on a prenoetic level.

Heidegger's account of Dasein's temporality seems quite removed from the experience involved in neonate imitation. Indeed, on Heideg-ger's description, it's difficult to classify the neonate as an instance of Dasein, ontologically or experientially. If Dasein is *das Man*, the infant has not yet had the chance to become *das Man* since it is only at the beginning of a socialization process. If Dasein has the possibility of authenticity as an alternative to inauthenticity, the infant has no such possibility. It can hardly be authentic or inauthentic since the possibility of its own death is not yet an issue for it. Perhaps the very young Dasein is not Dasein at all. Of course, my intention is not to make neonate experience a test case in any way. Yet returning to this example can help to throw some light on the precise nature and limitations of Heidegger's claims. Heidegger, like Husserl, wants to speak of a temporality that operates as a formal structure of human existence. We might, then, ask in what sense neonatal experience has the kind of formal temporal structure that Heidegger describes, or to what extent that structure develops only in social relations with others.

There is very little indication of an answer in Heidegger. What we can say, however, is that the kind of temporal structure he describes belongs to a relatively mature and already socialized Dasein. Between the time of birth and the time when authenticity becomes an issue, Dasein undergoes a socialization process and enters into the temporal structure that Heidegger describes. The temporality of inauthenticity is the product of a generalized other. Since authenticity is a possibility only insofar as it involves a transformation of inauthenticity, it would seem that what Heidegger calls primordial temporality is not primordial in any ontogenetic sense. Ontogeny and ontology are somewhat askew in Heidegger's phenomenology. In one sense, however, this suggests that Dasein's ontological structure, and the formal temporal structure that belongs to it, originate in social experience, and do so in different ways and with different results, depending on the nature of the society within which one is raised. "Temporality has different possibilities and different ways of *temporalizing* [*zeitigen*] itself"—that is, temporality develops differ-ently in different cases (1962, 351). Even if one always finds oneself in a certain disposition and with certain possibilities, the particular nature of Dasein's dispositions and projections will depend to a great extent on how one has developed in the social setting. For Heidegger, historicity must be shaped by a particular historical content. In some sense, then, content helps to shape the formal structure of temporality.

Heidegger takes pains to distinguish his account from anything resembling a Husserlian one. Still, in the end, Heidegger retreats from questions about Dasein's relations with other people by focusing on Dasein's *ownmost* authentic temporality. Since his analysis of inauthenticity involves getting lost in others, his analysis of authenticity is carried out in terms (like "selfhood," "self-projection," "for-the-sake-of-oneself," "ownmost possibilities," etc.) that never seem to relate back to other persons. In its authenticity, Dasein never comes "face-to-face" with anything except that which belongs to its ownmost existence.[8] By moving the focus from the sociality of *das Man* to Dasein's ownmost being-towards-death, the retrieval of authentic temporality is reminiscent of the *epoché* through which Husserl too claims to uncover a "more original" temporality independent of the temporality of others.

Perhaps it is right to say that the return to the sphere of one's ownness in order to retrieve authentic time leads Heidegger back toward a Husserlian transcendentalism. Habermas goes too far in identifying the Heideggerian with the Husserlian account of the other, but he may be right to say that Heidegger "still remains caught in the problems that the philosophy of the subject in the form of Husserlian phenomenology had presented to him" (1987, 137). In this judgment, however, Habermas is not in disagreement with the later Heidegger's own self-critique (Heidegger 1972). Of course, long before Habermas noticed this about Heidegger, Levinas had written several books that, in their own way, explicated this problem in Heidegger.

Diachrony and the Transcendence of the Other

As early as 1930, in *Théorie de l'intuition dans la phénoménologie de Husserl*, Levinas notes a certain lack in Husserl's phenomenology, a lack that Heidegger had called to Levinas's attention. Husserl had ignored, in his analysis of time-consciousness, the historicity of consciousness—in simple terms, the relation of consciousness to its life-history; in Heideggerian terms, the existential manner in which Dasein is its past. Levinas notes that Husserl "never discusses the relation between the historicity of consciousness and its intentionality, its personality, its social character" (1973, 156). In his later works Levinas constantly attempts to elucidate what is involved in this lack, especially in terms of other persons, even while going beyond Heidegger's ontology.

On Levinas's reading, in the structure of Husserlian intentionality, the other person is subsumed into the realm of the ego; it appears as another of the same, an alter ego. It appears only on the noematic horizon at the end of my vector of consciousness. The other is already mine, deprived of its real alterity, insofar as it is contained or represented in the noema of my consciousness. In contrast, for Mead, the ego is already subsumed into others; the ego is nothing other than the uniquely particularized other. For Heidegger, precisely because the ego (Dasein) is already subsumed into the other (*das Man*), the task is to alter the subsumption, to retrieve authenticity out of inauthenticity, in a sense, to move back toward Husserl's starting point. For Levinas, in contrast to all of these approaches, the task is to undo the very conception of *subsumption*. First, the other cannot be taken up or fused into intentional consciousness; it cannot be reduced to a noematic correlate or noematic sameness. In effect, the relation between the ego and the other cannot be viewed in terms of intentionality, "for this Husserlian term evokes the relation with the object, the posited, the *thematic,* whereas the metaphysical relation [with another person] does not link up a subject with an object" (Levinas 1969, 109). Nor, second, does the ego find itself comfortably embedded within the economy of the other. The idea of the internalization of the generalized other, the emergence of self from social relations, still represents a fusion, albeit anterior to Husserl's intentional sublation. Third, Levinas rejects Heidegger's alteration of this fusion, the retrieval of authentic time as being-towards-death. This principle of individuation encloses us "within the immanence of the *Jemeinigkeit* [ownness] of *Dasein*" and therefore, according to Levinas, remains under the spell of a philosophy of presence in which "sociality is completely found in the solitary subject" (1978, 95; see 1987, 115–16).

To these conceptions of immanence, fusion, and ownness Levinas opposes a philosophy of alterity developed in terms of transcendence and exteriority. The other person remains always other, withdrawing beyond my grasp, always exterior, never reducible to intentional immanence, never me. In opposition to Heidegger's *Mitsein*, a notion of being-with contained in a collectivity that is already a "we," Levinas contrasts "the I-you collectivity" which is prior to the "we" and which is based on "the fearful face-to-face situation of a relationship without intermediary, without mediations" (1978, 95). Alterity is not reducible to alter ego, which is simply another way of saying "the same." Rather, the same (the ego, the we) is disrupted by something that it cannot accommodate, by an exteriority that always transcends noematic identity. In contrast to Heidegger's view, the face-to-face relation is a heterogeneous, asymmetrical relation in which the face of the other person is never brought under control, is never made comprehensible, but always withdraws into a mystery or an infinity beyond my comprehension. The other person thus introduces another extra-intentional dimension into my existence.

"Like is known by like"—the first expression of the concept of intentionality uttered by Empedocles, taken up by Aristotle and then by the Scholastics, finds its way into Brentano's psychology and thence to Husserl's phenomenology. It expresses both the essence and the inadequacy of intentionality: that the other is reduced to the same, that we only recognize *ourselves* in the other person, that the other person can only be for us an alter ego, reduced to a conscious presence, the present. Intentionality grants a privilege to the present. In doing so it reduces the other to the same, and understands the past and the future as modifications of the present (the "former *now*," the "not-yet *now*"), that are accessible only in the present. Diachrony is reduced to synchrony. Even if by intentionality Husserl is able to move beyond the cognitive paradox that reduces the reality of succession to *real* simultaneity in the present, he nonetheless does not escape a reduction of past and future to an intentional simultaneity. "Every anteriority of the given is reducible to the instantaneity of thought and, simultaneous with it, arises in the present." Intentionality reduces "to the instantaneousness of thought everything that seems independent of it" (Levinas 1969, 127).

Levinas asks whether "this gathering of time into presence by intentionality, and thus [whether] the reduction of time . . . to presence and representation is the primordial intrigue of time" (1982, 103). He answers "no." He finds a different model of temporality at work in a relationship that cannot, without loss, be reduced to an intentional one—the unrepresentable relation between "I" and other, which is "a for-the-other older than *consciousness of* . . ." (1982, 106). Here he lays the foundation for a critique of intentional time-consciousness by delineating a past that "had neither been present nor re-presented by anyone—the immemorial or an-archic past," and a future "which no one anticipates" (1982, 102). A past that escapes retention, a future that withdraws from protention, cannot be brought under control within a manipulatory specious present, as Mead might contend.

The past that escapes retention Levinas calls "the ethical past." It does not consist in an event that I can recall. Rather, I am thrown into the *always already* responsibility of being-for-others which is " 'my business' outside of all reminiscence, re-tention, re-presentation, or reference to a remembered past" (1982, 112). This past is "my *nonintentional* participation in the history of humanity, in the past of others, who 'regard me.' The dia-chrony of a past that does not gather into re-presentation is at the bottom of the concreteness of the time that is the time of my responsibility for the Other" (1982, 112).[9] The face, the temporality of the other person, *concerns* me, but without my being able to get an intentional grasp on it—without my being able to reduce it to a definable noema, without my being able to limit it to a present or to a past that I know. It is something that makes a demand on me as having been there even prior to me, in what Merleau-Ponty had called a "time before time," a temporality "beyond reminiscence" (Levinas 1981, 30). I am subject to the other person *prior to* my ability for ethical deliberation and without a prior conscious commitment. Ethical obligation is not a matter of decision; I do not decide to be ethically obligated or not. "The past has the significance of an inveterate obligation." I am bound by a past that is not my own, that "thinks itself—without recourse to the memory, without a return to 'living presents' " (1982, 113).

The ethical future strongly contrasts with "the synchronizable time of re-presentation, and with the time offered to intentionality" (1982, 114). This future is not formed on the horizon of my protention or as a horizon of my ownmost possibilities. Moving the focus from my *own* death and authentic temporality (Heidegger), Levinas emphasizes that the other person's death opens for me the realization of a future that is beyond my death, beyond what happens to me, beyond the ordinary, natural future. The future that never comes, that never will come, is the unreachable, ungraspable "oncoming character of the Other," the other qua future, always "on the verge of the present," but always escaping intentional presence, and forever deferred.[10]

The other, to the extent that it can be made the representational content of our intentional experience, to the extent that it can be "invested in a noema which is correlative to a noesis and cut to its measure" (1987, 133), can be enframed within commonsense time. In that case the content of experience, the other qua phenomenon, would not disrupt ordinary succession. But to the extent that the other person cannot be reduced to representation, to the extent that the other person introduces an irreducible difference in point of view, a difference in the ordering of the world, simple succession is disordered. Husserl's rule of intentionality, "all consciousness is consciousness of something," is broken by the experience of the other person, violated by a temporality on the "hither side" of intentionality (Levinas 1981, 38). Husserl's intentionality, Levinas says, is "neutralized and disincarnate"—without desire (1978, 37). Desire of another person, for example, in love, is permanent and impossible to satisfy—it has no noematic fulfillment—it "launches forth into an unlimited, empty, vertiginous future. It consumes pure time" (1978, 44).[11]

124

Subjectivity, then, is not a self-identical immediacy in the living present, but is produced in the circumstance of a discontinuity that opens up within the present. The present can only be a temporal "interval which separates the same from the other" (1981, 24). If some being, some other person, is manifested to the experiencing subject—and if that is what constitutes experience—this happens, not in identical presentness, but in a delay, a deferred extra-intentional expansion of time. Intentional experience itself rests on a prenoetic dimension; it has the structure of a question-response that involves a separation, an articulation within being, a "getting out of phase which is precisely time, that astonishing divergence of the identical from itself" (1981, 28). This "getting out of phase" is shot through with the immemorial past and the withdrawing future—dimensions not included but missing from and missed by what Husserl would call primal impression. Already built into primal impression, and even more basic than the *différance* that Derrida attributes to retention and protention, there is an implicit differing that can be explicated in terms of sensation. The sensory impression differs from itself, "is other within identity," since, insofar as it presents something, there is an *écart,* a separation between it and the something. Not in phase with itself, intentionality always already involves prenoetic elements. The *Urimpression,* even "before" it begins to flow into the seeming seriality of time-consciousness, is *always already* caught up within a divergence, out of phase with itself.

One can find something of this divergence in the face-to-face of neonate imitation. For the newborn to imitate the facial gestures of another person, the infant already has to have something like a primitive self-consciousness which involves three factors (Gallagher 1996). First, a primitive, proprioceptive sense of its own body. It needs to have some sense of where to locate the structure on its own body which corresponds to the structure that it sees on the face of the other person. Second, a capacity, already established at birth, to discriminate self from non-self. In this context the term "self" does not signify a fully developed phenomenon, but a primitive sense of self that is tied to the infant's proprioceptive awareness of its own body. Its ability to imitate, and to improve its imitative performance over time, which implies a recognition of the difference between its own gesture and the gesture of the other, shows that it must be aware of the other as different from itself, at least in some rudimentary way. Third, the infant also must have a capacity to recognize that the other person is of the same sort as itself. This is evident from the fact that infants do not imitate nonhuman objects or movements other than human movements (Legerstee 1991).

The infant recognizes the other's face as belonging to the same order as itself, and it can do this only on the basis of some built-in genetic inheritance, a past that is not reducible to its own short span of time. A face resonates in human experience in a way that entirely transcends intentional accounts.[12] At the same time, in that moment of imitation, the face of the other already appears as something different and irreducible to the infant's own sense of self, no matter how primitive the latter is. This idea, like Levinas's conception of the irreducibility of the other to the self, contrasts with an entire tradition of philosophy and psychology that stretches from William James's notion of the infant's world as a "blooming, buzzing confusion," to Wallon's conception of "syncretic sociability," which Merleau-Ponty adopts and describes as follows: "there is not one individual over against another but rather an anonymous collectivity, an undifferentiated group. . . . Syncretism here is the indistinction between me and the other, a confusion at the core of a situation that is common to us both" (1964, 119–20). On this view there seems to be, in the infant's phenomenal experience, a complete lack of differentiation between itself and the other. The fact of neonate imitation overturns this syncretism and inserts an irreducible difference between self and other.

Despite ontologically irreconcilable differences between one's self and the other person, Levinas, like Heidegger and Mead, wants to retain the transcendental imperfection of the "always already." It is not the case that the first and only sustainable meaning of the other is instituted in a relation as the thing-that-escapes-my-intentional-act; rather, I am *always already* within a prenoetic relation with the other. For Levinas this already established responsibility to the other person is the original ethical relation. If it is to be maintained, the other cannot be reduced to the same; nor can the same be made an instance of the other. Justice is not harmony; rather, we must strive for justice within the heterogeneity of our relations.

Prenoetic temporality (which Levinas calls "diachrony") involves proximity, exposure, and vulnerability which are "irreducible to consciousness of . . . , and describable, if possible, as an inversion of its intentionality" (1981, 47)—an inversion of intentionality insofar as subjectivity is decentered by a responsibility for (response to) the other person impressed upon the "I" by the other. This is not a responsibility that I could retrieve as my own invention at a prior age; it is irrecuperable, lost in a "lapse of time that does not return" (1981, 9). Diachrony involves nonsynthesis. In diachrony, identity is assigned to the ego from the outside, not constituted in the self-constitution of time-consciousness. I am not a self-constituting flux; I am a subject who is *subject to* time, a subjectivity who ages, not in an attitude of being-unto-death, but in "a lassitude, a passive exposure to being which is not assumed, an exposure to death" (1981, 54).

In whatever way one steers a course among these various post-Husserlian approaches to time and alterity, whether from Mead to Heidegger or from Heidegger to Levinas (and we note that one need not treat them as isolated islands of theory) one will not be able to avoid the storm of protest launched against Husserl's concept of intentionality upon which depends his analysis of time-consciousness. Our intention is not to seek an easy synthesis of the several theoretical adventures we have been following, or to ignore the dangers implicated in a number of these theoretical turns. These approaches do, however, indicate a common direction. If we find ourselves already immersed in others to such an extent that we tend to think and act as others do (Mead/Heidegger), and if this represents a danger of losing sight of our authentic relations to others (Heidegger/Levinas), then what seems clear is that the Husserlian concept of intentionality, which reduces otherness to noematic sameness, is inadequate to account for either alterity or time.

PART 3

POST-HUSSERLIAN TEMPORALITY

Intentionality and Interpretation

It is ultimately because I am an open intentionality that I am a
temporality.

—*Jean-François Lyotard,* Phenomenology

Time is not a line, but a network of intentionalities.

—*Maurice Merleau-Ponty,* Phenomenology of Perception

Even today, this term "intentionality" is no all-explanatory word
but one which designates a central *problem.*

—*Martin Heidegger, Foreword to Husserl,* Vorlesungen zur
Phänomenologie des inneren Zeitbewusstseins

I f we take our direction from the various studies of the prenoetic
dimensions of existence outlined in the previous chapters, at least
two possible lines of thought are open. The first, a more conservative
course which we attempt to follow in this chapter, involves expanding
the analysis of intentionality to include the effects of various prenoetic
and hermeneutical elements of experience, and in this way provides an
account of how such elements qualify or condition intentionality and
temporal experience. This requires complicating the Husserlian model
with considerations about language, tradition, embodied sensuousness,
and alterity. The second and more radical course, which we reserve
for the next chapter, involves moving away from the phenomenological
paradigm, and trying to explicate a different way of thinking about
human experience, starting where our expanded model fails to provide
an account.

Beyond Narrow Views of Intentionality

Conceived as a relation (whether real or nonreal) intentionality follows
a geometrical rule: the shortest distance between two points is a straight

line. Intentionality is, as Brentano suggests, "a direction upon an object," a vector, a directionality without curves. There are seemingly no twists or turns between the knower and the known. Furthermore, it is a unidirectional "ray," a one-way line, a "mixed," nonreciprocating relation. I view the object; the object does not view me. At the beginning of this line, consciousness appears out of nowhere, as an absolute starting point of experience, *spontaneous,* a sheer act of the ego; and it is *given* the world *immediately.* In the immediate straightforward clarity of intentional consciousness, the world is present for me when I look in its direction, when I turn toward it (Husserl 1962, § 28).

For Husserl, intentionality does not distort; it delivers the world in a straightforward manner. Consciousness is a clear intuition. Even when perception is not clear, that very lack of clarity is clearly given. The very idea of a perceptual horizon defines consciousness as a directionality of the straight and narrow kind: while I am turned toward the object of my attention, I am not turned toward objects in the immediate background. Intentionality is an attending to (*Erfassen*) something, a paying attention to (*Achten*) that brings the something to direct veridical presence.

The noetic schema

If Husserl gives up the noetic schema (the schema of apprehension–content of apprehension) in his reflections on time-consciousness (see chapter 3), he does not always give it up in his other diverse reflections. Generally it remains the basic mechanism that explains the intentionality of consciousness. The noetic schema allows for there to be—is that by which there is—an appearance; it constitutes the intentional act that brings an object to phenomenal presence within consciousness. Yet, isn't all of this made more complex when one introduces the genetic aspects of time-consciousness, since the structures of noetic schema and intentional act are already being synthesized in the flowing stream of retentions and protentions? To isolate the essential structures of intentionality, however, Husserl abstracts from the temporal flow and provides a "static" analysis. Notwithstanding this simplification, we should note several complexities involved with both Husserl's explication and the intentionality that he explicates.

1. Husserl originally explained time-consciousness in terms of the noetic schema. Retention, for example, was said to be a type of apprehension of contents. As we have already noted (in chapter 3) he abandoned this idea because it involved the cognitive paradox, the real presence of past sensations, or specifically, LA2, the simultaneity of sense-data which were actually successive.

2. In his explication of retention and protention he replaces the noetic schema with a simple, and more directly functional or operative intentionality. Retention, for instance, is a form of intentionality, and its content is no longer real (*reell*) sensations. Rather, retentioning maintains the past phase of consciousness in *intentional* presence.

3. Act-intentionality is explained as dependent on the noetic schema, and as constituted within the flowing structure of time-consciousness. But both the schema and the temporal structure of the flow involve an operative intentionality that is not explained by anything more basic. So intentionality itself is an irreducible principle that explains almost everything else, including the retentional-protentional structure, the apprehension, and the intentional act, but excluding hyletic (sense) data.

4. Finally, although primal impression clearly involves intentionality, it is not clear whether its intentionality can be modeled on the noetic schema. Primal impression is not an act of consciousness, but is part of the structure of an act. Does its intentionality function like the direct grasp of retentioning, or does it take on the structure of the schema? Is primal impression an apprehension of a real (*reell*) content?[1]

When Husserl explains intentionality he provides a static analysis that focuses on the intentionality of an act of consciousness, usually perception. When he explicates time-consciousness, however, he takes intentionality as basic and irreducible. He never explicitly or precisely delineates the relations between act, apprehension, and primal impression despite the fact that they all fall on the noetic side of intentionality. Both primal impression and apprehension seem to be part of the structure of the act. But it is not clear whether primal impression is a type of apprehension, or apprehension is a type of (or depends on) primal impression. Could it be that they are identical intentionalities explained first as primal impression in genetic analysis and then as apprehension in static analysis?

I am inclined to take this latter view.[2] Furthermore, on this view, I think that Husserl provides a valuable clue to the nature of operative (as well as act-) intentionality in his description of how apprehension works in the schema. *Auffassen* means not simply to apprehend, but "to interpret." For Husserl apprehension *interprets* the sense-content. Hyletic contents, he says, receive "an objective interpretation. . . . [I]ntentional characters like a perceptual [imaginative, memorial, etc.] interpretation lay hold of them, and as it were animate them" (1970a, 573; see 539, 565). The conscious appearance of an object depends on an interpretation of sense-content. The model of interpretation implied in the schema, however, is still, according to Husserl, a one-way bestowal. He calls the content "dead material" that the interpretation enlivens, animates, brings to life (1962,

§ 86). We will need to explore further this sense of interpretation, and the notion of hyletics, in order to expand the model of intentionality. But first, there is another dimension of intentionality that we must not ignore.

The noema

No account of the temporality and especially the duration of an act of consciousness is possible without reference to the noema involved.

—A. Gurwitsch, "Husserl's Theory of the Intentionality of Consciousness"

As we noted earlier, there is still a conflict of interpretations concerning Husserl's concept of noema. One group of scholars follows a reading suggested by Gurwitsch; another group develops an interpretation proposed by Dagfinn Føllesdal.[3] Gurwitsch takes his point of departure from the problem of perception as it is explicated in Husserl's *Ideas,* and equates the noema with the "perceived as such." For Gurwitsch this means that the noema is a perceptual sense (*Sinn*). More precisely, it includes the perceptual perspective in which the object appears. The fact that Gurwitsch focuses his analysis on perception leads his critics to view his interpretation as overly narrow. Still, Gurwitsch does acknowledge the fact that noemata belong to "the sphere of sense [*Sinn*]" and that in this sphere they are atemporal, i.e., independent of "the concrete act by which they are actualized, in the sense that every one of them may correspond, as identically the same, to another act, and even to an indefinite number of acts" (Gurwitsch 1966, 133; see Husserl 1965, § 133; and Solomon 1977).

Føllesdal, in contrast to Gurwitsch, takes his orientation from the field of logic and focuses on Husserl's analysis of judgment. Føllesdal views the noema as if it were the sense (*Sinn*) of a linguistic expression generalized to nonlinguistic acts. On this view, the noema is primarily a logical meaning, like Frege's concept of *Sinn,* which can be explicated in contexts of perception, memory, imagination, thinking, judging, or other noetic acts. Still, whether in perception or judgment, noemata are *abstract*—they are not spatial objects, they "are not experienced through perspectives," and despite Husserl's contention that they are the "perceived as such," they are not perceived through the senses (Føllesdal 1982b, 77).

This conflict of interpretations between Gurwitsch and Føllesdal has been rehearsed numerous times in the literature, so I will not develop it further here. Nor will I try to adjudicate the dispute by appealing to Husserl's text—others have shown that his text lends itself to both interpretations. Rather, since my intent is to develop a post-Husserlian conception of intentionality, the expanded and enriched concept of the noema that I will propose in the next section will be somewhat different from both Gurwitsch and Føllesdal, and somewhat unfaithful to Husserl's intent. The orientation that I will take, which cannot be reduced to either the perceptual or logical fields, but which cuts across both, can be expressed as follows: the noema, indeed, as Husserl, Gurwitsch, Føllesdal, and everyone agrees, belongs to the sphere of meaning (*Sinn*). But whether, in any particular case, it is a perceptual meaning or a linguistic meaning, as a meaning it is always *hermeneutical*. This, I think, is an inescapable fact, and it holds within itself certain disagreeable implications that both Husserl and Frege, in their various projects, always tried to discredit. Frege, with whom Husserl had corresponded extensively, is most often cited in this context by Føllesdal and others (Føllesdal 1982a, 1982b; Dreyfus 1982; Mohanty 1982). The intent of Frege's logical distinction between *Sinn* and *Bedeutung* (sense and reference) as two different kinds of meaning, finds some expression in Husserl's concept of noema, namely, that the noema is an atemporal *Sinn* and is therefore an apodictic basis of truth and identity.[4] The direction in which Frege and Husserl move, that is, away from psychologism and historicism, is also directly away from a certain threat posed by temporality, a threat that Husserl had discerned in another of his correspondents—Wilhelm Dilthey.

Perhaps, in a counterdirection to Husserl, one should consider the concept of noema, not in terms of the *Sinn-Bedeutung* distinction, but in terms of a distinction made by students of Dilthey between *Sinn* and *Bedeutsamkeit*—sense and significance—meaning that is atemporal and meaning that undergoes temporal change.[5] What if the noema appears to be an atemporal *Sinn, only* in contrast to the constant and homogeneous intentional flow of consciousness, but is otherwise conditioned by significance, that is, by the hermeneutical and prenoetic situation of the perceiving or judging consciousness?

Prenoetic and Hermeneutical Constraints on Intentionality

Certain aspects of the historical and systematic definition of intentionality can be further developed along lines that would help to explicate intentionality as an interpretive process. Consider, for example, the idea, found in Aquinas, that intentionality is a relation to something that is always beyond the knower, something that is never completely under the knower's control, something that is never completely reducible to the knower. On this model of intentionality, that which is known is never completely known; and the knower, qua knower, remains incomplete insofar as there is always something more to know. For Aquinas this is an expression of the temporality (understood as the finitude) of human nature. It implies not that some "transobjective" *ding-an-sich* is introduced into the intellect, but that the knower always falls short of the transobjective, always remains in a state of desire, unsatisfied by its object. Thus, on one side of the relation, the knower is not a subject complete within itself. The knowing subject is not a transcendental ego that generates the intentional process ex nihilo. Intentionality has its being within contexts and perspectives that cannot be reduced to isolated subjectivity. On the other side, the object can never include all horizons that would constitute its complete sense. In more precise terms, since, within the intentional relation, there is never a complete knower or a complete known, the relation should not be viewed as one existing between subject (understood as fully constituted, independent entity capable of entering into or not entering into such a relation) and object (understood as fully constituted, independent entity that can be known or not known).

To pursue these ideas and to develop a hermeneutical concept of intentionality one could follow the course outlined by Heidegger in *Being and Time* (1962, esp. §§ 29–34). It may be more fruitful for our analysis, however, to explore the interpretational nature of intentionality within the Husserlian framework already provided. Without attempting to offer a complete analysis, it is still possible to outline a hermeneutical approach to intentionality by considering the dimensions introduced into experience by the prenoetic factors of embodied existence, historical traditions, language, and our relations with other persons.

The process of interpretation is never without constraints; it never happens in a vacuum. The interpretation process that occurs even in the most basic intentional performances of perception, not to mention what Husserl would consider the higher level, more complex acts of judgment, memory, imagination, etc., is conditioned by the situation of the interpreter and his or her conscious existence. In effect, conscious existence is always already embodied, historical, linguistic, and intersubjective.

The body

On the underside of intentionality, so to speak, within the noetic schema, apprehension interprets hyletic (sense) data. For Husserl this seems to be a straightforward process, yet there are a number of questions he leaves unanswered. One concerns the ultimate nature of hyle. Husserl does indicate that hyle is unformed, real (*reell*), and therefore nonintentional material that operates as contents in the noetic schema. Hyletic data, however, are not perceived; they operate prereflectively, pre-objectively. According to Husserl, hyletic data can be made the object of a reflective act that abstracts them from their role in the schema (see 1962, § 150; 1977, 163). In effect, hyletic data are abstractions when reflectively lifted out of the intentional process, and here too Husserl cautions about the possible distortions introduced by even the most careful reflection.[6]

The most peculiar and paradoxical distortion that could be introduced into hyle by a reflective process involves the attribution of meaning. According to Husserl, hyletic data are without meaning, without either *Sinn* or reference (see, e.g., 1991, 94). This is what it means to say that hyletic data are nonintentional. They do not have a reference to anything. In the noetic schema they become informed with meaning and thereby help to constitute noematic appearance. But in themselves they are "irrational stuff without any sense" (1962, § 86). This makes it difficult to reflectively thematize hyletic data in themselves, since reflective consciousness is itself a noetic process that interprets, that is, imposes sense on its object.[7]

The idea that hyletic data have no implicit meaning and are without reference would seem to indicate that they are entirely neutral, and thereby open to any noetic interpretation whatsoever. They would be, so to speak, contentless content. In this case, the interpretation bestowed upon them by apprehension would be completely arbitrary. But this seems to contradict other comments Husserl makes in regard to hyle. For example, he states that hyletic data are data of color, tone, smell, etc. In this case, however, hyletic data of color must already refer to or signify some specific color, and this, in itself, provides some constraint on apprehension. Husserl also indicates that hyletic data are found already organized as members of a sense-field or sense-Gestalt (1970a, 1973b). Furthermore, they belong to different sense-modalities (1977). So, for example, a visual field can be discriminated from a tactile field, an acoustical field, etc.

In traditional theories sense material is frequently associated with the human body. Husserl was aware of this (see 1965, § 85), but his phenomenological method ruled out any attempt to explain hyletic data in this way. Under the rule of the *epoché* he would consider hyletic data "purely subjectively, therefore here without thinking of the bodily organs or of anything psychophysical" (1977, 167). He was not interested in pursuing a naturalistic, nontranscendental science that would clarify "the 'external conditions' to which the occurrence of a datum of sensation is subject" (1991, 115). Max Scheler calls these external conditions "extra-intentional" and indicates that they include the body, among other things: "precisely the things that are bracketed in the *epoché*" (Scheler 1973, 55). The exclusion of extra-intentional conditions by the *epoché* leads to the various perplexities and doubts raised about hyletic data and, I want to suggest, an oversimplified conception of intentionality. A theory of intentionality that develops its transcendental "mechanics" without considering extra-intentional conditions represents intentional experience as coming from nowhere. Simply stated, one needs to show how the human body constrains human intentionality from the bottom up, from the hyletic process conceived as an embodied process, to the spatial perspectives that define the perceptual noema.

The following abbreviated considerations have been worked out elsewhere in greater detail (Gallagher 1986a, 1995). They represent a way of thinking about the hyletic process as a lived process of the body. First, what Husserl calls "hyletic data" are indeed, and as he admits, reflective abstractions. But they are not arbitrary inventions or fictions. Rather there is some experience or process from which they are abstracted. Second, Husserl himself provides some clues about the nature of this process. His examples of hyle include pain, tickling, warmth, and other somaesthetic experiences. These examples do not belong to the transcendent objective order. They are neither qualities of an objective entity nor phenomenal representations; rather, they are experiences connected with bodily processes. Third, a hyletic process, as an original process lived through by the body, is transcendent (and irreducible) to consciousness, yet it does not belong on the side of the object or the noema. Of course one can objectify it and represent it as belonging to an objective body. But its first (prereflective, pre-objective) actuality belongs to a lived body that lives out its processes in a prenoetic fashion.

The effects of hyletic processes can be traced from (1) their prenoetic, uninterpreted physical advent in the body, through (2) their role in the extra-intentional (subpersonal, nonconscious) behavior of the body in the physical environment, to (3) their constraining function in perceptual consciousness. Hyletic processes take place in the body and are lived through in a nonconscious fashion. Certain physiological processes are lived through in this way. Examples include the automatic rhythms of respiration, blood flow, and heartbeat. The fact is that such physiological processes accompany and condition every behavior and consciousness. Every situation I find myself in is defined in some fashion by the self-regulating processes of the body. Consider how the body copes with its environment through autonomic responses to nonconscious but meaningful content. In multichannel selective listening experiments, for example, changes in the body's autonomic nervous system are recorded as responses to semantically defined target words that occur in the ignored or unattended channel. Such responses occur despite the experimental subject's failure to report the occurrence of the target words by means of a manual or vocal gesture (Allport 1988; Corteen and Dunn 1974; Forster and Govier 1978).

Above a certain threshold, such responses have a significant effect on my behavior. Pain, for example, even before it is consciously recognized as pain, may motivate changes in bodily behavior. In the case of eyestrain, for instance, I, or more precisely, my *body*, without my explicit awareness, moves closer to the reading surface, my *eyes* squint, my *fingers* start to trace the lines of text. Even prior to explicit consciousness, my body interprets its environment. It makes meaningful, subconscious movements. It takes up a meaningful position. The body's interactive interpretation of its environment is not noetic; it is not performed by a knowing subject, but by the body itself, living through its hyletic processes, dealing with its physical environment.

These extra-intentional, prenoetic performances of the body condition the way in which we perceive the world. Again, in eyestrain, prior to the phenomenal pain, prenoetic hyletic processes cause me to perceive the lighting as too dim, the text as too difficult. Hyletic processes are not interpreted as phenomenal pain in the first instance, but are translated into perceptual changes relative to the immediate environment. This in turn motivates changes in bodily behavior: I move closer to the desktop, I squint my eyes, I use my fingers to follow the lines of text, etc. (see Buytendijk 1974).

One could go on to consider differences introduced into perception when the perceiver is fatigued or physically stressed. In cases of chronic fatigue, for instance, patients complain of "brain fog," by which they mean disorganization in both cognitive and perceptual behavior. Fatigue can slow down reaction time and cause perceptual misjudgments with respect to distance. Consider the impact of hunger and thirst on perception. Psychologists are fond of pointing out that food looks more appealing when we are hungry than when satiated. Various kinds of cognitive dispositions can be correlated to the different ways that the body lives through its hyletic processes (Gallagher 1986a, 1986b). But this means that the world is delivered to noetic apprehension *already interpreted* by the body's prenoetic hyletic processes.

On the basis of such considerations, we can press forward to the following conclusions. First, the hyletic processes of one's own body have an extremely important part to play in providing an already meaningful experiential sense-field, a field already "interpreted," shaped, or processed by the body in its environment. Second, this already structured (formed, interpreted) hyletic experience is still an abstraction from a larger, integrated process in which experience acquires more "layers" of meaning. This way of putting it, however, is not precise, or, perhaps we should say, is too precise for a process that is by its very nature ambiguous. I open my eyes and I see a tree at the side of the road. This intentional experience is not composed of "layers" of meaning built upon one another. It is more of a holistic process than a set of integrated steps. Here we run into another of the distortions introduced by reflection, which Husserl was so keen to warn about.

History and the process of tradition

> Establishing a tradition means forgetting its origins, the aging Husserl used to say. Precisely because we owe so much to tradition, we are in no position to see just what belongs to it.
>
> —*Maurice Merleau-Ponty,* Signs

Merleau-Ponty here reminds us of a hermeneutical principle that applies equally to all intentional acts, not just to reading a text. Our understanding is always historical, always informed by traditions, and is so in such a way that we tend to forget that it is. If we take into account the historicity of consciousness, then intentionality cannot be viewed as a straightforward, unbiased process. I see a tree as a tree because I am already familiar with what a tree is. This may simply be the result of my past experiences, my personal history, although even here one must consider the role language plays in making it more than just "my" experience (see below). If, however, I see a tree as a *malus pumila* my perception is informed by a scientific tradition. If I hear a new melody and recognize it as an Irish ballad or an Italian sonata, my perception is informed both by my own personal history (my familiarity with such musical forms) and by the historical traditions that define such musical forms. If I describe my perception in these cases as starting at the point of an act of apprehension constituting a meaning, I overlook an operative, prenoetic history that is built into the noetic act of apprehension.

With the phenomenological *epoché* Husserl intended to eliminate the effects of this operative history, and thereby to escape historicist relativism.[8] In the end, in his posthumously published book (1970b), he invoked the concept of the lifeworld to address this problem. The lifeworld in which we live is already sedimented with meanings. Perception does not take place outside of a shared culture that conditions our ways of experiencing the world. The internalization of cultural traditions and biases shapes our perspectives so that the purity or innocence of apprehension is undermined. Of course, one may argue that precisely such historicity is what motivates and justifies Husserl's attempt at the *epoché*, but whether becoming aware of and bracketing historical presuppositions actually neutralize their role in intentional processes is another issue.[9] Can reflection on history lift reflecting consciousness out of history or reduce the hermeneutical effect of history?

What Husserl calls "genetic analysis" allows him to note two important aspects of the historical effect. First, he notes that each consciousness stands within a historical situation along with its intentional object "in such a fashion that every single process of consciousness, as occurring temporally, has its own 'history'—that is: its temporal genesis" (1969, 316). Second, he notes that history has an influence on subsequent experience. Husserl refers here to the "apperceptional aftereffect" of previous experience on subsequent experience (1969, 317). Experience is cumulative in some regard. On this basis he can explain how we can come to know the previously unknown; previous experience provides certain categories that allow us to recognize similar determinations in new objects. Husserl even goes so far as to speak of an unconscious, both as defining the limits of retentional consciousness, and as constituting a horizon that "accompanies every living present and shows its own continuously changing sense when it becomes 'awakened' " (1969, 319).

Still, for Husserl, this influence, this process of historical effect, seems perfectly rational, following consistent and stable rules of retention and reflection. Moreover, the sedimentations of meaning that result from the retentional process still remain within the possible regard of reflective or recollective acts: reflection can "reach back and seize them again." Sedimented meanings constitute a stock of knowledge for the knower; they are "an intellectual acquisition that is at his free disposal whenever he pleases" (1969, 321). Even to the extent that these meanings come back to consciousness through a "passive recollection," they do so following eidetic laws governing associative intentionality (1969, 322). For Husserl, then, the historical effect is a controlled, or at least a controllable, effect. Through a critical reflection the thinker can "will to liberate himself from all prejudices" which arise "out of a sedimentation of tradition" (1970b, 72; see 370).

We can see here that the issues raised in Husserl's later philosophy complicate his earlier analyses of intentionality. We can no longer be satisfied in ignoring or bracketing the historical effects that shape intentionality. David Carr summarizes Husserl's mature position in this way: "For here Husserl recognizes that it is not enough simply to turn our backs on history—*our* history—in order to move toward a non-relative truth. We must work our way through it in order to escape it" (1987, 93). Carr's interpretation, however, raises a question about the possibility of such escape. He points out that Husserl reaches the concept of the historicity of consciousness only through a synthesis of his investigations into genetic temporality and intersubjectivity (Carr 1987, 78ff.). This means that, since one's own personal history is always conditioned by that community of others among whom one lives, "*our* history" includes elements that go beyond the intentionalities of individual consciousness, and that these elements "outrun what is directly given." Despite Carr's own sympathies with the Husserlian project in this regard, his analysis indicates those elements that are uncontrollable, and that place human consciousness in a field of relations to what is always beyond the knower, never completely under the knower's control, never completely reducible to the knower. Merleau-Ponty points us in a more precise direction: "We are in the field of history as we are in the field of language or existence" (1964b, 20).

Language

At the conclusion of the first of the *Logical Investigations* Husserl states his position on the question of language very clearly: There is, he says, "no intrinsic connection between the ideal unities which in fact operate as meanings, and the signs to which they are tied" (1970a, 333). Language plays no essential role in the constitution of intentional meaning; the noema can have its existence independently of the signs that may express it. This is an old story, clearly told by Augustine, and then again by Descartes. Thought is nonlinguistic; meaning and articulation are independent. Language is an accessory feature to intentional life. Husserl and his followers, even those who want to regard the noema on the model of linguistic meaning, hesitate to abandon the priority of the intentional over the linguistic. Would it not make things easier if when Føllesdal indicates that "the noema is a generalization of the notion of meaning," he could say "*linguistic* meaning" and refrain from diminishing its linguistic aspect?

Ronald McIntyre and David Woodruff Smith come very close to doing this. They maintain two propositions. First, "every linguistic meaning is a noematic *Sinn*." This is perfectly Husserlian, since noematic meaning remains the larger genus to which linguistic meaning belongs. Second, "every noematic *Sinn* is a linguistic meaning." But not really. When you look closely, after making this claim, McIntyre and Smith shy away from maintaining it. Rather they reinforce a weaker thesis: "Husserl's thesis is that *every* noematic Sinn is in principle expressible in language."[10] Only in virtue of being expressed can a noematic meaning be considered a linguistic meaning. The noema is not intrinsically linguistic, but only potentially linguistic. Despite their claims, such expressibility is hardly an "*identification*" of noematic *Sinn* and linguistic meaning.

For McIntyre and Smith, maintaining the Husserlian doctrine does provide the advantage of a certain consistency with John Searle's theory of intentionality. He, much like Husserl, would deny any intrinsic connection between meaning and language.

> By explaining Intentionality in terms of linguistic acts, I do not mean to suggest that Intentionality is somehow essentially linguistic. The analogy between speech acts and Intentional states is drawn as an expository device, as a heuristic for explaining Intentionality. Once I have tried to make the nature of Intentionality clear, I will argue that the direction of dependence is precisely the reverse. Language is derived from Intentionality, and not conversely. (Searle 1982, 260)

In spite of this similarity to Husserl, Searle does recognize something that Husserl, Føllesdal, McIntyre, and Smith fail to even consider, namely, another aspect of language that could be at stake in the question of intentionality. "I have not said anything about the social character of many of our Intentional states. Many of our Intentional states require forms of social interaction—in particular, language—as a necessary condition of their existence" (Searle 1982, 275). Precisely because of this exclusion of the social, or more generally, the hermeneutical character of intentionality, Searle is able to simplify the story and treat intentionality as a simple notion not open to further analysis.

If one excludes or ignores hermeneutical aspects of language, focusing exclusively on the expressibility of noematic meaning, the concept of intentionality is oversimplified. Still, we can steer in a different direction if we attempt to answer the question "*Why* is noematic meaning expressible?" The answer: noematic meaning is expressible because it is already linguistic. To see this, one needs to look back along the intentional stream to find out how language plays a role in the very constitution of the noema. This is what Husserl denies and what Searle only hints at. The hermeneutical aspect of intentionality that we need to focus on is not found in the issue of expressibility, but in the *anterior relation of language* that makes all interpretation linguistic.

Commentators on Husserl (e.g., Smith and McIntyre 1982) often like to provide a spatial diagram of the structure of intentionality in which the basic components are

Ego — Noetic Act ——— Noema ——▶ [Intended Object]
       (Perception)

If we look for language in this diagram, Husserl and his followers would place it to the right of the noema, or, more precisely, northeast of the noema, because language does not block or interfere with the nonlinguistic intentional relation to the intended object. That is, the ego perceives or conceives its way, nonlinguistically, through to the noema, and then, after thought is already formed, one has the option of formulating it in language. The hermeneutical tradition, however, would place language back to the left of the ego, or at least to the left of the noetic act. Thinking, or even perceiving, does not occur outside of certain linguistic constraints that operate in our experience from the very start. As Mead pointed out, the ego itself is socially and linguistically constituted.

I am conscious of the tree by the side of the road. Following Husserl's line of thought, this has meaning for me that doesn't seem to depend on language. That is, the fact that I know *this* as a tree and *that* as a road does not require that there be a sign hanging on the tree that reads "tree," or one on the road that spells out "road." We perceive things, not texts. Language doesn't operate as an intermediate between the perceiving subject and the perceived object, but it is external to the knowing act and operates as a tool that the subject might use to express the object's meaning, or the inner thought. Other theorists, however, tell us that to fail to find a sign "out front," out there between the perceiver and the object, does not mean that language plays no role in cognition, but that we are looking for it in the wrong place. Language functions "behind our backs," but in an anterior way, before we know it, prereflectively. We can never arrive at meaning without it. We perceive and think and get to meaning only within language.

Meaning depends on language. Various arguments to this effect have been put forward by Mead, Dewey, Merleau-Ponty, Gadamer, Levinas, and many others. These thinkers, although taking different points of departure, come to the same conclusion, that the relation between meaning and language is not an external, causal one, but intrinsic. For Dewey "meanings do not *come into being* without language" (1977, 477). In the process of communication, words not only express meaning, but primarily constitute it. Think of the ordinary conversation. We often sense that meaning is brought into existence in the very speaking. I do not think first and speak second; meaning is created in the speech extemporaneously; it is improvised on the spot. But even if I am trying to be careful and I "think before I speak," the thinking process itself is a form of speaking, an inner dialogue, a conversation (Mead, Gadamer, Levinas, and even Dennett agree on this). Thinking itself is a linguistic event, a linguistic practice. Language, as Merleau-Ponty indicates, in the first order "does not translate ready-made thought, but accomplishes it" (1962, 178).

The following reflection may help to make this clear. I hold out in my hand an object of a kind you have never seen before. The thing is so extremely odd looking that you may be tempted to say it has no meaning. I need to explain its function or nature to you in order for it to make sense. I tell you its meaning. In some sense, that meaning may be constituted by the particular thing's function or place in nature, and so we are led to the idea that its meaning is independent of my explanation. And certainly it is independent of the particular words I might employ to express it, since I could use different words, or even words in a different language. Moreover, suppose that I don't speak your language, and that I have to communicate the odd thing's meaning by showing you how it is used. For the sake of an example, let's suppose the object is a pogo stick—something that you are completely unfamiliar with. I gesture in its direction and you shrug your shoulders. Of course we are already using a form of gestural language, but that doesn't help me explain the meaning of pogo stick. So I take the stick and start hopping around on it, thereby demonstrating it's meaning. This would be a demonstration, a denotative definition, rather than a gesture. So I have conveyed the meaning of this thing without the use of language, and its meaning seems to depend on the particular use that someone puts it to. In every way, its meaning seems independent of language. But is that really the case?

When you "got" the meaning, what did that "getting" actually mean? Isn't meaning itself always relative to an act of understanding, or to a socially constituted understanding, just as movement is always relative to an observer, hypothetical or real? When you got the meaning, you got the context. But, just as your looking (your observation of my demonstration) was not a blank stare, your understanding was not a wordless prehension. You no doubt explained to yourself, in your own words, in your own language, within your own mind, what you saw. Even if this was not an interior dialogue in any explicit sense, it involved putting the demonstrated event into a context that could only be framed by categories and concepts that you had learned from previous experience—e.g., person, ground, spring, jump, play. These concepts, however, are socially constituted. You did not invent them on the spot, or even in your previous experience.

You "got" them in some linguistic/communicative context. You may even have stored them and/or retrieved them as meaningful schemas by some linguistic mechanism. If we take away that backdrop of categories and schemas that help us to make sense out of what we experience, then there would be no possibility of meaning. My demonstration would be as meaningless as the odd looking object we started with.[11]

Going beyond the Husserlian model, we need to look for the anterior functioning of language, not in the resulting noema, although we can find clues there, but at the beginning of the intentional process, and already influencing the noetic apprehension. According to Husserl, noetic apprehension involves the bestowal of meaning. It is an interpretation of something *as* something. If noesis, then, cannot be a formless intuition, we must ask: Where does it get the form that it imposes? Is it innate? Do we have here a Platonic recollection, or a Kantian a priori? Or does it depend in some fashion on the available meanings already operating in language. As we saw in the previous chapter, it's not quite right to say, with James, that the infant is born into a "blooming, buzzing confusion." But if there is some lack of semantic organization in early infancy, developmental psychology tells us that the principle of organization that will start to make sense out of the world is language. In the neonate imitation experiments, the experimenter must first attract the child's attention, and this is done by the voice. The child does not first interpret language; language—including preverbal linguistic behavior, watching the signs made by others, and listening to the voice of others— allows the child to first interpret the world.[12] In perception, we do not come face-to-face with brute, unarticulated fact. The perceptual world is already structured and articulated in the language that we find ourselves immersed in.

Others

Studies of infant imitation conducted by Meltzoff and Moore challenge James's famous notion of the "blooming, buzzing confusion" of earliest experience, and suggest that what Husserl calls "intentional transgression" is operative from the very beginning.[13] As we have seen, from birth infants are capable of imitating a variety of facial gestures. That means that experientially, and not just objectively, we are born into a world in which others help to define the possible themes of bodily activity and intentional behavior. The same studies of newborn imitation, however, put into question what Merleau-Ponty describes as a "precommunication phase." The latter idea assumes a complete lack of differentiation between the infant and the other in earliest experience, and a gradual discrimination between self and other starting to develop only at three to six months. In contrast, the infant's capacity for imitation, or more precisely, the way this capacity is structured, including the newborn infant's ability to correct its imitative movement, implies the infant's recognition of the difference between its own gesture and the gesture of the other, and indicates a rudimentary differentiation between self and non-self from the very beginning. Furthermore, the neonate's capacity for imitation suggests that this earliest period is not a "*pre*communication" phase, but is already an experience of preverbal communication in the language of gesture and action.

The problem of intersubjectivity ceases to be a problem once we understand that consciousness develops, from the earliest experience, within a socially structured and linguistic framework. Individual consciousness is always already related to other persons. Others cannot be relegated entirely to the objective side of intentionality; they have an influence at the very beginning of the process, conditioning my individual apprehension of myself and of the world. Language is something shared; linguistic meaning is a social phenomenon. I perceive the world as others perceive it, in the same categories, in the same terms, because they have been providing me with these categories and terms from the very start, and all along. Even in its very formation, my intentionality is intertwined with the intentionalities of others.

The other that we must consider is not "the appresentatively experienced Other" that Husserl describes in the *Cartesian Meditations*. This would be to reduce others to an intentional content of consciousness. The communion that we want to explicate here is not the "intentional communion" of absolutely separate monads that, for Husserl, is a product of intentional life (1970c, 129). In contrast to treating intersubjectivity as a particular and usually secondary problem of intentionality, we need to see intentionality as a particular aspect of intersubjectivity. Instead of worrying about an "intentional community" that is the product of intentional life, we need to elucidate a prenoetic community that is a presupposition of intentional life. Interpersonal alterity is already within "the monad," which means that the monad is not really monadic. The ego is really a peculiar form of participation in alterity. Mead, Heidegger, and Levinas all agree on the priority of our relations to others over our relations to ourselves. Before another person is *intentionally* "given" to *me*, I have already been taken, taken up and taken over by others, appropriated within a generalized other. Merleau-Ponty explicates this alternative to Husserl's view: "Our relationship to the social is, like our relationship to the world, deeper than any express perception or any judgement. . . . The social is already there when we come to know or

146

judge it. Prior to the process of becoming aware, the social exists obscurely as a summons" (1962, 362).

Our primary relationship to the other is not reducible to an I-Thou relation, a "con-frontal" relationship, but involves an anterior one, like our relation to our own body, to history, and to language. We are caught up in these relations before we know it. Thus, our primary relation to others cannot be adequately modeled on dialogue or conversation. Before I can speak in a conversation, in an I-Thou dialogical relation, I must have already been caught up within social relations; I must have already emerged from others. The problem is not how I can be conscious of others, but how others already predetermine me as a social creature. To explain subjectivity in terms of the I-Thou or ego–alter ego relation is to begin too late in the process. Originary sociality is not the relation by which subjects are given to one another; rather, as Lyotard puts it,

> the meanings of the Other for me are sedimented in a history that is not first of all mine, but a history of many, a transitivity, where my own point of view is only slowly drawn (through conflict, of course) from the originary interworld . . . the Other and I have been and remain comprehended within a unique network of behavior, and in a common flux of intentionalities. (1991, 100, 103)

There is no mysterious process here. The social sciences provide evidence for this anterior relation of others. Think of educational experience. Language is "given" to us by others, and through language we learn everything we can.[14] Other persons can make us see the world differently or in the same terms as they see it. Much of what I know I have learned from others directly. More than this, however, everything that I know I have come to understand through the terms and categories that I have inherited from others. My cognitive schemas, my presuppositions, my learning methods are all socially constructed. I perceive a world with other persons in it; but not simply that. More generally, my prior experiences with others will determine in numerous ways the way that I will perceive and understand, in similar and dissimilar situations, people that I newly meet. My perception itself is shaped by the indications of other people, for example, in what they take to be important or unimportant, ordinary or extraordinary.[15] I see things as others see them; I look for things that others look for.

I am in a world, not only *with* others, but because of the influence of others. The way in which I am *with* others depends on this anterior network of intersubjectivity. It is a process through which I find myself already within a social matrix that involves class and economic position.

That I belong to a certain social class is reflected in the language and the categories that I have at my disposal. Sociological studies of the language of schooling clarify this issue. An individual is defined by specific linguistic resources and a particular cultural capital that he or she inherits from others (family, friends, teachers, etc.) who can either reinforce or transform that capital (Bernstein 1961, 1977). My imagination, my intuition, my basic intentionalities are conditioned not only by such class-related social conditions, but by the national culture in which I am raised. Because I live with others in a specific society and culture, when I open my eyes to look for a restaurant, a barber shop, or a gas station, my eyes are not trained (and I don't expect) to find a trattoria, a coiffeur, or a petrol stop. I look for signs, I perceive the world, already made familiar within a particular social context. In a foreign country, my perception requires translation, at least of a minor sort.[16]

A Hermeneutics of the Noema

The hermeneutical nature of intentionality can be clearly discerned in a remarkably clear passage by Gurwitsch, in which he sets out a number of prenoetic effects that impact on perceptual intentionality.

> Let the thing perceived be a tree. This tree, at any rate, presents itself in a well-determined manner: it shows itself from this side rather than from that; it stands straight before the observer or occupies a rather lateral position; it is near the perceiving subject or removed from him at a considerable distance, and so on. Finally, it offers itself with a certain prospect, e.g., giving shade, or, when the subject perceiving the tree recalls to his mind his past life, the tree perceived appears in the light of this or that scene of his youth. What has been described by these allusions is the *noema of perception*—namely, the object just (exactly so and only so) as the perceiving subject is aware of it, as he intends it in this concrete experienced mental state. (Gurwitsch 1966, 132)

Gurwitsch never pursues a hermeneutical explication of the noema, yet, in his description he touches on many of the elements that would need to be considered if we were to follow this route. They include (1) the limitations imposed on intentionality by embodied existence—limitations that operate as the conditions of possibility for perceptual perspectives. Thus a perceptual noema is never without the constraints of a figure-ground spatial Gestalt. (2) Practical interests that condition our perception and/or understanding of any object. The tree promises shade or fruit; the *malus pumila* offers itself with scientific clarity. The perception or understanding of the tree and its potentialities depends on the particular use, purpose, or project the subject has in mind. (3) The contexts and perspectives provided by personal history or larger traditions with which and within which we operate. On the one hand, I take it to be the same ancient tree that my grandfather planted, that I climbed as a child, and that my daughter now climbs. As a botanist, on the other hand, I classify it according to traditional morphological categories.

We can clearly see shifts of significance in these various perspectives. The tree perceived as such is in one instance "the tree over there," in another instance "the tree next to me." It is the tree that offers shade or the tree that I can climb or the tree that I can classify. The same tree in each case changes its significance for me. Husserl and his followers always grant to the noema this tension between identity and corrigibility. A noema has an unchanging and identical nucleus of meaning that can withstand numerous perspectival variations. These variations, however, only appear as magical transformations until we take into account pre-noetic constraints like embodiment and history. Precisely because our intentional experience is constrained by such factors, intentionality is not simply "consciousness of something," but always "consciousness of something *as* something." I am, in various instances, conscious of the tree *as* X, where X signifies "tree to be climbed," "tree to be classified," "tree from which to get fruit," and so forth. Simply put, this means that the noema is always an interpretation, i.e., a product of a process of interpretation. Its status as *Sinn* is first of all hermeneutical, and only because of its hermeneutical status can it be explicated as logical meaning, perceptual meaning, and so forth.

The analysis offered by Smith and McIntyre of the "conception-dependence" of intentionality provides another way to understand the intentional relation as a hermeneutical relation. An intentional relation is one that depends upon intending something "*under a particular conception of the object*" (Smith and McIntyre 1982, 14). Husserl states that "an act's phenomenological content . . . not only determines *that* it apprehends [*auffasst*] the object but also *as what* it apprehends it, the properties, relations, categorial forms, that it itself attributes to it" (1970a, 589, trans. revised). On this basis Smith and McIntyre suggest that the traditional statement of intentionality be embellished: "*intentionality is the consciousness 'of' something 'as' conceived in a particular way*" (1982, 14). This is the hermeneutical "as" once again. There is never anything like a direct, innocent apprehension of X; intentionality always involves the interpretation of X as some kind of Y. Some category or perspective will always be in operation; the *as* will always constrain the *of.* The conception, category, or perspective will include "background information or beliefs about the intended object, presupposed but not actively articulated in the intention" (Smith and McIntyre 1982, 15).[17]

The phenomenologist might object that precisely these beliefs have been put out of effect by the phenomenological *epoché.* But is this possible? If so, then the phenomenologist could never start a description *of* something—the noema would never be a *meaning*—since descriptives themselves are never ex nihilo but always depend on background knowledge, as well as on language.

Føllesdal also provides some direction for a hermeneutical approach, for example, when he speaks of the "explosion" of the noema. Background perspectives provide a "predelineated pattern" that sets up expectation. If this pattern is not met with, we can easily get a misinterpretation (Føllesdal 1982, 80). This is a much more general structure than Føllesdal's remarks indicate. In effect, all intentional experience involves a projection of meaning that is either fulfilled or unfulfilled. This is part of the structure of what is usually called the "hermeneutical circle."

Cognitive psychologists offer an explanation of the hermeneutical projection of meaning in slightly different terms. Their concept of the *cognitive schema,* however, is not incompatible with the notions of hermeneutical circle, horizon, or conception-dependence.[18] According to the concept of the cognitive schema, our intentional experience is informed by background knowledge organized into patterns. We rely on these schemas or patterns to acquire new knowledge. They not only assimilate new information but also accommodate unexpected results, transforming or revising themselves in the case of an unfulfilled or disappointed interpretation. Richard Anderson explains the schema in terms reminiscent of Husserl's account of *Abschattungen* or perceptual profiles: "people have no trouble visualizing that an object is a cube even though several of its faces are not in view. The schema which accounts for what is directly perceivable entails expectations about unseen features" (1977, 417). Like Husserl's concept of horizon, the schema supplements the missing profiles with a pattern of meaning.

In different instances the object intended may be identically the same, but there may be differences in the background knowledge employed. These differences may depend, for example, on differences in the expectations, purposes, or projects of the perceiver. In such cases, the same object may be intended but "in a different way" (Husserl 1970a, 588). The "*of* something" remains the same, but the "*as*" varies. I perceive the tree *as* (that is, under the description of) *malus pumila;* or I perceive the tree *as* a source of apples. My perception or conception of Greenland (to use one of Husserl's examples [1970a, 590–91], that is also borrowed by Gurwitsch [1982] and cited by Smith and McIntyre [1982, 16] to make the same point) upon my first visit there is quite different from the expert explorer's perception or conception (or even my own upon subsequent visits). I may stand in exactly the explorer's physical place and perceive the same things, but our background knowledge is quite different so we intend different things—our respective noemata diverge. Smith and McIntyre rightly relate these considerations to the incompleteness of perceptual intentions, the perspectival and horizonal nature of perception, and, consequently, the indeterminacy of the intentional object, all of which are due, we could say, to the hermeneutical constraints introduced by "conception-dependence," background knowledge, schemas, the finitude of the perceiving subject, and so forth.

The schemas that organize intentional experience and make it rational are themselves constrained by prenoetic or hermeneutical factors of language and historical traditions. They depend on our prior experience and the more general experience we gain by being members of a linguistic community. Furthermore, schemas are not just cognitive. They may be practical (schemas of developed skills and practical habits) or emotional (based on both idiosyncratic and cultural patterns), or normative, and so forth.

Husserl liked to point out the complication introduced into intentionality by noting that the noetic act could be of different types (perception, memory, judgment, emotion, etc.), while the noema remained identical or changed with the act; or that the noematic content may fluctuate with or stand its ground against fluctuations in hyletic data. But consider another level of complexity introduced by hermeneutical constraints. I open my eyes and I see the leaves of a tree shimmering in the sunlight. Hyletic data fluctuate, according to Husserl, and noematic variations take place although the noematic nucleus remains "the tree perceived as such." I perceive the tree, but I can also make a judgment about it or compare it in memory to the tree as it appeared last winter. Seemingly I can control much of this complexity. I can decide to open my eyes or keep them shut; I can choose to compare the tree with its winter variation. Hermeneutical fore-structures, however, introduce new levels of uncontrollable complexity. I see the tree and all sorts of "information" may come flooding into the intentional process. My intentional act of judgment may be twisted by sedimented prejudices of an intellectual nature (as when the botanist, for example, cannot help but see the tree as *malus pumila*) or by the insistent effect of prior emotional experience, or by an aesthetic mood associated with Impressionist paintings. My socially conditioned past may come flooding into the present intentional structure directing it toward an unanticipated future. All of this goes well beyond, but also conditions the retentional-protentional performance of consciousness. Here, however, I want to postpone considerations about time-consciousness which are clearly in order (see chapter 10).

Even given these hermeneutical dimensions, isn't it still possible to understand the noema, qua interpretation, as a *Sinn* in the Husserlian sense? Gurwitsch and Føllesdal could even be made somewhat consistent on this view. To do this one would have to adopt a conservative hermeneutical approach and claim that interpretation is capable of attaining the unchanging meaning (*Sinn*) of the object. Certainly this would be Husserl's view. By careful and methodical procedure one would control the variables and arrive at the invariable. Husserl's notion of eidetic reduction is the very model of a conservative approach to interpretation. All of this would be possible, however, only if we kept Husserl's analysis of time-consciousness within its proper Husserlian bounds. Remember that the noema, as an intentional identity, is constituted within the flow of consciousness. Husserl provides for the possibility of the identity and stability of meaning by means of the retentional-protentional structure. But to what extent would any of this be possible if we paid heed to Derrida's concerns about the difference and nonidentity lurking within the structure of time-consciousness, or gave serious hermeneutical weight to prenoetic factors such as embodiment, traditions, life histories, and so forth?

It is also possible to take a hermeneutical approach to these issues that refuses to discount temporality, that places *Sinn* under the control of significance, and intentionality under the constraints of prenoetic effects. Such an expanded approach might undermine the intentions of Husserl, as well as of Gurwitsch and Føllesdal, and complicate both intentionality and time-consciousness, yet it would not be totally incommensurable with the concept of noema as they outline it or with the more general concept of Husserlian intentionality.

9

Beyond Intentionality

The expanded model of an intentional flow of consciousness set in the context of prenoetic and hermeneutical effects may be capable of accounting for the more complex temporal experiences left unexplained by narrow theories of intentionality. But with the introduction of extra-intentional elements, the phenomenological paradigm itself is thrown into question. Isn't it possible that the flow of consciousness is really an abstract metaphorical locus, a Humean or Derridian fiction that hides a dispersal of experience occurring across a variety of prenoetic dimensions? Would it not then be possible to develop a different approach that would include experiences and conditions of experience that are excluded from even an expanded phenomenological-hermeneutical model? Whether we say that the exclusion of such conditions occurs because of the methodological procedures of phenomenology, or because of the limitations of reflection, or because of the inadequacy of metaphors such as theater or flow, makes little difference; in practical terms it amounts to the same thing. Of course, one might rightly ask whether any interpretation or paradigm is ever completely adequate, or whether any methodological procedure guarantees complete understanding. At best we may only find an interpretive model that will allow us to view things differently and if possible with a higher degree of inclusiveness with respect to extra-intentional factors.

Prenoetic Dispersals

For Husserl the retentional-protentional structure of consciousness explains how we can perceive an identical thing over time and how personal identity over time is possible. His notion of identity, however, is a formal one—a formal intentional identity floating on a sea of real (*reell*) change. Yet Husserl's concepts of horizon and lifeworld implicitly

152

contain prenoetic elements. Husserl and his followers would want to make these elements (potentially, at least) transparent, controllable, and in the end, governed by intentionality. On this view, horizon and lifeworld are accounted for in terms of hidden intentionalities that potentially can be made explicit, rather than extra-intentional forces that are continually effaced in any attempt to grasp them reflectively, or at least in any attempt to totalize them. Phenomenological method would simply neutralize the historical effect of the lifeworld, and turn it to eidetic account. Thus, the lifeworld, as Husserl construes it, does not introduce irreducible complexities into intentional experience, but collaborates with and complements intentionality.[1]

Once we take prenoetic content (embodied perspective, background knowledge, schemas, and so forth) into account, however, the concept of identity, like intentionality, becomes much more complicated. We can begin to see these complications by exploring two propositions: (1) The explanation of why I perceive (or conceive) X to be X cannot be fully explained by Husserl's model of time-consciousness; (2) Ambiguous and incomplete identities that include prenoetic factors actually undermine the well-ordered operations of time-consciousness.

Of course (1), standing by itself, does not amount to an objection against Husserl's analysis. His phenomenology of time-consciousness was never meant to explain why something is perceived as a particular something. Rather it was meant to explain why anything can be experienced in an orderly (rather than chaotic) fashion. But (2) qualifies (1). It suggests that even with regard to the formal temporal structure of experience, content matters.

With regard to the first proposition, to explain how I perceive some object, X, to be X, a particular and identical thing, we need to consider further the hermeneutical "as." We perceive X *as* X. It is not enough that retentional consciousness provides a formal synthesis of identity. The identity of X *as* X also depends on background knowledge, cognitive schemas, and so forth. But no single intentional act, and no finite number of intentional acts, contain the complete background knowledge (or set of schemas) required to know X fully. The intentional act remains always incomplete, open-ended on the prenoetic side, and the intended X is never completely determinate. Smith and McIntyre (1982) call this a "dispersed identity." Since the schema or category under which one intends an object necessarily involves more than what is explicitly present to consciousness at the moment of intending, they argue that identity "is best understood as dispersed, as it were, throughout a network of background beliefs about the intended object."[2] On the Husserlian view, however, background beliefs themselves are part of intentional life, and can always be reflectively explicated. A less conservative hermeneutics, however, suggests that intentional identity is always dispersed across extra-intentional difference. Identity is a construction that is not only never complete, but is never completely reducible to the intentional realm. Rather, what passes for identity is dispersed across a prenoetic network of historical traditions, languages, and social relations. Such prenoetic factors have effects that can complicate, twist, or disrupt the intentional identity of the intended object and the determinacy of the noematic meaning.

Is it possible for the retentional-protentional structure of time-consciousness to hold together, to synthesize an identity in the face of the prenoetic dispersal of experience? If the *content*, the intentional meaning, is not entirely or completely contained within an absolute presence, or a well-defined noema, but is distributed in indefinite ways across prenoetic factors that operate in and beyond intentional experience, then the purely formal, synthetic identity accomplished by time-consciousness, rather than constituting intentional identity, hides a dispersed semantic field. One ends up with a Humean/Derridian fiction without appeal to a separate or external faculty of imagination. The fiction is inscribed in the network, at the intersection of prenoetic lines.

The onslaught (or perhaps, in some cases, the covert and quiet invasion) of prenoetic forces (that is, the constraints imposed by body, history, language, and alterity) is not brought under control by the passive synthesis of time-consciousness. Rather, such forces disrupt the well-ordered flow, and introduce dimensions that escape the rules of retention and protention (this is the sense of the second proposition). This disruption is not the exceptional case but the result of the constant introduction of difference into identity (although it is frequently hidden by abstract reflection and phenomenological methods, and it may manifest itself more clearly in exceptional cases). It has an effect not only on the identity of the intended object, but also on the intentional process itself and on the identity of consciousness—on personal identity. Indeed, in Husserl's terms, identities constituted in transverse intentionality (which accounts for the continuity and identity of the intended object), and in noematic structures, are breached precisely because *horizontal* intentionality (which accounts for the identity of consciousness and on which transverse intentionality depends) is already disrupted by prenoetic effects that involve the body, history, language, and others. Accordingly, not only is personal identity a dispersed identity, but the metaphor of the flow of consciousness, and its phenomenological description, seem inadequate to capture more than just the abstract end-results of human experience.

The challenge here is to introduce a more inclusive metaphor, to think differently about "experience" and "temporality." These concepts are themselves in question, of course; yet it is difficult (perhaps impossible) to think about such things without them, or to think of either one separately. In this regard it might be instructive to consider James's conception of a "tissue of experience" that involves "relations that unroll themselves in time," that is, his conception of radical empiricism (James 1976, 29).

James, shortly after the publication of *The Principles of Psychology*, begins to shift away from the phenomenological paradigm, and specifically from the model of consciousness. Still, he finds it difficult to give up the term "experience," which he characterizes as something like a network: "Well, the experience is a member of diverse processes that can be followed away from it along different lines" (1976, 8). The different lines turn out to include both a subjective line (experience considered to function as "consciousness") and an objective line (experience considered as part of the physical world). But, moving away from the traditional concept of an "inner duplicity" of experience, James construes experience as an intersection of many relations so that "you can take it in disparate systems of association, and treat it as belonging with opposite contexts" (1976, 8).

James's concept of "pure experience" involves the collapse of several different dimensions. First, a collapse of the intentional relation, or the noesis-noema distinction: "In its pure state, or when isolated, there is no self-splitting of it into consciousness and what the consciousness is 'of' " (1976, 13). Rather than an intentional relation James posits an identity between the experience and the experienced; one "primal stuff." Second, a collapse of the specious present: "The instant field of the present is at all times what I call the 'pure' experience" (1976, 13). This is not to deny temporality, but to confine *pure* experience to a momentary present, to simultaneity. Only when it is past, and only in reflection, is experience distinguishable into consciousness and object. Finally, a collapse of the universal: "there is no *general* stuff of which experience at large is made. . . . Experience is only a collective name for all these sensible natures, and save for time and space (and if you like, for 'being') there appears no universal element of which all things are made" (1976, 14–15).

James's notion of pure experience, however, does not provide a model that would account for prenoetic effects. Rather than collapsing intentionality into identity, the recognition of the role played by prenoetic factors motivates us to view intentionality as more complicated, more ambiguous, and more dispersed. Further, to consider experience as primarily a momentary and simultaneous event would be to reassert LA1 and to lose the explanatory power that Husserl had gained with his concept of intentionality. Although we want to move beyond intentionality, we do not want to move back to a nonintentional model. It is also clear that although James wants to move beyond a universal conception of experience, he retains certain universal aspects, notably time. In contrast, we want to view time not as a universal or a priori form, but as constituted in the particular; and constituted differently in every case, because it gets constituted in a situation constrained by prenoetic effects.

To be fair, however, James's notion of identity is more complex than the collapse of the intentional relation might indicate. Although he insists on pure experience as the one primal stuff "of which everything is composed," he also insists on a knowing relation that is itself "part of pure experience." Moreover, it is not impossible to characterize this relation as an intentional one, but involving an intentionality that is in no need of a noetic schema or a transcendental ego (1976, 263–70). One of the tenets of radical empiricism, then, might be formulated like this: within the "identity" of pure experience the intentional relation emerges as a differentiation. One might also say that the "identity" of pure experience is dispersed by time; once it is pushed into the past, the once present is differentiated into a plurality of experiences, opened to a multiplicity of interpretations, destined to participate in an inordinate number of pasts. Furthermore, the denial of universality means that the "identity" of pure experience is always already dispersed into particular instances of experience. On every level, the identity of experience is a dispersed identity, that is, an identity that is always differentiated, a specious identity.[3]

The idea is not to dismiss the notion of consciousness—even James retains it, conceived as a function—but rather, to view consciousness as an abstraction from, and a product of a much more complicated prenoetic system. Experience is too neatly packaged in the philosophy of consciousness. Even conceived as a flow, it is too neatly tied together by the intentionality of retentioning. But to shift the paradigm from consciousness to a prenoetic network does not mean that we shift away from consciousness altogether. Rather, conscious experience is pictured as embedded in a dispersed network of prenoetic relations, the principle of which is not chaos, but a very high degree of irresolvable complexity and ambiguity.

If experience is modeled as embedded within a complicated system of prenoetic relations, part of the complication is due to conscious activity itself, and to choice, and human agency. The network I want to describe does not deny human agency. It is not that we are completely caught up and passively determined in a system that is structured without our complicity.[4] The correct metaphor for this network which includes consciousness is neither a one-way dispersion of electronic signals (broadcasting station to a receiver), nor a two-way system confined to existing circuits (telephonic dialogue), but an ill-defined, unstable, open system that learns or fails to learn, moves or is moved in unexpected or expected directions, with some degree of predictability, which means also some degree of unpredictability. New circuits emerge, or can be created within the network because experience is not entirely determined. Consciousness, including the constituted self within the network, the "I" who is dispersed across this open system of embodied existence, historical traditions, linguistic and social relations, is not entirely free or entirely determined.[5]

One might try to map out this non-Cartesian experience on Cartesian coordinates (fig. 9.1) Prenoetic dimensions define the axes. If the language axis represents the amount of control I have over my language, and the tradition axis represents the amount of constraint placed upon me by a particular tradition, at some point I (represented by the curve Pt1–Pt2) may be caught between what I want to say and what a certain tradition (for example, a metaphysical or literary, or scientific tradition) may enable me to say. At one time (t1) I may choose to use language in a relatively nontraditional way (Pt1); at another time (t2) I may be forced to let traditional terms define what I want to say (Pt2), and how I experience the world. What we would also want this graph to express is the fact that traditions tend to be both preserved and transformed through language, at the same time that language is shaped by tradition. The x and y axes would themselves fluctuate and curve (in a non-Cartesian fashion, over the long term and within stricter parameters than the ones defining an individual's curve). Perhaps a particular tradition constrains language in some regard, or a language constrains the effect of a tradition. At any particular time I find myself constituted within these constraints; and/or I may help to constitute them.

Thus the fuller picture could only be inadequately drawn in a Cartesian system, even with a plurality of axes in a multitude of dimensions. Not only language and traditions, but personal histories (including the Freudian unconscious), physical (embodied) situations, other people, political, economic, and cultural practices and structures—all would require their own axes. And we would have to define the complex relations that exist between these dimensions and how they come together in an individual person at any particular time. I am free to act only under the constraints of these various prenoetic factors, yet through my activity I transform these factors into variables since I have the ability to alter them simply by being in their path. In this complicated model, we can find individuality, but an individuality that is also completely social, historical, linguistic, and so forth, and that cannot be defined by any simple dialectical relation. The individual cannot be represented as an

Figure 9.1

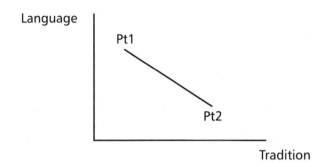

abstract point, but, on a two-dimensional graph, only by a curve. In the fuller picture the individual opens into planes and dimensions dispersed across a multitude of variables.

Radical experience is not reducible to a flow of consciousness. It would have to include structures and temporary events that may not flow at all but position themselves like rocks that disrupt the stream. This is a network of ill-defined and changing relations, not a flow; a multiplicity of currents crossing and differentiating. What it is in one case cannot be generalized to cover all other cases. It is experience open to a disparity of interpretations, experience that has many different identities, or a dispersed identity. In this context, the flow of consciousness could not be pictured as self-constituting, but as the product of various tributaries, and nontributaries, "diverse processes," and "disparate systems" (James) of historical traditions, physical positions, linguistic practices, social relations, and so forth. Some of these prenoetic elements may be incommensurable with others, so that in the end the logic of the intentional flow (its retentional-protentional structure that blends everything into a formal, temporal order) is only a phenomenological reflective reading that hides paralogical experience.

Parachronic Effacements

Husserl, in his final works, comes close to allowing for the effects of prenoetic factors in his concepts of horizon, lifeworld, "habitus" of background cognitions, and "traces" of forgotten but latent lived experience (1970c, § 32; 1973b, 122–23). Still, even in these cases, phenomenological reflection is portrayed with the capacity to explicate the relevant pre-noetic factors, retrieving them for full consciousness, turning them to intentional account. On Husserl's view, the ability of phenomenological reflection is guaranteed by the fact that even prenoetic processes are in some way intentional and follow the essential and fixed laws of retention and protention (1973b, 110–11, 279). Thus, even in those cases where Husserl and his followers want to introduce the seemingly unphenomenological into phenomenological analysis, phenomenology remains victorious.

The unconscious, for example, is, for Husserl, the product of intentional processes. On his account, a judgment sinks back in retentional consciousness.

> It then sinks ever further into the background and at the same time becomes ever more indistinct; the degree of its prominence gradually lessens until it finally disappears from the field of immediate consciousness, is "forgotten." It is henceforth incorporated into the passive background, into the "unconscious," which is not a dead nothingness but a limiting mode of consciousness and accordingly can affect us anew like another passivity in the form of whims, free-floating ideas, and so on. (1973b, 279)

Nonetheless, according to Husserl, unconscious effects, like historical, linguistic, and social effects, are *managed* within the realm of intentionality. We manage them as a computer might manage information: through memory and manipulative software. They remain as possessions of consciousness, "ready for a new associative awakening. We can turn again toward what is awakened in the form of a whim, a free-floating idea; we can bring it nearer, make it more distinct; and, finally, by renewing its articulated accomplishment under certain circumstances, we can restore the judgment to self-givenness" (1973b, 279). Thus, in various phenomenological approaches, the unconscious is reduced to a form of intentionality. Indeed, according to one account, we are conscious of unconscious contents, albeit as allusionary.[6] Reflection, on this view, allows us to manage unconscious contents. Just as Freud would require psychoanalysis, conceived as a science, to escape unconscious effects, so a phenomenologically guided psychoanalytic reflection must methodically make such effects transparent.

For the phenomenologist, then, reflection is considered a powerful tool, despite Husserl's own admissions about the distortions introduced by reflection. Reflection, Husserl indicates, adds something to phenomena, even if it is only differentiation where there is no differentiation. But Husserl does not go far enough. Not only is reflection an intentional act within the flow of consciousness, having its own retentional-protentional structure, as Husserl admits, but reflection itself is necessarily constrained by prenoetic factors. Quite clearly, what we call "phenomenological reflection" has its meaning only within a well-defined philosophical tradition and could not operate outside of a linguistic community. Nor is it accomplished by disembodied egos whose cogitations are free of spatial metaphor. Phenomenology clearly overestimates the power of reflection. Reflection does not free itself from prenoetic prejudices simply by becoming aware of them. Furthermore, it is uncertain whether reflection is even capable of making conscious all such prenoetic effects. We can express this in the following way: reflection is always hermeneutical.[7]

It is this intersection that I am most interested in exploring—where reflection with its hermeneutical limitations attempts to confront the prenoetic factors that condition and displace intentional experience, including reflection itself. This is where consciousness ceases to be transparent, where self-understanding comes to the realization that it does not understand itself, where the meaningful horizon continues to recede, where the habitus transcends my reflective conception of it, where the traces of latent experiences themselves remain latent. Here reflection fails to comprehend. Intentionality is not enough.

There are many prenoetic limitations on intentionality: the effects of the unconscious, embodiment, language, historical traditions, political and social structures, and so forth. We will take three examples for further consideration. They involve indeterminate events that cannot be represented in the theater space of the mind; happenings that go beyond intentional experience and yet condition that very experience. They are not chosen arbitrarily. The first may be viewed as something that escapes retention, namely, what Lyotard calls a "nonreversible forgetting," a past that is not past. The second is something that transcends the intentionality of the living present, namely, what Levinas calls "the face" of the other person. The third outstrips protention; Heidegger describes it in terms of "being-towards-death." These three aspects of existence—a future that outruns all expectation, a present that effaces itself toward infinitude, a past that eludes memory—disrupt the intentionality of consciousness, overflow the banks of the intentional stream. They involve experiences that take no object; experiences that cannot be put in the form: "consciousness of *something*," or even in an expanded, hermeneutical form: "consciousness of something *as* something."

Historical effect

Neuropsychology and hermeneutics, two very different disciplines, provide ways to think of how the past escapes retention yet continues to affect present experience. Neuroscience and neuropsychology offer some very fine-grained details of how retention works; hermeneutics can help us to generalize and to see some practical implications.

I want to start with an observation that seems to go directly against one of my earlier claims, namely, that content has an effect on the formal structure of time-consciousness. Ernst Pöppel (1994) distinguishes between neuronal system states of approximately 30 msec that are the subpersonal quanta of primary conscious experience, and the neuronal mechanism responsible for the temporal integration of these states into a successive order within approximately 3-second frames or "operational windows" of temporally extended subpersonal processes (correlated to an experienced specious present). For sake of clarity I will refer to a 30-msec system state as S, and an operational frame or window as W. Pöppel provides evidence to suggest that the integration and ordering process which produces W is "pre-semantic and, thus, independent from concrete events" (1994, 194). In other words, the mechanism that is responsible for the microgenesis of what Husserl would call retention, functions automatically to produce a formal unity of approximately 3 seconds, regardless of the content that is being experienced.

Pöppel proceeds, however, to contrast this content-independent retentional mechanism with a semantic binding that comes into effect in time frames over 3 seconds duration.[8] It's also possible, however, that W varies and may be of magnitudes as short as 0.5 seconds (Varela 1998). In other words, beyond the magnitude of W (0.5 to 3 seconds) the coherency (or lack of coherency) of phenomenal experience may depend on content. If the retentional function, described by Husserl, extends beyond the magnitude of W (0.5 to 3 seconds), then content apparently would have an effect on the retentional process. If we think of retention, as Husserl does, on the intentional level, then the often cited experiences of time seeming to slow down or speed up, when subjects are respectively bored or having fun, may be just such cases in which the retentional structure is affected by content.

Pöppel's theory of temporal binding does help to make sense out of many of our experiences. Evidence about intersensory differences with respect to the specious present suggests that the retentioning process varies intermodally. Precisely the integration or binding across sensory modalities is one of the things Pöppel is trying to account for in microgenetic, neuronal terms. Recall the example of Plumer's duck in chapters 2 and 4. If we're holding a duck and it quacks, we feel the movement of its diaphragm, see its mouth open, and hear the quack simultaneously. Neuroscience tells us, however, that the information coming from different senses is processed in a distributed manner and not necessarily synchronically. The temporal binding problem concerns the question of how all of this information is collated and delivered to (or translated into) experience simultaneously. According to Pöppel, subpersonal neuronal mechanisms in some automatic fashion collate the nonsimultaneous processes, treating them as simultaneous within S, which in turn, along with other Ss, is positioned in a successive order of such states in W.

This model may even help to explain some intrasensory perplexities. In the *phi* phenomenon, for example, a subject is presented with two spots of differently colored light, lasting 150 msec each, flashed in 50-msec sequence. The time frame of the presentation is such that the perceiving subject experiences not two separate dots in sequence, but a moving dot that changes color in midstream. If a spot of one color is flashed at point A, and a spot of a different color is flashed 50 msec later at point B, the effect seems to be that the subject is conscious of the second color at a point between A and B, and at a phenomenal time that seems prior to the time the second color was actually flashed at B. The end point of the event seems to gain some representation at the midpoint of the experience (see Dennett 1991 for a good, although controversial, account). The retentional-protentional order seems to be twisted in this case. On the phenomenal level, I seem to be retaining something that has not yet happened.

Yet one can make sense of this aspect of the *phi* experience by appealing to the S and W mechanisms of temporal binding on the subpersonal level. S may be of magnitudes that vary from 30 to 100 msec (Varela 1998). Assume in the following that S1 and S2 have magnitudes of 60 msec each, and that S1 begins 35 msec prior to the beginning of the 50-msec interval between the flashing of a red dot and a green dot. Everything in S1 is treated as simultaneous. S2 begins 25 msec after the onset of the 50-msec interval, and ends 35 msec after the flashing of the green dot occurs. If everything in S2 is treated as simultaneous, and if W orders things as they should be, S1 followed by S2, it seems clear that the perceiving subject will continue to see the red dot during the first part of the interval, and will start to see the green dot around the midpoint of the interval. This explains the timing of the phenomenon if not the apparent movement involved.

This theory of temporal binding does not solve all problems, however. It should be noted that a great deal more information is retained on the subpersonal level than ever reaches consciousness. A. J. Marcel (1983) suggests that the capacity of nonconscious or subpersonal representations is not limited to the same extent as conscious experience. It follows that, somewhere between the subpersonal processes involved in S and those involved in W, or between W and conscious experience, much of that information is filtered out. Whatever the mechanism of selectivity is, it would need to operate on the basis of semantic aspects rather than nonsemantic aspects. The presemantic mechanism leading to the order of W, as proposed by Pöppel, does not account for the fact that only some informational events (Ss), namely, those having semantic relevance to intentional states, get retained for consciousness, and other events which are semantically irrelevant for the current situation are retained but remain on a nonconscious level, either as simple Ss or already as sequentially ordered in W. It may be possible that the retentional mechanism responsible for the temporal integration of material within W is not simply a passive collector that orders and transports everything to consciousness. If that is the case, if the integration process in W is already selective, then some information would remain outside of the sequential order provided by W. If this is not the case, there must be some other process that selects out material from that which is already ordered in W.[9]

Consciously, we can entertain only one interpretation at a time, even if nonconsciously numerous interpretations are possible (Marcel 1983). What, then, drives the selection for conscious representation? In some way, and at some level, the microgenesis of retention must be shaped by extraformal, and perhaps intentional/semantic aspects. What I see or hear or feel is often determined by what I am looking for, or listening to, or desiring, or doing, although that is often subject to distraction. My interests or my circumstances, which are defined semantically, help to determine how certain information gets retained—either consciously, or subconsciously, either within an otherwise formal sequence, or out of sequence.[10]

Importantly, what remains below the threshold of consciousness, retained at some subpersonal level (either outside or within the formal order of a past W [call it W_p]), can have an effect on the intentional content of consciousness at some time subsequent to W_p. The phenomenon of perceptual masking offers some interesting evidence in this regard. Marcel (1980) has shown that words presented at a subliminal level, and therefore not consciously registered, are nonetheless retained at the subpersonal level and can interfere with later conscious experience. For example, if the word "palm" is presented subsequent to the masked presentation of the word "hand," its interpretation differs from the interpretation it receives when it is preceded by the masked presentation of the word "tree." Past semantic content which is registered and retained on a subpersonal level, but does not enter consciousness, can prime or inhibit later cognition. Semantic content that is never retained at the level of conscious experience, because it never reached presentation in consciousness, can exert itself in a way that might override the effects of ordinary and orderly retention on the intentional level.[11]

Temporal masking can also occur. The tonal arrangement of sounds presented in a sequence can affect the perception of that sequence. If in the sequence of sounds ABCDBA, the tone A is of a particular low frequency, and B is also a low frequency, the order of C and D will be masked. In some cases, the order of C and D will not be distinguishable, or C will appear to come before D; and in other cases, varying the tones, D will appear to come before C (see, e.g., Bregman and Rudnicky 1975). It's not simply that the conscious retention of A and B determines the phenomenal order of C and D, for the later sounds of B and A are also required for the masking effect. Rather, the subpersonal processing of these sounds, the timing of the relevant Ss, and their arrangement within W, will result in one interpretation rather than another. In effect, not unlike aspects of the *phi* phenomenon, the subpersonal processing of auditory information relevant to sounds that follow C and D in the objective sequential order will determine the way C and D play out on the conscious level.

The role of certain prenoetic factors in such phenomena can be seen in cases of auditory fusion. Two words (e.g., "back" and "lack") presented in close sequence can be heard as one ("black"). But this depends not only on the relative interval time, but on factors such as the subject's fatigue level, and on linguistic rules ("back" and "lack" fuse to "black" but not to "lback") (Marcel 1983). What happens to retention in such cases? If the subsequent word was "rack" instead of "lack," or possibly if the subject was more alert, the word "back" would be retained in its properly discrete sequence, and not fused. Thus, in the case of auditory fusion, retention seems to collapse into primal impression or is overruled or undermined by factors that pertain to perceptual (in this case linguistic) content or to prenoetic embodiment (e.g., fatigue).

Much of the neuropsychological discussion depends on evidence gained in relatively abstract experimental situations. Similar conclusions, however, can be reached in an examination of practical understanding and everyday experience. Philosophical hermeneutics can help to bring us closer to the pragmatics of the lifeworld.

Hermeneutics, in its traditional practice and theory, explicates that which is capable of being brought to intentional presentation and especially that which is in danger of falling away from presentation. It is, as Gadamer points out, "an effort to grasp something vanishing and hold it up in the light of consciousness" (1976, 21). Interpretation thus counts retention and memory among its conditions of possibility. It also suggests that some things are beyond retention and memory, and beyond the scope of hermeneutics in this traditional sense; those events that have already vanished and that cannot be recollected—more precisely, those vanished events that nonetheless still have an effect on intentional presentation and interpretation. In the most precise terms, we are concerned with the insistent past that invades intentional life yet evades reflective consciousness.

Gadamer's hermeneutics, especially his discussions of historical effect, *Wirkungsgeschichte,* and the limits of hermeneutical reflection, offers some important help for understanding how past occurrences continue to have an influence on intentional consciousness. Some of these occurrences belong to our own individual experiences, others have cultural significance, and still others transcend both individuals and particular societies. It may also be the case that through historical study or hermeneutical reflection some of these influences can be brought to intentional presentation and in some sense can be brought under scientific control. Memory and historical consciousness can turn some of these influences to intentional account. But whether we successfully become aware of (construe or reconstruct) such influences, or fail to become reflectively aware of them, they nonetheless continue to operate in an anterior way and to have an effect on intentional structure that is irreducible to intentional presence. Whether or to what degree phenomenological or hermeneutical reflection is powerful enough to neutralize the operation of these influences is open to debate. Here it is sufficient to say that in a particular intentional operation a certain tradition or bias, or a certain social-economic structure, may continue to operate, to have an effect on consciousness, unbeknownst to consciousness.

Good examples of historical events that have determined present practices are often uncovered and retrieved by historians. The historian James Burke has created an interesting career tracing obscure connections that link events together in often unsuspected and amazing ways. But for every question that a historian is able to answer, there are many other questions that cannot be answered, or perhaps cannot even be raised, simply because no documentation, no trace exists. The personal histories of our ancestors, now completely forgotten, may continue to shape our lives profoundly.

Very similar considerations are relevant to thought and language. Categories that we use today, sometimes the most basic ones that shape our present thoughts, have histories that in some cases can never be fully reconstructed. If language had an origin, the very events of that origin are unrecoverable and yet, in some way, are inscribed in human genetic materials, their effects completely conditioning our understanding of the world.

Thus, not every historical effect can be brought under reflective, intentional control. Consciousness cannot make itself completely transparent to itself. "Reflection on a given pre-understanding brings before me something that otherwise happens *behind my back*. Something—but not everything, for what I have called the *wirkungsgeschichtliches Bewusstsein* is inescapably more *being* than consciousness, and being is never fully manifest" (Gadamer 1976, 38). Historical effects, then, can be *relative refractions*—traditions, linguistic structures, social-economic forces that are hidden, yet operative within intentional life—part of the realm that we have called the prenoetic. The reflective consciousness that could make one of these effects its object is itself conditioned and constrained by other hidden, prenoetic aspects. This is the finitude and the historicity of intentionality.

If, with Aristotle, we say that in some sense time is a measure, an intentional enumeration, then the past is enumerated and domesticated by the various intentionalities of memory, custom, and historical science. Yet just these intentionalities operate like filters blocking out pasts that would register only on different scales. Events confined in prenoetic dimensions escape the order of time-consciousness because the temporal system of reference that we customarily employ simply filters out that which cannot be marked on any particular intentional time scale. We are led here to a very speculative question—speculative because we have no way of answering it. Consider the totality of events that would be counted using every possible intentional scale. Would it not still be possible that certain, prenoetic effects would escape the standard space-time frameworks set up by time-consciousness? Are there events that are irremediably absent and yet continuously efficacious for intentional life?[12]

Under the heading of historical effect we can include those events (or "nonevents") that remain beyond the reach of intentionality, unmastered by even the most powerful reflection, inaccessible to scientific testing. Immediately we think of the unconscious, composed of both personal and impersonal pasts that continue to shape the individual, that continue to have their effect over and above intention or will. Childhood experiences that shape our habits and thought-patterns, and that are "personal" in the minimal sense that in the forgotten and irretrievable past they happened to a "me" that I no longer am, are also more than personal insofar as they partake of a cultural dimension. My posture and gait, my thinking and seeing are in some way personal, but also culturally conditioned within experiences that escape retention and memory, yet continue to have efficacy.

Beyond the categories of the personal and the original, there are pasts that, if they had not been, would change everything: those things that seem part of human nature now, that come to us from a past long forgotten, and so, in effect, without a discoverable origin, a past we did not have and yet a past that we carry around with us and that continues to have an effect. We cannot, for example, genuinely conceive of the advent of language, or what may have been left behind, or what may have been transformed by that advent. In the attempt to conceive of such an event, the event takes on the character of a Kantian Idea, beyond intentional presentation, and distorted by our own linguistic conception. In this case, however, it would always already, in an anterior fashion, regulate intentional life. Such an event is, in Lyotard's phrase, "refractory to all functions of presentation," and by this very resistance proves itself indubitably (1989, 405).

The effacement of the other

"Look for nothing behind phenomena: they themselves are what is to be learned" (Goethe 1963, 17). Goethe expresses well a motto of phenomenology. Would it always be metaphysics to claim that behind a phenomenon there is something more, something in excess of that which appears, and something for which the phenomenon itself is only a sign, a trace that gives evidence for what effaces itself in the appearance? Metaphysics, perhaps, if it is *being* beyond the sign. Levinas, however, speaks of "*signification* beyond *being*." The face of the other person presents itself to intentional consciousness, and yet withdraws from intentional presence. The withdrawal of the face, Levinas says, "is not a negation of presence, nor its pure latency, recoupable in memory or actualization. It is alterity, without common measure with a presence or a past assembling into a synthesis in the synchrony of the correlative" (1981, 90). The face of the other escapes the schema of time-consciousness, and reveals the inadequacy of intentionality in its most vivid moment of primal impression. In Levinas's metaphor, the present becomes an abyss "where synthesis and contemporaneousness are refused" (1981, 89). Faced with the face, intentionality "defects," falters. The other person offers to intentionality only a trace of that which could not be contained or summarized in the phenomenon of the other's face, that which is "disproportionate to all measure and all capacity, the trace of the infinite signifying diachronically exactly through these ambiguities" (1981, 91).

We may be able to grasp what Levinas means by considering cases in which a person's face does not operate as a face normally does. In Möbius Syndrome, first described by the nineteenth-century German neurologist, Paul Möbius, subjects are born unable to move any of the muscles of facial expression, or to move their eyes laterally. They are unable, for example, to smile or move their lips, to raise their eyebrows, or close their eyes tightly. People with Möbius have drooping, wide eyes, and a narrow open mouth, and the face appears to have a masklike quality. In addition they are unable to perform sideways movement of the eyes, so that they have to move the whole head to look to the right or left (Cole 1997b). As might be expected, Möbius patients have difficulties with respect to social and emotional development. Patients report a certain lack of dimension to emotional life, or a dissociation from feelings, which tend to be reduced to intellectual attitudes. To another person the Möbius face presents an interpretational difficulty. One needs to search its masklike quality for signs that transcend its mere physical appearance. The problem with the Möbius face is that it doesn't efface itself; it impedes the normal communicative lines that lead in the direction of the other person. This lends some support to the idea that, as in the case of neonate imitation, what one normally sees in a face is not its purely physical appearance, but its gesture, its expression, or more precisely, the other person's gesture and expression, and one's own possibilities. These attributes and processes are not reducible to things that are entirely present. Unlike the Möbius face, the face is normally a sign, leading beyond its mere physicality.

The effacement happens beyond intentionality and cognition in what would be an ethical relation, a relation that might involve sexuality or justice or communication, but in a way that would not be reducible to noetic-noematic, subjective-objective correlation. In the face-to-face of such a relation I do not *know* the other in any sense of imposing a form upon a sensible content, or of constituting a noema within a noetic schema. It remains primitive in comparison to intentional maturity; it takes shape, or more precisely it refuses to take on shape, at the level of hyletic experience. In Husserl's terms, as Levinas points out, sensation or *hyle* "participates in the meaningful only inasmuch as it is *animated* by intentionality, a constituted immanent time according to the schema of theoretical consciousness of . . . in retention and protention, in memory and expectation" (Levinas 1981, 65). But outside of intentional animation my experience of the other person in an immediacy of sensuousness (enjoyment, suffering) eludes the determinacy of meaning. Intentionality prevaricates in the face of affective sensibility by treating it as information for processing in a schema that bestows meaning. In the bestowal of meaning, in the conferral of myself (the same) on the other, intentionality destroys the alterity of the other person, reduces otherness to sameness, and difference to identity.

Within the intentional relation, knowledge tends toward the totalization of its object, ties it down in time and space. In the face-to-face, however, one is never even sure the other person is "there." Donna

Williams, an extraordinary woman who suffers from a form of autism, describes an extreme instance. "He kissed me—or perhaps I should say that he kissed my face, as I wasn't in it at the time."[13] Autism may involve extreme problems in connection with "disconnected faces," but the uncertainty of the other person's presence is a constant possibility even in everyday, nonautistic relations.

What effaces itself in the presence of the face, that is, in our attempt to know the other, is not a past or a future that could be retended or protended by time-consciousness. In the movement of effacement the presented other involves a future we can never experience comprehensively or synthesize, something that continually escapes, never to be caught up with, never fulfilled. It does not flow away in a stream that could be remembered by consciousness. Our relation to the presented other is prior to the present in a way that cannot be recovered; it involves a past that we cannot remember, like our birth. The mother has the child prior to the child having a past. The face of the mother, Lyotard remarks, will be forgotten "because it will not have been inscribed" (1989, 217). More generally, it is difficult to inscribe any face, and perhaps even impossible to inscribe our own. Witness the anxiety experienced when we have difficulty remembering how a deceased loved one really looked. Witness, also, our dissatisfaction with most photographs of those whom we "know well," especially photographs of ourselves. A photograph or a portrait that can somehow acknowledge (not capture) that which is beyond the intentionalized face, or that can acknowledge the movement of effacement, is sublime art. The face-to-face is not reducible to photographic intentionality; it cannot be totalized or summarized, collected, caught, or represented. At best the face poses a *persona* that has no identity and that cannot be played out on a theater-stage of consciousness.[14]

Experiences associated with the face of the other person are, for good reason, similar to an experience that the phenomenologist has at the very center of the vortex of intentional consciousness, an experience that completely outstrips the power of reflection and that demonstrates the inadequacy of reflection for an essential phenomenological task. I refer to the attempt to grasp reflectively the transcendental ego. In the first edition of the *Logical Investigations* Husserl asserted that for him it was not possible to find in consciousness a transcendental ego, and that any attempt to do so would result in an objectified empirical ego. Although Husserl later changes his mind, both figuratively and literally in this case—claiming "I have since managed to find it," and "how can we avoid assuming a pure ego?"—it is clear that reflection allows him only to make the assumption (see 1970a, 549 n. 1, 544 n. 1). The earlier Husserl rightly takes an appropriately Kantian position against the possibility of intuiting the formal ego. The ego effaces itself before reflection; reflection falls short, intentionality fails at the very center of intentional consciousness.[15]

Attempting to grasp reflectively the transcendental ego of one's own stream of consciousness has a structure similar to attempting to see one's own, or even another's face. My own face, like the face of the other, is a transcendental in the sense that it lies beyond the capability of intentional grasp.

Memento mori

It is always possible to treat death as an objective event and to place it within a time series. My death (or another person's death) occurs some time *later* than my birth or another person's birth. If yesterday was my thirtieth birthday, my death will occur some time *after* my thirtieth birthday, and always, some time future to this present moment. On the one hand, I can always conceive of my death, or another's death, as an objective event, and thereby make it into an intentional object. On the other hand, however, death is something more than an objective event in serial time, more than a conception, more than an intentional object. In actuality, death always escapes intentionality; it always operates beyond the constraints of an intentional consciousness. Death is the end, the finish, but not the completion of intentionality. Death itself, as it *is* in itself (and these words do not correctly capture it) is indeterminate and incomprehensible; it becomes impoverished and distorted if reduced to an intentional object.

Death is not something we can conceive in itself, as it actually *is* or could be. Indeed, death is not an *it* and perhaps escapes any positive ontological categories. The word "is" may be inappropriate to death. Although common sense and predicate logic allow us to say that a person "is dead," death is not a predicate that can be attributed to a subject; it is a matter neither of common sense nor of logic. There is no positive image of death that would suffice for death itself. Every attempt to comprehend death results in classifying it in terms of life: thinking of either "life coming to an end" or "continued life beyond death," the negation of life or the reaffirmation of life, the negation of the person or the nondeath of the person. In either case, Epicurus's adage is appropriate: "Where death is, I am not; where I am, death is not." This seems to be the case both existentially, as Epicurus intended, and with respect to designing a theory of death.

In many ways this thought runs counter to Heidegger's existential conception of death, which he summarizes in this way: death "reveals itself as that possibility which is one's ownmost, which is non-relational, and which is not to be outstripped" (1962, 294). But is death, as Heidegger contends, a *possibility*, or something we can be *capable* of? (1971, 178). Everything about death is uncertain, except the certitude of it. A possibility is something that may not happen; but isn't death beyond possibility because it is certain? Death is not even "the possibility of impossibility" (Levinas) but the certitude of impossibility, a certitude of not-being rather than a "possibility-of-Being" (Heidegger 1962, 294), the certitude of nonexistence rather than "the uttermost possibility of existence" (1962, 299). *It* is certain, even if *I* am not certain. Furthermore, death can be neither "*my ownmost* possibility," nor *my ownmost* actuality since, in death, "*my ownmost*" is dissipated: "where death is, I am not." Although dying, or a hypothetical death that is not yet, may be mine, death itself is not mine since in death the *me,* the *I,* is absolutely dispersed. Even if being-towards-death is inevitably mine, death itself is never in any case mine. It is not a possibility of being for me, because it is neither a mere possibility nor mine.

Again, in opposition to Heidegger, we could say that there belongs to Dasein, as long as it is, a not-yet that it will never be (cf. 1962, 286), even if it is and has to be *towards* its not-yet, in the sense of being-towards-death. The being-towards of being-towards-death is a form of intentionality that reduces death to a possibility and an intentional object. I can have an intentional relation toward a possibility that I have, I can plan out some project and go on to realize it or not, but I cannot have an intentional relation to death. Even in the case of suicide, the act of killing myself is cut off from death. I can have a relation to the project of killing myself; but in death the project and the relation dissipate as Dasein dissipates. As Levinas expresses it, death "is the impossibility of having a project" (1987, 74). Death is not a totalizing of Dasein, as Heidegger recognizes, but an absolute dispersal. It is not something "still missing" from Dasein (1962, 286), as if it were the final part of a puzzle. Rather, it is such that when added to the puzzle, the puzzle is not completed but destroyed. In death there is no puzzle left, no Dasein, no possibilities.

By the proposition that death is nonrelational Heidegger means that the intentional relation of being-towards-death individuates Dasein. "When it [Dasein] stands before itself in this way, all its relations to any other Dasein have been undone" (1962, 294). Dasein is thrust back onto its isolated ownness as it confronts the certitude of death. Heidegger's analysis here is disputed by Levinas. For Levinas, death is "refractory to the intimacy of the self with the ego to which all our experiences return" (1987, 69). Death is not constituted in an intentional relation; at best, "the subject is in relationship with what does not come from itself. We could say it is in relationship with mystery" (1987, 69). This relationship to the mystery of death does not individuate or isolate the subject, rather it throws the individual into a relation with something "absolutely other."

The solitude of the ego is not authenticated by death, but shattered by it. Not death but being-towards the certitude of death makes possible ethical relations with other persons. I ought not to remain indifferent toward others who, like me, are mortal. The relation I have toward the certitude of death calls me to a relationship toward others who share the same fate (see Marx 1987; Wyschogrod 1990).

Even within the ethical relation, however, death maintains a certain nonrelational character, not as Heidegger contends, with respect to other persons, but with respect to one's own person. Death, as Levinas suggests, is something "in relation to which the subject is no longer a subject" (1987, 70). Being-towards-death is not a relation that I have with death itself, but with some idea of death. If being-towards-death opens up possibilities of ethical relations between others and myself, death itself closes down all such possibilities. Insofar as I am, I can have no relation to death itself; insofar as there is death, it can have no relation to me. Death itself effaces the possibility of any relationship with it. This is why Epicurus's adage captures the paradox of death: I exist in an impossible relation with death.[16] The subject will certainly die, but it will never be dead, or exist in death. Death is not a negation of a relation; it is not nonrelational, it is arelational, it is beyond both intentional and metaphysical relations.

This means, not so much as Heidegger puts it, that death cannot be outstripped, but rather, that death outstrips the subject. Heidegger would be right to say that being-towards-death, and dying itself are such that they cannot be outstripped, that is, avoided. Death itself, however, is always avoided insofar as where Dasein is there is no death, and where there is death Dasein is not.

Historical effect, the other person, death: these are things reduced and distorted if objectified in intentional consciousness. As such, they escape subjective control and operate rather as prenoetic dimensions that disrupt intentionality before it begins, decenter it at its very center, and disperse it at its end. These dimensions constitute transcendentals beyond intentionality, yet not without effect on intentionality, shaping and limiting our existence, and making up, along with other constraints, the prenoetic network that transcends and yet carries human subjectivity.

The Inordinate Reality of Time

McTaggart, in his essay of 1908, "The Unreality of Time," famously renewed a traditional disputation about the ontological reality of time. The issue can be traced back to Augustine and even to Aristotle, who made the soul an essential player in the institution of time. McTaggart joined the ranks of many theorists who reduce time to a subjective construction, a form of intuition or a function of cognitive faculties like memory and expectation. Although Husserl, in his phenomenological enterprise, attempts to avoid metaphysical judgments about the reality or unreality of time, he too finds himself caught in certain metaphysical presuppositions about presence and actuality that seemingly lead to a notion of time reduced to a construction of intentional consciousness. And, before we forget that this view is not an exclusive purview shared only by would-be rivals from the camps of idealistic psychologism and phenomenology, let's remind ourselves that modern physicists are not exempt from claiming that time is a subjective construct. Einstein, for example, not only makes time relative to the position and velocity of the observer, but proposes that time is a mode of thought rather than a condition of existence.[17] Space-time is a theoretical model, not an ontological reality.

We can, of course, find opposition to such views. In the Newtonian universe as well as in the Leibnizian universe, time is independent of subjectivity, respectively in either an absolute, metaphysically real way, or in a relative, mathematically ideal way. Common sense and naive realism, too, do not fail to recognize time's objective nature.

Do these alternatives, then, exhaust the possibilities? Is it, accordingly, impossible to avoid thinking of time in the metaphysical framework of subjective versus objective—categories that are of one system insofar as they are defined in terms of each other? The system of intentionality certainly reflects this metaphysical structure. Time is either constituted within the noetic framework of conscious acts floating on the retentional-protentional flow, or it is objectively present in the world revealed as an intentional correlate. It may be that when thinking about time it is difficult if not impossible to escape this metaphysical thought, and that any alternative proposal will necessarily be tied to a subjective-objective dualism, or to a sense of unreality-reality. Is it not possible, however, to propose an alternative that acknowledges the prenoetic dispersals and parachronic effacements considered above, and that moves us beyond the intentional model?

Starting from a reflective intentionality one is led to cast time in terms of either subjective ideality or objective reality, either specious present or real serial flow. Such reflective fixations, however, lead us away from a certain facticity that cannot be reduced to experiential presence or objective succession. Reflection requires, as Merleau-Ponty indicated, forgetting or repressing the "non-knowing of the beginning which is not nothing, and which is not the reflective truth either, and which also must be accounted for" (1968, 49). What is the facticity, the anteriority that is not nothing, but that eludes reflective and theoretical analysis?

The reflecting phenomenologist, like the theorizing physicist, and everybody else, is already submerged in a localized and temporalized factical existence. What appears to be the presence of absolute subjectivity, appears so only because of an immense network of effects that intentionality does not so much represent as conceal. Intentionality can only function as it does by occluding prenoetic effects, diverging from them, leaving them unpresented, unrepresented, invisible. The body in the act of perceiving, the anterior effects of history and language that shape experience, the alterity that disrupts the identity of self-consciousness, are all effaced in the noetic-noematic structure. There is, in this sense, a latent, anterior, pre-intentional dimension of experience missed by the phenomenological focus on the noetic *act* of consciousness.

That these factors are anterior means that they have an influence, a real effect on temporal form. Anteriority also means that they are already there, already operating as factors established in a past that is different from the past that we can make the theme of reflective intentionality. The body, for example, in its habitual schemas—in its gait and posture, in its autonomic functions—retains a past that falls short of explicit, intentional memory; yet this is a past that helps, in a real way, to define the very possibilities of the present. This past falls short of an explicit act of remembering; it transcends intentionality in the sense that I, as an experiencing subject, am not required to have a conscious act of recollection in order for this past to be operative in the present. This past does not recede into a remote past; it does not take its orderly place in an objective B-series. And like the specious present it seems to collapse the neat distinctions of the ordinary and orderly A-series. There is here a certain inordinate reality that does not follow the rules of seriality.

Prenoetic pasts encroach and intrude upon primal impression, not in the form of a frontal imposition of an objective or intentional time; rather, the temporality involved in prenoetic effects intrudes *a tergo*. Some of these pasts are a matter of forgotten autobiography, others a matter of common cultural practices. Such pasts are never present for intentional consciousness, but play out their effects on consciousness while they remain effaced in the form of the perceiver's body schema, or embedded in the environment, in language, in social custom, and so forth.[18] Time, in this prenoetic sense, transcends and has a reality beyond intentional consciousness, not, however, in the direction of what is usually regarded as objective reality, "out there" and open to the careful regard of intentional examination. Rather, the reality of time must be sought in the direction of prenoetic—corporeal, historical, linguistic, and social—effects. These effects operate from a past that is not under noetic control, a past so far beyond the reach of memory that our reconstruction of it can only remain incompletely explicated in a hermeneutical approach. Yet, this is a past that remains significantly operative in our present cognition and action. The ordering of consciousness into an intentional temporalizing structure geared into the surrounding world depends on an embodied and effective past, continually operating in the prenoetic background.

Similar things can be said of a future that constantly escapes intentional control. This cannot be a future that is laid out at the far end of objective seriality, or a future made intentionally present within the protentional grasp of consciousness. Nonetheless, a prodigal and improvident future, that which is not yet and is completely indeterminate affects our possibilities and constrains what we can project from out of the present. That this is the case we have seen in considerations about death, a not-yet that never will be something for intentionality, a nonphenomenon that nonetheless limits the directionality of intentional life since we are always "toward" it even if we are running away from it. I find myself caught up in a relation with something absolutely other to existence—and this is a condition that conditions my existence and my relations with other persons.

Time has real effects; it has reality, not in the traditional metaphysical sense of being something *in itself,* objective, on the *far* side of phenomena. Nor is this temporality something that can be reduced to noetic structure or noematic content, a time limited to the irreality of consciousness. Its reality is hidden in transintentional effects.

Time on this conception is not susceptible to McTaggart's arguments about the unreality of time. McTaggart claims that time, in the form of the A-series (past-present-future), is unreal because it involves a contradiction: any event is characterized by all of the incompatible determinations: past, present, future. A future event, for example, will be present and then past. He considers the obvious response that no event has incompatible A-characteristics at the same time—it can only have them successively. This seems obvious from the required use of different tenses in statements about how a particular event can have such incompatible determinations. But, according to McTaggart, this riposte is viciously circular. Tense depends upon the A-series, and we end up escaping the initial contradiction of incompatible temporal determinations by an appeal to either a second-order contradiction (incompatible tenses) or an infinite regress from A-series to A-series. As Mellor clearly puts it, "the truth conditions of tensed sentences are either tenseless or self-contradictory" (1981, 101). McTaggart solves this paradox by making time purely a matter of an Augustinian psychology—the distinctions of past-present-future arise on the basis of the cognitive functions: memory, perception, and expectation. But this only leads to a different paradox, the cognitive paradox, which, as we saw in chapter 2, McTaggart was willing to live with.

In the time-order of his text, just before his suggestion about the psychological nature of time, McTaggart considers a possible objection to his claim that objective time-determinations involve contradiction. He had demonstrated that the A-series cannot be explained without assuming the A-series (as it is involved in tense). Doesn't this prove "not that time is invalid, but rather that time is ultimate?" Isn't time so ubiquitous and inescapable that it would be silly to reject its reality? McTaggart easily handles this objection by pointing again to the irresolvable contradiction that makes the validity of the objective reality of time impossible. "It cannot be valid of reality if its application to reality involves a contradiction" (1908, 470).

This leads us further back to an earlier part of his argument, and to an assumption that he made even earlier than that—an assumption that continues to have an effect even if it is hidden in the background. McTaggart assumes, of course, the principle of noncontradiction: a thing cannot be and not be *at the same time*. Doesn't this last phrase begin to unravel McTaggart's argument? Isn't this the seed of its own deconstruction? Time is so ubiquitous that it infects the very principle that McTaggart uses to reject its ubiquity. If time is unreal, then the principle that McTaggart assumes in the demonstration of its unreality is itself undermined. The argument that the reality of time is invalid is itself invalid unless one assumes the reality of time.

This response to McTaggart is neither original nor the final word. Others have considered it and have gone on to reformulate the principle of noncontradiction without the presupposition of time.[19] For our purposes this response is also a detour away from the question of a prenoetic reality of time. All such considerations about McTaggart's argument are still concerned with the issue of the objective reality of time. I want to suggest that regardless of what McTaggart's argument means for the objective reality of time, in one sense his argument actually proves the prenoetic (pre-objective) reality of time. The proof is not that McTaggart necessarily wrote his argument one word at a time, one part of the text necessarily earlier than the other; nor the requirement that the argument be constructed one premise or syllogism at a time in the order of a B-series. Nor do I mean simply that McTaggart's argument was made sometime in the past, relative to all of our present perceptions. These are precisely the sorts of things that McTaggart wanted to reduce to psychology. The fact that text has a temporal structure, and that the event of his argumentation becomes ever more remote in the past; these facts reflect the objective temporal characteristics that lead to contradiction.

It might help us to put this issue into slightly different terms. One way to define the reality of time is to claim that time is real if it has an existence independent of the observer, the perceiver, the epistemological and psychological subject. Newton, for example, claimed that time was independent of everything—without relation to anything external to it. On this view, time exists outside of any context. In relativity theory, time is contextualized to the extent that in some respects it is not independent of the observer and other factors such as distance, velocity, and gravity.

McTaggart argues that time is unreal in the sense that it is just psychological—that is, completely confined to the context of subjective cognition. His evidence for this is to be found in the contradictions associated with tensed statements. Much of the critical discussion following McTaggart focuses on the status of tensed versus tenseless statements, or propositions and their truth conditions considered as objective facts. To take up the argument in that way, however, requires accepting not only certain logical assumptions, like the principle of noncontradiction, or the assumption that there is a complete description of reality (see Dummett 1960), but also certain ontological assumptions involved in the standard subjective-objective distinction, as well as a certain traditional view of language.

The very fact of making assumptions, indeed, the unavoidability of making assumptions not only in logical argumentation, but in more general communicative actions, indicates a context that transcends the individual subject. The assumptions are not the inventions of McTaggart. They are, in some respects, the products of historical effects. No thinker thinks in isolation; no argument is constructed without some temporally prior contexts of thought, and language, and history that are beyond the individual thinker. Can anyone doubt that McTaggart, in formulating his solution, saw the light only by being in the shadow of Augustine? And isn't Augustine's solution worked out in the shadow of a certain conflict between a preestablished theological framework and certain doubts raised by skeptics and Stoics? And should we then not name a set of other traditions that provided the framework and the cause for doubts that Augustine inherited? And could we not trace these traces back until we lose them in a variety of prehistories that still seem to have their effects on our current deliberations?

McTaggart denies the reality of time. Regardless of how we formulate this fact in language (to satisfy some we should have to say, "It was the case that McTaggart denies the reality of time," and for others, "It is the case that McTaggart denied the reality of time"), doesn't his argument actually show that temporality is unavoidable, since even the language that is used to attempt to resolve difficulties and contradictions contained in explanations of time is itself caught up in its own temporality? Even Mellor, who argues that tense is unreal, that is, has no basis in objective reality, admits that it is impossible to avoid tensed statements. And this is the case, he claims, because intentionality is unavoidably tensed (1981, 6, 78ff., 99–100). That which accounts for the temporality of intentionality, however, does not lie purely within the realm of intentionality, but extends back into prenoetic effects that are more than intentional structures or psychological constructs.

Such effects are inordinately temporal; some set of them is unavoidable; many times they remain hidden. It is not just that an inheritance from the past invades our present experience and is passed on to future generations in our belief systems and institutions. More than that, our experiences and communications are shaped, semantically twisted, and often unpinned by that which cannot be presented or represented, by those dimensions that transcend the capabilities of retention and recollection, and by an indeterminate excess that cannot be protended. Time is real to the extent that there are real prenoetic temporal effects. The evidence for this is not to be found in objective reality, or in the truth-conditions for tensed statements, but in the temporal effects of prenoetic and hermeneutical constraints on experience. These effects transcend subjectivity, and cannot be brought under subjective control. They are both relative to, yet independent of "the observer" (the epistemological subject, the perceiver, the ego, the self, etc.) in the sense that they refer us to a larger context than subjectivity—a context (network, system) within which subjective experience is shaped by contents and factors that outstrip subjective control. Thus, we cannot name or explicate all of the temporal effects that make argumentation and communication possible, and temporality is not confined to the context of subjectivity—that is, it is not reducible to psychological, cognitive, or intentional operations.

Inordinate Temporality

Faced with a prenoetic network distributed across the effects of history, language, social and cultural traditions, embodiment, the unconscious, and so forth, is it possible to develop an expanded analysis of the experience of the flow of time? In light of the parachronic effacements of temporalities that are dissipated in history, other persons, and the mystery of death, is it not impossible to develop a single consistent theory that would adequately account for the full complexity of the experience of time? I want to answer yes to both of these questions. On the one hand, following our considerations in chapter 8, I think it is possible to develop a more sophisticated, hermeneutically enlightened conception of temporal experience that would complicate, but also serve, scientific investigations of cognitive behavior. On the other hand, following our considerations in chapter 9, I want to suggest that no one theory, no one paradigm, not even a hermeneutically enlightened one, will ever be able to account fully for temporal experience. In this case, the best we can do is to allow for a plurality of theories, a variety of accounts that will demonstrate in different ways the inexhaustible parachronicity of experience.

Phenomenology, Psychology, and Subpersonal Effects

The modern conception of the flow of the conscious stream no doubt reflects the idea of an objective flow of time, Newton's *tempus quod equabiliter fluit*. And no less than the Kantian form of intuition, the stream of consciousness operates as a formal organizing principle. The stream, as Husserl puts it, flows just as it flows, regardless of the content of experience. The retentional-protentional temporal structure of consciousness is a formal rule that organizes content. Still, at the fringes of this formal structure, Husserl, no less than James, admits that in some sense the

content of experience may impinge upon the autonomy of the temporal
flow. Some things, because of their significance, remain in the retentional
train longer than others; protention can be extended in boredom or cut
short in surprise. James goes further along this line than Husserl when
he suggests that the flow speeds up or slows down depending on the
interest or lack of interest the subject has in the object of attention. Good
conversation can sometimes make time pass too quickly. Time flies when
you're having fun, and so forth.[1] How normal, and yet how similar to the
psychopathological in temporal structure, are experiences like reverie,
fantasies, lapses of memory, invasions of memory, and so forth?

Notwithstanding such annotations, it is clear that throughout the
history of the phenomenological paradigm, from Locke to Husserl, formal structure always rules over content. This is clear in Husserl's opposition to Brentano's view that the temporal element in consciousness is
in some way tied to sense and re-presented content. For similar reasons
Husserl opposed a position held by Paul Natorp. Natorp suggests that
consciousness consists in having contents, and that change in consciousness is due to change in contents. Not unlike Hume, Natorp insists that if
"anyone can catch his consciousness in anything else than the existence
of a content for him, I am unable to follow him."[2] Natorp thus reduces
the conscious flow to a flow of intentional or sense-content.

More recently, in a different context, David Wood has suggested
that the conscious present is not content-independent. The conscious
presence of a particular musical note, for example, would be "shaped"
differently from the conscious presence of the sound of ocean surf. "If
it were admitted that *some* 'content,' with contributions of its own to
make to the shape and scope of the 'present,' were always to be taken
account of, then one would have an argument for the *radical impurity* of
the present"(Wood 1989, 121). For Wood, however, the content under
consideration is limited to intentional content: "for some 'content' to
lend shape to the present, that content has to be grasped as such. . . .
For a tune to shape time it must be experienced *as a tuneful sequence*"
(1989, 121).

Husserl, as we have seen, argues against the possibility that formal
noetic and temporal structures of consciousness are in some way shaped
by content. He insists that content must be distinguishable from conscious
acts, that a particular content can be the object of a variety of acts, and
that acts, along with their contents, flow off in the formal stream of consciousness. His concept of the double intentionality of retentioning tells
us that the content flows only because the act, structured in a retentional
fashion, flows. Otherwise, content would simply appear and disappear
instantaneously. Thus, according to phenomenology, the temporality

of consciousness is a formal structure by which acts and contents are formally ordered: temporality is not derived from content; content is brought into the order of sense and significance only on the basis of the retentional-protentional structure.

Psychologists who offer a cognitive interpretation to account for various time distortions (the speeding up or slowing down of the flow of consciousness) remain tied to the same formalistic approach, even when they suggest that content makes a difference. To the extent that physiological models (biological clocks and oscillators, etc.) are unable to explain such distortions, the cognitivist falls back on a psychological explanation in terms of the *quantity* of conscious acts or contents rather than considering the possibility that the content-quality may be a controlling factor.[3] On at least one cognitivist account, content counts only because it can be counted, because it crowds our consciousness, or deserts it, not because it draws or fails to draw our interest. This sort of cognitive explanation is limited to the formal, quantitative, syntactic aspects of information processing, and fails to take into consideration the possible semantic effects of content.

In order to understand the semantic effects of content on the temporality of consciousness we cannot simply conceive of consciousness as a formal system that completely controls and organizes the temporal order of content. Rather we need to see that the "stream" (in this section we retain this metaphor) is not purely formal. Furthermore, we cannot focus on just intentional content, even in terms of its semantic quality. For Husserl, just as much as for Natorp and Wood, content means intentional content, content that we are aware of. They fail to consider the effects of what we could call "prenoetic content."

If we focus on a fuller formulation of intentionality, such as, "consciousness of something *as* something," then we may start to recognize the weight that needs to be attributed to intentional content—the something-*as*-something. Pursuing this hermeneutical *as*, however, leads us to acknowledge that there is a hidden basis for the projection of meaning. Consciousness, as an interpretive process, is not purely formal (if we understand this to mean independent of content), nor fully summarized by its intentional content, since consciousness is shaped by an excess, anterior content that it does not have under its intentional control.

Hermeneutical theory shows us that intentional *content* (what we perceive or judge or believe, and so forth) and the particular character of our intentional *acts* are shaped by prenoetic factors (like language and tradition). Beyond this, shouldn't we also say that the formal structure of such acts, and in particular their temporal structure, are also subject to prenoetic forces? To admit this is to give up the idea of a relatively autonomous subject. It would be to admit, not simply that *what* I believe shapes my act of belief, but that factors I am not even intentionally aware of can structure my belief at a very basic level, and that such factors can shape experience into something different than a linear stream.

"Content" is perhaps an inappropriate term in this context. In philosophical contexts, content tends to be viewed as the passive, controlled part of the traditional form-content distinction. The prenoetic factors that we are invoking here, however, do not submit to form so much as they disrupt, in both theory and practice, the form-content distinction. "Content" also traditionally signifies something contained, something immanent. For Husserl that can mean either intentional content or hyletic content (sensations); he argues against the idea of unconscious content. The prenoetic factors we have been discussing, however, are neither intentional nor equivalent to hyletic data, in Husserl's precise sense. They are neither contained in nor immanent to consciousness. Yet they have *effects,* and might better be called "*forces*" than "contents."

There is, no doubt, an interaction between intentional contents and prenoetic forces. The anterior function of language and social traditions constrain the significance of a particular content, which, in turn may add to or modify linguistic usages and social traditions. It may also be the case, as Natorp and Wood contend, that intentional contents have an effect on the temporal structure of consciousness. But why content X (e.g., a musical lament) shapes temporality in one way, while content Y (e.g., a stormy sea) does not, cannot be adequately answered on the level of intentional analysis; it can only be answered by inquiring into appropriate prenoetic backgrounds. If, as Wood argues, time-consciousness is disrupted by representation, i.e., intentional content, this can only be the case because a particular representation takes on a time-shaping significance on the basis of prenoetic forces.

Prenoetic forces not only operate as a basic sine qua non to intentional consciousness, conditioning and enabling its temporal order, but they can also invade and disrupt the ordering mechanisms of intentionality, including those responsible for temporal ordering. Such forces can be described in terms of a network of meaning-generating factors out of which a particular consciousness emerges, a network system that involves at least two different sets of forces that we began to explore in previous chapters. The first set includes subpersonal, hyletic (material) factors of embodiment and environment. Here one can describe effects on the structure of intentionality in terms of hyletic factors, body schema, and an organism-environment interaction. The second set of forces, which in contrast might be called "superpersonal," includes the hermeneutical effects of language, historical circumstance, culture, social relations, and so forth. In the remainder of this section I want to further explore certain subpersonal aspects, including what Husserl calls hyletic processes. I will reserve discussion of hermeneutical effects for the following section.

As we have already seen, the status of hyletic data in Husserl's phenomenology is quite complex. For our purposes, three interconnected issues are important. There is, first, the shift in the theoretical status of hyletic data for the explanation of time-consciousness. In his early analysis Husserl employed the noetic schema (apprehension–hyletic content) as the central component of his model of intentionality and as a controlling concept for the account of time-consciousness. Later he abandoned this theoretical construct in his analysis of time-consciousness, although he never gave it up completely in his account of intentionality. Second, the status of hyletic data as nonintentional, *reell* elements of consciousness is made ambiguous by Husserl's contention that we are aware of sensations, that they are incorporated into the stream of consciousness in a way that makes them accessible to a reflective intentionality (e.g., 1991, 131). This, in effect, turns hyletic content into intentional content for phenomenological reflective regard. Third, the ontological status of hyletic data remains unresolved. Are hyletic data, as Husserl claims, *reell* elements in consciousness, or are they misplaced theoretical constructs?

I have already suggested that the hyletic factors that shape experience do not consist of *reell* content contained in consciousness; rather, they consist of prenoetic processes of bodily existence (see chapter 8; Gallagher 1986a). Physiological changes in the body not only have physical results describable in purely physical and objective terms; they also affect intentional experience—either allowing it to continue in a way consistent with its contemporary course, or causing a noticeable change in experience. Physiological processes, insofar as they have an effect on intentionality, are prenoetic hyletic processes. In some cases hyletic processes noticeably affect the temporal structure of experience. As such, their exclusion from considerations about time-consciousness, which commentators unanimously view as a valuable development in Husserl's later analysis, and which allows Husserl to perfect the phenomenological paradigm of time-consciousness, is nonetheless a mistake that helps to explain the inadequacy of Husserl's theory in the face of post-Husserlian objections.

On Husserl's analysis, hyletic contents follow the intentional flow and are organized by apprehensions that interpret their place subordinate to intentional meaning. In contrast, if hyletic processes are prenoetic, subpersonal operations of the body, then they condition intentional experience, and rather than being under the complete control of consciousness, fitting neatly into its temporal order, they have the potential to disrupt or reconfigure the intentional stream. This view, furthermore, suggests that there are other temporal orders, other sets of rhythms that belong to the body—a biological time, or multiple biological times measured by biological clocks that have an effect on time-consciousness.[4] These include diurnal or circadian temporalities worked out in relations between the body and its environment. As long as these biological clocks are synchronized and maintained at a normal rate, the intentional flow can proceed at its ordinary pace. In some cases, however, such processes can interfere with the orderly flow of consciousness. Either the processes are in sync or they begin to interrupt each other. One can point to psychosomatic symptoms in which intentional content, laden with emotional values, throws off the normal rhythms of the body, which, in turn, take their effect on intentional order. Think, for example, of the increased heart-rate and rise in blood pressure, as well as the mistiming of action that can accompany anger. Other examples include stress, lability, stagefright, and the flutter of the heart involved in some love experiences. Time passes differently in such experiences.

We can be more specific than this. The interference and disruption of the orderly and ordinary flow of the stream of consciousness by subpersonal forces is easily and empirically demonstrated in fields such as psychopharmacology and psychopathology.

Chemical changes in the body caused by the ingestion of drugs or the chemical imbalance of illness not only have an effect on the content of experience, but clearly alter the experience of time. Psychotomimetic drugs, such as LSD, mescaline, and psilocybin, produce physiological changes evidenced in a desynchronizing of EEG rhythm, increased muscle tension, and an acceleration in the rate of metabolism. The hyletic effects of such physiological changes include changes in the way subjects consciously experience their bodies, including complaints of dizziness, weakness, tremors, nausea, drowsiness, and blurred vision. Subjects also experience altered shapes and colors, difficulty in focusing, and sometimes synaesthesia (Hollister 1978). In such cases, subjects suffer from disordered temporal experience, including abnormalities in the sense of time-velocity, time estimation and temporal orientation (Barr, et al. 1972; Hollister 1978; Laurie 1971; Mayer-Gross 1964; Ornstein 1969; Tinklenberg, et al. 1972). Cannabis intoxication results in increased heart-rate and abnormal EEG rhythms, disturbances in perceptual experience, and distortions in time estimation and time perspective, including flashbacks (Bech, Rafaelsen, and Rafaelsen 1973; Jones 1978; Laurie 1971; Meyer 1978; Ornstein 1969; Tinklenberg 1972). The opiates produce hyletic changes associated with slower respiration, lower body temperature, and abnormal EEG patterns. These correlate with changes in intentional experience: itching, nausea, feelings of warmth, light-headedness, dizziness, and perceptual disturbances, as well as an experiential expansion of time (Fink 1978; Friedman 1990; Mansky 1978; Whitrow 1963).

The same kinds of correlations between physiological, hyletic, perceptual, and temporal experiences can be found in psychopathological disturbances. In schizophrenia, for example, physiological changes are evidenced by abnormal EEG patterns, increased muscle tension, higher heart-rate and blood pressure, as well as abnormalities in the autonomic nervous system. Hyletic and perceptual changes are evidenced in a variety of body-image disturbances, somatic passivity experiences, the lack of external focus, and auditory hallucinations. Such changes are correlated to difficulties in temporally indexing events, distortions in time estimation and temporal velocity, the curtailment of coherent future time perspective, and a confusion between past, present, and future. Similar correlations can be found in the symptoms of depersonalization, hypochondria, depression, Korsakoff's syndrome, and in various neuroses (Crain, Goldstone, and Lhamon 1975; Goldstone and Goldfarb 1962; Kolb 1959; Melges and Freeman 1977; Minkowski 1970; Pontius 1977; Rosenfield 1992; Rutschmann 1973).

Still, one might object, such accounts of *abnormal* hyletic processes and their correlation to the disruption of orderly temporal experience seem to presuppose and even verify the idea that a formal seriality of the conscious stream is the norm.[5] The fact is, however, that the very notion of an orderly stream can be put into question even within the category of the normal. Normal interruptions or distortions may not be the radical or noticeable kinds documented in psychopathological or psychopharmacological studies, but they can be significant enough to challenge the general laws of time-consciousness. In certain contexts hyletic processes associated with hunger or pain can, like boredom, make the experienced sense of time seem to slow down. When the embodied subject gets tired, loses the ability to concentrate, or begins to fall asleep, disruptions of the orderly flow of consciousness are quite normal. Thus, even granting the concept of a stream of consciousness on the intentional level, we can point to a variety of normal and abnormal interruptions of that stream connected to bodily-hyletic processes. In some cases these processes can even have the effect of reserializing the intentional flow, relative to objective measurements.

Daniel Dennett provides an explanation of how a lack of synchronization between physical (neurophysiological) processes and intentional sequences may be part of a reordering process built into normal experience. We can make good use of his analysis here precisely because it is conducted in a mix of metaphors that cut across the brain-consciousness distinction. On the one hand, he clearly wants to frame his explanation in terms of brain processes, yet he knowingly employs intentional language to help out his descriptions. Thus, he talks of "decisions" or "judgments" made in the cortex, but qualifies it immediately as metaphor. He also employs concepts like "content" (intentional or semantic), "interpretation," and "memory" to describe neuronal states or processes (1991, 134–35). Although, for Dennett, consciousness emerges as an excess of brain activity above a certain critical threshold, there is no clearly drawn line that defines the threshold. Thus, his descriptions of brain states seem, in some respects, to equally describe intentional states.

Starting with good neurophysiological evidence, Dennett holds that when a visual stimulus causes a multiplicity of nonserial neuronal activities across a variety of different parts of the cortex, over a period of hundreds of milliseconds, this process yields an apparent narrative stream of intentional experience. Still, he explains, because of its multiplicity it is not precisely like a linear stream: "at any point there are multiple drafts of narrative fragments at various stages of editing in various places in the brain" (1991, 113, 135). The processes that produce this narrative stream are complicated even more by the different rates at which different types of input are processed in different parts of the brain. The amazing thing is that, however it happens, perception usually makes sense. Dennett unabashedly insists that the fragments of information "*are* narratives: single versions of a portion of 'the stream of consciousness' " (1991, 135).

Dennett is consistent with Husserl in his claim that the intentional stream is not defined independently of our reflective grasp of it. Reflective or experimental probing modifies the temporality of experience, as well as the semantic content of the narrative. Could we not go further and say that reflective probing actually modifies temporal experience so that it only appears to be a stream or well-regulated narrative? The idea would be that reflection imposes a certain streamlike, narrative structure on conscious experience. Short of this, Dennett suggests that a continual revision of "the narrative stream" takes place based at the level of underlying neurophysiological processes. The temporality of the neurophysiological processes, however, may be quite dissimilar to the apparent temporality of the stream of experience, since "these two time lines may not superimpose themselves in orthogonal registration" (1991, 136).

Such disequilibrium is not a pathological or even uncommon event. It can occur spontaneously, without any explicit act of reflection. Dennett borrows on this idea to explain the *phi* phenomenon. In the *phi* phenomenon, remember, two separately spaced, differently colored dots (red and green, for example) are shown to subjects in rapid succession, red first, green second. Rather than seeing two dots, however, subjects actually perceive one moving dot which remarkably changes color (from red to green) at a point in time phenomenally *prior to* the flashing of the green dot. In this case, Dennett explains, experienced (intentional) temporality is quite different from objective (brain) temporality: "even though the (mis)discrimination of *red-turning-to-green* occurred in the brain *after* the discrimination of green spot, the *subjective* or *narrative* sequence is, of course, *red spot, then red-turning-to-green, and finally green spot*. So within the temporal smear of the point of view of the subject, there may be order differences that induce kinks" (1991, 136).

One cannot help but think of the similar strangeness of the perfectly normal state of vision called physiological diplopia. At certain points in our visual foreground things are visually doubled when we focus on something in the background. We don't ordinarily notice this. In effect, we edit it out because it would be too disruptive or disconcerting for our visual experience. This ability to edit or rescript is an example of a prenoetic operation carried out by the body outside of intentional consciousness, but nonetheless having its effect (a very beneficial one) on intentional consciousness.

Just as physiological diplopia is a normal condition for our visual perception, so what Pöppel (1994) calls "temporal diplopia" is a normal condition for all perception. That is, given the different processing speeds of our different sense organs, and the distributed module processing that takes place in the brain, all perceptually relevant information is not centrally available in precise simultaneity. Objective simultaneity is constantly displaced by a simultaneity that is pieced together by the perceiving organism (Pöppel 1988). The brain is constantly rescripting (perhaps on the model of Ss and Ws that Pöppel suggests—see chapter 9) and recasting a phenomenal time-stream out of its own prenoetic time. Thus, the kind of unnoticed, and in principle, phenomenologically unnoticeable, temporal kinks described by Dennett with respect to the *phi* phenomenon, are really characteristic of all experience. In effect, a rescripting that includes a "backwards projection in time" takes place; a "revised draft" is constructed with a quite incongruous temporality relative to the objective sequence. Dennett represents this as a fold in the experience of time (see fig. 10.1).

It is not just the formal, syntactic processing of information, or the quantity of that information, that fully determines the neurological timing in such cases, since the particular fact and specific nature of the processing is a complex one that depends on, for example, what moves or doesn't move in the environment, what I'm looking at, what I recognize on the basis of such-and-such past experience, how I feel, and so

Figure 10.1

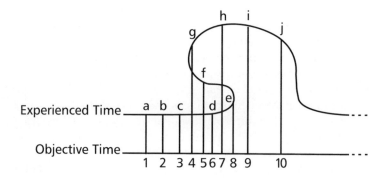

forth. In other words, both prenoetic forces and intentional content will help to determine the neurological timing, and the curves on Dennett's graph. To express this in Husserl's terminology one would have to say that the nature of the retained content actually twists the retentioning process. Because the series does not run off in a veracious way, perception involves a productively illusory component. We experience these motion and color illusions, which are also time illusions, every time we watch television or a motion picture, favorite places inhabited by *phi* phenomena. Somewhere between the video display and our awareness temporal relations are rescripted in ways similar to rescriptions that take place in recollection or in unconscious effects. Given the way in which our brains process information, however, such time illusions are an essential part of all sense perception and much, if not all, of cognition.

The temporal order of experience is modified, or disrupted not only on the microchronological, neurophysiological level, but also on a more holistic, but still subpersonal, level. Changes at the level of the body schema, for example, changes in posture, have been shown to have an effect on thought-content and the configuration of the stream of consciousness. Not only the frequency of shifts in mental content, but the percentage of thoughts that focus on present circumstances in contrast to past experience or future projections of meaning are affected by body posture and movement—walking versus reclining versus sitting (Pope 1978).

It is also the case that the body, in its habitual schemas, retains a past in excess of explicit memory, but one that nonetheless helps to define the present. This past falls short of an explicit act of remembering in the sense that I am not required to have a conscious act of recollection in order for this past to be operative in the present. Edward Casey provides an example of the body's keeping of the past:

> Consider only the way the body keeps the past in a veiled and yet entirely efficacious form in its continuing ability to perform certain skilled actions: I may not remember just how, or even when I first learned the breaststroke, but I can keep on doing it successfully—remembering how to do it—without any representational activity on my part whatsoever. (Casey 1983, 80)[6]

In a case like this, that is, in cases of bodily schematic operations and habitual behaviors such as swimming, walking, gesturing, maintaining posture, and so forth, the serial order of experience is difficult to discern. Experience does not recede into a remote past. Rather, the present is built up upon a past that remains unconsciously in effect.

Human posture and gait, as well as the possibilities that are built into them—possibilities that include human reason (see Straus 1966)— are not, of course, my own personal accomplishments, although my personal experiences modify certain general possibilities. Body schemas are in some respects innate, in some respects the product of an ancient evolution, and in some respects the result of social practices that may be long forgotten.[7] Such would be a past that we have never experienced, a past so far beyond the reach of memory that our reconstruction of it is confined to theory. Yet, this is a past that is still operative in a significant way in every step we take and in every action we perform. Precisely so, it is also a past that helps to define our possible futures.

Thus, we are forced to acknowledge that the temporal ordering of consciousness depends on an effective bodily past, operating in a prenoetic fashion. This means, however, that what appears as a temporally well-ordered experience in which the past flows off through a retentional train, and the future dawns at the edge of protention, is, on a different level, already compromised by a past that will not go away.

Hermeneutics and Superpersonal Effects

A second set of prenoetic forces to be considered might be termed "superpersonal forces." They are evidenced in the hermeneutical effects associated with background presuppositions tied to the language, culture, and historical circumstance in which our intentionality finds itself embedded. A number of theorists employ the concept of pre-intentional "background" to account for the possibility of intentional experience. Wittgenstein's (1953) concept of "forms of life," Searle's (1983, 1992) notion of "background," and related concepts found in a variety of thinkers all share a kinship with what Husserl calls the "lifeworld." Despite the importance of these concepts, and various discussions of them in the fields of cognitive science and hermeneutics, their relation to the temporality of consciousness has not been made clear. We can explore the actual workings of these prenoetic effects by focusing on two themes: memory and language.

Memory and the effects of the past

Behind the notion that perception does not simply and straightforwardly "take" its object, but, more specifically, "gives a take" on it, that is, constitutes or construes its meaning in a constructive process, stands an important temporal relation: perception is not clear and present intuition but is infected with memory. Not memory as simple recollection, or a straightforward intentionality of the past. Husserl has already shown us that this would be a full-blown act on its own and that the act of perception does not include a second act of memory within it. But neither is this memory a retention, in Husserl's sense of a straightforward intentionality of the past. Rather, the memory that constrains our perception is more like the notion of historical effect in hermeneutics. What I see with my eyes is neither a pure intuition of intentional consciousness nor an imposition of an already established world. What I see with my eyes is already informed by the impact of my previous experiences; my present is already informed, made ready by a past that is not made present but that, in some sense, makes the present. This is not a past that trails behind in a retentional train, but a past that operates in an anterior fashion to constrain the present. My present is the product of historical effects working behind the back of intentional control.

The experienced present is not part of a stream that flows from a past-present into a now, structured to retain in successive order that which has just passed. Rather, the contents of present experience elicit effects whose origins are long since past, well beyond the reach of retention or even recollection. Such pasts, then, are not present *for* intentional consciousness, but play out their effects *on* intentional consciousness in such a way that intentional consciousness gets constituted in them. But where, one needs to ask, are such effective factors stored? If they are beyond retention and recollection, then they are not in any memory banks that intentional consciousness would have access to. If "storage" is the metaphor that we favor, then perhaps the best we can do is to say that prenoetic effective factors are stored in the operations of the per-ceiver's body schema, in the environment, in the obscurities of forgotten autobiography, in language, in social custom, and so forth.

As we noted above, the prenoetic past is not kept or stored in recol-lective memory, but has its operant existence in the interrelations of body and environment. The habitual memory of the body is supplemented by a past that is kept in the things that surround us, in places and landscapes.[8] The fact that intentionality always takes place in a place, the fact that consciousness is always situated, provides convenient storage for the past. Folk psychology tells us too that places are often full of memories. One might object, however, that the very idea of the past stored in a place cannot be taken literally, any more than the claim that the past is stored in language and social practices. What is at stake in such an objection, however, is not the mnemonic efficacy of bodies, places, and practices, but the very idea of memory "storage" which is itself metaphorical. Literal claims are not intended in this sort of discourse.

Recollection itself, in the sense of an act of remembrance on the strictly intentional level, is not necessarily dependent on memory storage. We do not simply call up a stored piece of information. An individual's memory is not similar to a computer's memory bank. Data are not stored in an isolated bank that is accessed only when the right buttons are pushed. Human memory, unlike computer memory, is invasive and "leaky." It tends to be already, and to some extent, uncontrollably interac-tive with a full intentional system. Certain aspects of the past can invade or infiltrate my present thought, without being invited.

Keith Oatley associates this kind of infiltration with what he calls "Woolfian consciousness," named after the novelist Virginia Woolf, who often portrays it in her narratives. He cites a passage from Woolf's *Mrs. Dalloway* describing the stream of consciousness of the protagonist walk-ing on London's Bond Street viewing shop windows that displayed only one item each.

> "That is all" she repeated, pausing for a moment at the window of a glove shop where, before the War, you could buy almost perfect gloves. And her old Uncle William used to say a lady is known by her shoes and gloves. He had turned on his bed one morning in the middle of the War. He had said "I have had enough." Gloves and shoes; she had a passion for gloves, but her own daughter, her Elizabeth, cared not a straw for either of them. (Woolf, cited in Oatley 1988, 372)

Woolf tries to capture how perceptual, motor, memorial, and associative contents tumble in a disorderly way into the phenomenal stream. Memory (of Uncle William) here interrupts and invades an ongoing consciousness (of the store window).

In contrast to Husserl's contention that, in the act of remembering, earlier consciousness is completely reproduced or simply repeated with formal modifications (see 1991, 44ff., 184ff.), cognitive psychologists, from the time of Bartlett (1932), have argued that, in remembering, certain aspects of the past are constructed rather than stored. The constructive process, however, is not something that is restricted to intentional control—it's not purely a process of inductive inference. The recollected past is the product of a present selective and constructive interpretation that is informed by future concerns and practical interests, but also by the prenoetic forces of an invasive past that outstrips intentional parameters. Thus, for example, witnesses with different cultural backgrounds will have quite different recollections of the same event (Connerton 1989, 28). It has also been shown that for normal memory the emotional aspect of the remembered experience or the emotional state of the person at the time of the remembered experience, and even the proclivity to remember on the basis of visual image may interfere with the accuracy of memory and may contribute to high levels of construction and confabulation (Reisberg and Heuer 1992). It is also possible that memory deteriorates in terms of accuracy, and is constructively enhanced as time passes. Thus, the remembrance of an event one day after the event can be quite different from the remembrance of the same event three years later, even with respect to major features. And despite the difference in memories, subjects are still highly confident in the accuracy of the later reports (Heuer 1994).

How memory actually works, readied by the concerns and interests of the present and future, supplemented by imagination, and, like other intentional experience, shaped by a prenoetic past that affects, but is not itself under the control of, intentional representation, attests to something bordering on reinvention or reconstruction, rather than repetition or reproduction of the past.[9] Here, quite clearly, in the case of memory, the prenoetic past does not coincide with the representational past.

This is an instance of a more general rule. There are aspects of construction and selectivity in all forms of intentionality. Generally, the temporality of the intentional object is not strictly parallel to the temporality of the consciousness of the object. This, Meinong notes, is clear "in the case of the dreaming subject" (see Husserl 1991, 231 n. 50). In other words, the seriality of the manifest dream-content does not necessarily parallel the temporally compressed dream-act. Freud, of course, makes a number of interesting suggestions about the temporality of the dream. Simultaneity on the manifest level of the dream, for example, may represent logical connection on the latent level (Freud 1965). If this is the case, simultaneity in the dream is invented or produced by an effect that falls quite short of intentional representation. Freud also discusses chronological reversal in a way that suggests that consciousness may be construed as a stream for reasons that go beyond the reflective grasp of phenomenology (1965, 363).[10]

The insistence of prenoetic pasts is asymmetrically countered by an indeterminate future that we first project and subsequently suffer. Practical interests motivate actions that hold within themselves futures that will be closed off by those very actions. Each action, having a finite effect, in one sense allows for a degree of control over the actor's future, but only by being exclusive and letting alternative possibilities slip uncontrollably by. Expectation is not a well-ordered foresight of what is to come, but an attempt to come to grips with the indeterminacy of what may or may not happen. Protention is less an a priori intentional structure than an imposition on intentional experience. Limited in scope, intentionality is both defined and swallowed up by all of the futures that it does not trace out. Even as, moving toward a projected goal, within the confines of a well-thought-out plan, we confirm ourselves in our actions, our confirmation is always an acknowledgment of that which is constantly closing in, drawing the lines that delineate our fortune. Our fortune or misfortune is always something that starts with what we inherit from the past, and ends with whatever the future holds or withholds.

Linguistic effects

Language also contributes to certain prenoetic effects on intentionality. David Wood's analysis of the temporality of language offers an important corrective to the standard view that treats intentional experience as a well-ordered succession or stream. In his examination of temporal variations within linguistic experience he explicates a variety of complex serialities implicitly structured by language—repetitions, syntactic order, and the multiplex seriality of textuality (1989, 338–39). As he admits, however, these notions are still caught up in the order of linear time. Discontinuities and interruptions within textuality get us closer to nonserial, nonlinear temporality. Wood importantly notes that all of the temporal complexity found in textuality and the experience of reading narrative can be read back into other forms of intentional experience.

> Not only is the reader already lodged in a multiplicity of time tracks (writing a book, moving, struggling to defeat illness, digesting a meal,

waiting for a phone call, wondering about salvation, imagining unlikely possibilities, remembering his/her childhood) but these can impinge on the practical business of getting through the book, on the understanding of what the book is about, of what the characters are doing. . . . If there is no narrative except in relation to a reader, then the reader's range of temporal insertions is a vital element. (1989, 354)

This claim seems phenomenologically verifiable even without Wood's detailed analysis of the temporal structures of language. As I sat and read Wood's account, for example, my own intentional life was assaulted by, shaped and deformed by a complex and conflicting set of temporally indexed events. I sat reading at my breakfast table drinking tea, anticipating a meal, while, on my left, my attention was constantly being interrupted by my two young daughters who were interacting with each other while half-watching a much too disruptive television program that followed its own interrupted seriality, while, on my right, two other family members were planning out the day in a conversation in which I sometimes participated. My reading, in this context of interruptions and simultaneous occurrences that drifted in and out of my intentional experience of Wood's text, was not a mental recitation of his words as they were lined up on the page, but included a critical questioning that asked what was right and what was wrong with his analysis. My thoughts were influenced by a certain philosophical tradition, as well as by certain domestic arrangements. There were also ill-defined lines of reflection interspersed between distraction on the left and right—a reflection that started to take this complex situation as a possible qualification of Wood's analysis, and a reflection that started to marvel that despite the degree of intentional disruption something coherent was emerging—that is, Wood's argument and my objection to it.

What Wood says about language holds for consciousness generally. It is hardly an orderly successive flow. It's at least a complex "hodge podge" of multiple serialities that often disrupt one another. My intentional focus on the text was a hard win from a dispersal of attention across the room, the television, and the various conversations hovering in the background or interrupting the foreground. To Whitehead's famous claim that "it's always one damn thing after another," one could respond, "would that it were so simple." Phenomenological descriptions can lead to the same conclusion that Wood draws from his linguistic analysis:

The multiplicity of only contingently coordinated timetracks is surely not restricted to avant-garde literature, but a perfectly common experience. One need only think of the way we weave together a life of reverie, of

dream, of different kinds of perceptual experience . . . a whole variety
of *activities,* some nested within others. . . . The claim is . . . that "lived"
experience is already impregnated with those very reflective structures
elaborated in textuality in general and narrative in particular. (1989,
358–59)

The "multiplicity of time tracks" is not something limited to the event
of reading a text. Even if I am alone in a quiet circumstance, in a
nondisruptive environment, my "train" of thought is frequently, if not
constantly derailed, interrupted by the constructions of memory, the
hypotheses of imagination, the projections of expectations, the reveries
of fancy, the reversions of reflection, and so forth. Indeed, my thoughts
seem to take on a clear linear order of succession only as they get written
down, in the form of textuality, in the orderly structure of narrative.

Consider the description of a compact four seconds of reflective
thought described by Galen Strawson (1994, § 1.7).

Some time ago, I turned a page in a book and saw a black and white
photograph of a crowd of people crushed against a wall in a football
stadium. Too fast for subvocalized words my mind flashed with the
thought (1) "I'm glad it wasn't me." For a moment this thought was
completely self-concerned. At the same time (2) a grasp of the experience
of the trapped people became present, producing (3) a strong feeling of
sympathy. Concurrently, there was (4) an impulse of contrition about the
occurrence of (1). This blurred with (3) and was simultaneously genuine
and apotropaic.

This is just the start, approximately one-tenth of the entire description
which runs on through fifteen identifiable thoughts. We can pick it up
toward the end.

There was a sense in which the (12) awareness, familiar from many past
occasions, didn't occur spelt out in thought. Nevertheless its content
was in some way genuinely and fully apprehended by me. It flashed
on the mind as a familiar—wearisome—schema. And with it came its
usual accompaniment—itself a mere schema too fast for words—whose
content—to spell it out a bit—was (13) that although it is indeed
wearisome, this automatic activity, experience shows that the realization
that this is so is no remedy, and does not stop it happening. But there
was also, as always, a little accompanying shape of hope shadowing the
schema, a hope that (14) the ability to be completely aware of the set
pattern of what was going on might provide a way out of it. But the (13)

schema had already encompassed its by-product, the hope-shape, and it had already (15) reckoned it up and ruled it out.

Reflecting on his own description, Strawson notes,

> This, then, was some of the content of about four seconds of thought. Four seconds may seem too short a time, but it may well have been less than four seconds. The speed may be partly explained by the fact that the general pattern of thought was well worn. . . . Spelling out this content, it seems clear to me that I am doing just that: writing out content that was present to mind, not elaborating on it or adding to it.

One might argue against Wood that the distillation of intentionality that one finds in a text simplifies and hides the nonlinear course of the author's thought. If, with Gadamer (1989), we would agree that the text always goes beyond the author's intentions, we might also say that the text also always falls short of the complexity of experience that frames those intentions.

My objection to Wood is simply that his analysis of language is turned in the wrong direction when he claims to provide us with a new model of time. Although Wood recognizes the importance of language for an account of temporality, when he focuses on textuality he analyzes the wrong aspect of language; he attends to an already constituted product rather than to the constituting process. Textuality, like expressibility (McIntyre and Smith 1982) and more generally like intentionality, is already under the effect of a temporality that structures it. Anterior to either intentionality or textuality, language as a prenoetic force contributes to the institution of linear and nonlinear temporalities that are reflected in, because they have an effect on, intentional life, as well as in the structure of textuality itself.

Grammaticist philosophers like A. N. Prior (1968) sometimes come closer to the point. Prior rightly demonstrates that the very conception of the flow of time is a metaphor produced by the way grammar structures our language. Specifically, the stream metaphor is caused by the fact that certain expressions that look like nouns are actually concealed verbs, and certain expressions that look like verbs are actually concealed conjunctions or adverbs. But even if, through grammatical analysis, we get to the literal truth behind the metaphor, we do not escape the metaphor. Grammar continues to operate prenoetically to structure the various expressions of time-consciousness. This anterior functioning of language is not something that can be fully captured in either an analysis of textuality or in the logic of tense—phenomena that are already under its effect. It receives a clearer explication in a hermeneutical analysis that shows how language can both limit and enable our cognitive abilities.

I am, of course, overstating my claim here. I do not intend to deny that textuality has an effect. It's not the case that the anterior function of language operates in a one-way fashion, and that textuality is simply an inert product at the end of the process. Rather, it is quite possible that the linearity of textuality assists our reflective grasp of the structure of speech and thought. David Olson suggests that the advent of literacy historically leads to reflection on speech and its structure: "we introspect on language and mind in terms of the categories prescribed by our writing systems" (1994, 68). To the literate mind, speech and consciousness appear to be ordered according to a textual syntax.[11] Extending this idea, we could say that the temporal order of the mind appears to the literate introspector much as the linear succession of a narrative does. This may be a reflective distortion. On traditional views of language, where writing is understood to be the representation of words spoken, and speech is understood to be the externalization of thought, one not only might think of the written text as a spatialization of the temporality of speech and thought, one might reflectively read that spatialization back into the very structure of thought itself. Of course this modern view of the mind, as a succession of ideas, even if it is, in part, a bias of literacy, is an extremely beneficial bias for the advance of knowledge and modern science. Moreover, it may also be the case that literate reflection does not simply misconstrue the temporal structure of consciousness as a linear stream, but may in fact contribute to creating that structure, to making it real, since reflection obviously has an effect on how consciousness organizes itself.

The temporality that we find reflected in narrative is, on the one hand, an already composed temporality, organized and ordered by the linguistic structures that compose the orderliness of the text. It is a temporality already under the rules of poetic construction, tamed by a plot that places events in an orderly series. Paul Ricoeur aptly characterizes this effect: "*time becomes human to the extent that it is articulated through a narrative mode*" (1984, 52). One could also say, time is brought under the rule of reflective intentionality to the extent that it conforms to a flow-structure. This, indeed, seems to give time an orderliness that "presents a transcultural form of necessity" (Ricoeur 1984, 52), but it also tends to hide what was once a basic ontological question: Is time entirely contained and composed within the order—the narrative or intentional ordering—of events and experience, or is time something in excess of that order? Is the orderly structure of narrative or intentionality a necessary condition of temporal existence, as Ricoeur proposes, or is it more Augustinian?

As Ricoeur points out, Augustine views time as a threat, a negative excess that distracts and distends the soul, and therefore something that requires a cure, a poetic transformation. Augustine tames time by confining it to the mind, by putting it in a place where the *distentio* must follow certain cognitive rules. Ricoeur, likewise, suggests that the discordance of temporality is mended within the concordance of narrative structure (1984, 31). But what is it that is cured, what is it that threatens?

The composition of time in narrative and intentional structures is overtaken by prenoetic effects that cannot be reduced to a characteristic or a quality or even the formal structure of narrative or intentional life. Rather, temporality outstrips intentionality and exceeds the composure of narration to the extent that certain prenoetic factors have their effects. Prenoetic forces, like language, or that aspect of language that operates anterior to intentionality, carry their own inordinate temporal effects. As such, temporality is not reducible to a subjective flow. Temporality is more than a subjective stream could reflect; it shapes, and at the same time, tends to exceed the shape of intentionality.

Discourses of Time: Toward Joycean Theory

Just to the extent that temporality outstrips intentionality and is irreducible to any individual prenoetic force, so also it outstrips theory. Husserl thought that when we get right down to the very bottom of consciousness, into the very flux of existence, all names are lacking. This may be another way of saying that time is a mystery beyond our finite comprehension. Still, this may also be the most scientific conclusion. The evidence is in, isn't it? Neither philosophy nor science has ever been able to develop a complete and satisfactory explanation of time or time-consciousness. As scientific conclusions go, or sometimes go, this one takes us close to the point of either throwing up our hands in humble surrender, or embracing an ill-defined mysticism. I want to suggest a different tact, one that will not necessarily appeal to our strict scientific rationality, but one that should nonetheless appeal to our scientific arrogance. Perhaps the mystery of time is one that, like other mysteries, calls for a multiplicity of approaches. If we cannot devise a complete explanation of temporality, or a grand unified theory of time, perhaps many partial explanations and insights will allow us some scientific satisfaction.[12]

As a formal analysis of time-consciousness in the Lockean phenomenological tradition, Husserl's theory offers a more adequate account than any others found in that tradition. If we want to start by saying that our experience resembles an intentional stream of consciousness, or a "Joycean machine," Husserl's model has some profound insights to offer. At the same time it is only by going beyond the Husserlian account that we start to understand the complexity associated with the mystery of time. An exploration of prenoetic effects can lead us to further insights about the temporal relations that operate on and between history, language, embodiment, alterity, and our own temporally conditioned cognitive experiences. On this view, our understanding of time and temporal experience will not be misdirected by the variety of approaches found in disciplines such as social psychology, linguistics, anthropology, or the neurosciences, or by the multiplicity of experiences encountered in poetry, fiction, music, and the fine arts. Rather, each in turn, different arts and sciences, can shed light on the complexity of temporal experience. The only approach that might limit our insight would be one that insisted upon one true discourse, one overarching paradigm, one singular and unified theory of time to which all others would necessarily conform.

Beyond the scope of intentionality or phenomenological reflection we have considered various parachronic aspects of existence that cannot be reduced to the phenomenological paradigm. Such indeterminate effacements that cannot be represented in the theater space of the mind nonetheless condition that very experience. They indicate dimensions of a temporality that call for a discourse entirely different from phenomenology: a past that is not past; a present that refuses presentation; a future that outstrips protention. This is a temporality that overflows the banks of the intentional stream while it places limits on that very metaphor.

If there is a temporality that transcends all possible intentional standards of measure, that escapes the enumeration of memory, tradition, and historical science, that fails to register on the scales of phenomenology, then what could possibly allow us to think it? If there is an alterity that refuses to present itself, that causes consciousness to falter in the face of it, and that refuses to be contained in noematic presence, how can we respond to it? If something is more than what will be, something both more and less than a conception, something incomprehensible, how will it be possible to keep it in mind? These are parachronic effacements that escape the metaphor of the stream of consciousness.

Is it possible that art could capture something that phenomenology or the sciences miss? A close reading of Joyce reveals that what Dennett calls the "Joycean machine" is not the simple stream of consciousness that phenomenology and cognitive science make it out to be. The Joycean stream, as exemplified by Molly Bloom, is not characterized by seriality. There is neither a real nor virtual seriality at work in Molly's thoughts;

the content of the "Joycean machine" actually involves, in some sense, a disruption of formal seriality.

> who was the first person in the universe before there was anybody that made it all who ah they dont know that they dont know neither do I so there you are they might as well try to stop the sun from rising tomorrow the sun shines for you he said the day we were lying among the rhododendrons on Howth head in the gray tweed suit and his straw hat the day I got him to propose to me yes first I gave him the bit of seedcake out of my mouth and it was leapyear like now yes 16 years ago my God after that long kiss I nearly lost my breath . . . I was thinking of so many things he didnt know of Mulvey and Mr Stanhope and Hester and father and old Captain Groves and the sailors playing all birds fly . . . and how he kissed me under the Moorish wall. (Joyce 1914, 782–83)

Rather than being unidirectional, Joyce paints a picture of consciousness invaded by prenoetic forces that introduce twists and turns, rocks and undercurrents, tributaries and reversals, floods and islands. The "stream" does not have the formal structure of Husserl's rational seriality. A long duration across a variety of shifting events that confuse and conflate past and present constitute the dense content of a few seconds in Molly's mind. Only the necessity of the textual structure, the demand for a narrative train of words forces the author-phenomenologist to spread the content across a successive line.[13]

A comment from Virginia Woolf equally calls into question the phenomenological stream and Dennett's version of the Joycean machine.

> Examine for a moment an ordinary mind on an ordinary day. The mind receives a myriad impressions—trivial, fantastic, evanescent, or engraved with the sharpness of steel. From all sides they come, an incessant shower of innumerable atoms; and as they fall, as they shape themselves into the life of Monday or Tuesday, the accent falls differently from of old. . . .
> Life is not a series of gig lamps symmetrically arranged; life is a luminous halo, a semi-transparent envelope surrounding us from the beginning of consciousness to the end. (Woolf 1925, 154–55)

Like reflection, textuality is selective. Joyce's text appears to the reader as a stream of consciousness because it is written-out in a serial fashion; one thought after another. But content interferes with the form. Molly Bloom's thoughts are fused and confused in a very unstreamlike fashion, in a prereflective time that moves closer to the quickness of an instant than to the time it takes to read the text. The said sun that shines for Molly is not of the same temporal order as the sun that rises tomorrow, and the saying of the sun is of a different temporal order from the said sun. Except in the composure of the text, the one sun does not follow the other, nor does the saying follow the said. And in Molly's consciousness these thoughts are all jumbled together in an incessant shower of occurrence. More generally, in Joyce, the plot is overtaken by the inordinance of time. Serial time is simply one organization, one interpretation pulled out of the Woolfian rain.

If art, and even literary criticism, not to mention Derridian deconstruction, can enlighten and challenge our conceptions of time and consciousness, should we not allow them to do so? Perhaps Woolf's metaphor provides a different way of thinking about temporal experience. Instead of experience organized in a temporal stream, experience may be more like a rain against a finite surface, droplets of experience splashing together forming puddles of meaning which only sometimes flow together to create a short-lived stream. The serial temporality of the stream of consciousness is something engineered by reflection, a deferred imposition of order in which some droplets and puddles are forced together into a reflecting pool, streamlined according to a retrofitted meaning. Temporal streams are recursively constructed either by reflection or by textuality, by a kind of *scripting* that is closer to the ordinary conception of writing than Derrida's *arche ecriture*. Theory tends to follow the course of reflection, and reflection reviews, revises, and rewrites its object. Husserl had already cautioned us about this. Reflection is selective and the principles of selection are themselves caught up in a temporality that outstrips reflection. Despite his misconstrual of the Joycean machine, Dennett's analysis of the *phi* phenomenon indicates the possibility of a similar type of scripting on the level of hyletic processes, a spontaneous rescripting that includes a "backwards projection in time" a "revised draft" constructed with the incongruous temporalities of narrative fragments.

For the phenomenologist like Husserl, the phenomenological reduction would rule out considerations about prenoetic forces at work behind the back of intentionality. An investigation into prenoetic constraints would be considered a causal one, and therefore outside the realm of phenomenological reflection. Yet it is now clear that if the task is to understand the human experience of time we cannot narrow our investigations to the phenomenological approach, although we can treat it as one approach among others. In this sense, there is no one paradigm, phenomenological, existential, hermeneutical, cognitive, or otherwise, that would provide the full comprehension of temporality that science would demand. But as long as we do not think of a paradigm as defining the one and only framework appropriate for the explanation of a particular subject matter, then it is quite possible to pursue a plurality of models for the explanation of temporal experience, and to learn something from each. Although not limited to models that would address specific prenoetic factors, one may still find it useful, as one possible organizing principle, to view numerous approaches to the question of time and temporality in connection with the issue of various prenoetic effects.

For phenomenologists it has always been difficult to see how the various investigations developed even by social scientists, not to mention physicists and biologists, could somehow throw light upon temporal consciousness. But the very concept of "the prenoetic" allows us to see how only a disparate set of disciplines, a set of cognitive sciences and arts, can formulate appropriate agendas for the investigation of temporal experience.

The idea is not to line up all the theories that converge on some concept of a nonlinear scripting as opposed to the linear stream of phenomenology, in order to proclaim that we have finally discovered the truth about time. Rather, if time is indeed a mystery that resists final definition, if in the end all names are lacking, then we need a multiplicity of names, something like a *Joycean theory,* that is, an incomplete set of theories that keep each other off balance, that undermine the formation of a Grand Theory of time. We need the metaphor of stream as much as the metaphor of incessant rain. We need James and Husserl as much as Joyce and Derrida. To recognize temporality as a mystery does not entail giving up our attempts to explain it. Each discipline, each art, each science can develop its own interpretation and take up a position within a paralogical collection comprising the discourses of time.

Notes

1. In this regard, see the telling remarks of John Searle (1992, 127); also see Block (1990). For recent exceptions, however, see Ruhnau (1995); van Gelder (1998); and Varela (1998).

2. Slife (1993). We can add that even when time perception is the topic investigated, most studies assume a linear concept of time and only question how perceptual consciousness properly estimates or conforms to the parameters of that linearity. The literature in this area is quite extensive, but see, for example, Fraisse (1963). Friedman remarks, in this regard, that the dominant view in the psychology of time conceives the perception of time as foundational, and "rooted in the perception of moment-to-moment changes in our environment or consciousness of internal, clocklike processes" (1990, 6).

3. James cites most of these authors in a long footnote (1890, vol. 1, 632–34).

4. The concept of the specious present still has currency in the psychological literature under the title of the "psychological present" (see Block 1990). One also finds it described in terms of a neurological syntax in the works of Pöppel (1978, 1988, 1994; Pöppel et al. 1990). Mathematicians invoke the concept too. Bell (1995) suggests that synthetic differential geometry can provide a geometrical representation of the specious present. And in a recent internet discussion of Penrose (1994), Cooper (1995) proposes a mathematical theory of consciousness directly tied to James's notion of specious present.

Chapter 2

1. This and all of the other diagrams used or referred to in what follows present an unavoidable problem for representing time and/or the experience of time. Diagrams spatialize time and thereby introduce certain unintended distortions. For example, points D and E in figure 2.1 are meant to represent a future that is not yet in existence. The diagram makes it look as if such future points are already in existence just waiting their turn to move into the present. Thus I wish to note here that despite such spatializing distortions, my intention is not to commit what Kline (1983) calls "the fallacy of the actual future."

2. This is Mabbott's adaptation of Broad's diagram. It is essentially the same as Broad's. See Broad (1923, 349); Mabbott (1951, 158).

3. This is not the case in another diagram provided by Broad (1938, vol. 2, 281–88) where the height of the triangle represents different degrees of "presentedness," a concept he defines as "a psychological characteristic."

4. Depending upon the distances involved, it would not seem impossible at all if we think of time in terms of Einsteinian relativity and space-time. For an example of how an event might be past for one observer but future for another "contemporary" observer, see Penrose (1989, 200–201).

5. James (1890) cited evidence for this. More recently Ruhnau (1995) describes such intermodal differences in terms of a "coincidence threshold," that is, the temporal interval beneath which two stimuli are sensed as one stimulus. For auditory stimuli the threshold is approximately 2–3 msec; for tactile stimuli, approximately 10 msec; and for visual, approximately 20 msec. Also see Pöppel (1988).

Chapter 3

1. We should note, however, that when the German translation of James's *Psychology* appeared (James 1909a), Husserl, judging from markings in his copy of this volume in the Husserl Archives (Louvain, Belgium), seems to have reread only chapters 18 (*Erinnerung*), 26 (*Wille*), and the conclusion (*Psychologie und Philosophie*). It seems he never did return to the discussion of the specious present.

2. Gurwitsch also claims that "the parallelism and agreement between James's theory of the 'specious present' and Husserl's analysis of duration have been shown by A. Schutz" (1966, 304 n. 9). Schutz, however, does not make any claims beyond the suggestion that there is some agreement between James's notions of specious present and mental fringes and Husserl's concept of a temporal horizon. Moreover, Schutz is very careful in describing this agreement. He does not equate Husserl's description of the retentional-protentional structure of consciousness to the specious present, nor does he mention any similarity between Husserl's and James's diagrams. See Schutz (1966, 11).

3. To be fair I should note that Wälde (1985) was perhaps misled, in part, by my own suggestions (Gallagher 1979), which he cites in this regard.

4. John Brough's more recent translation (Husserl 1991, 22) uses the term "presence-time" to translate *Präsenzzeit*.

5. Stern (1898, 20–21). Husserl had underlined these important passages in his copy of Stern's *Psychologie*, which I consulted at the Husserl Archives.

6. We note that Wundt is also cited by James in precisely this regard (1890, 608 n.). James Ward's view was similar to the one proposed by Wundt. He held that the apprehension of a series involves a combination of "after sensations" or "primary memory-images" with percepts. In order for succession to be represented, Ward held that "we should have represented together presentations that were in the first instance attended to successively, and this we have both in the persistence of primary memory-images and in the simultaneous reproductions of longer or shorter portions of the memory-train" (1878–89,

64–65). Ward includes Volkmann (noting his Herbartian views), Lotze, and Wundt in his bibliography (1878–89, 85).

7. The details of his account can be found in the lectures and writings of 1905. See Husserl (1991, §§ 1–7, 16–17, 19, 30, 32–33, 41; parts of §§ 11, 14, 23, and 31; Appendixes 1–4; and Nos. 18–35). The dating of these materials is explained by Boehm (in Husserl 1966), Brough (in Husserl 1991), and Bernet (1985, xviii–xix).

8. Franz Brentano, *Psychologie vom empirischen Standpunkt,* cited in Chisholm (1960, 21). That Brentano views all relations to be mutual-real relations derives from his interpretation of Aristotle. See Brentano (1975, 18–19); also Mohanty (1971).

9. See Brough, Introduction to Husserl (1991) for this interpretation.

10. For a clear example of this earlier analysis, and a corresponding diagram, see Husserl (1991, 237–38). For a complete explanation of this change in Husserl's theory of time-consciousness, see Brough (1970, 1972) and his Introduction to Husserl (1991).

11. Based on the diagram in Husserl (1991, 29).

Chapter 4

1. There is no neat translation of "specious" from English to German. Some possibilities are *"scheinend," "äusserlich," "blendend,"* and *"bestechend,"* all having to do with appearance, brilliance, but also insincerity, corruption, delusion. As we have already seen, Stern's word and concept *"Präsenzzeit"* is neither terminologically nor conceptually the equivalent of "specious present." As noted above, Husserl read numerous chapters in the original edition of James's *Principles of Psychology,* shortly after its publication, including the chapter on "The Perception of Time." In Husserl's copy of this work he carefully underscored the term "specious present" and in the margin, in shorthand (although in this particular case it is undecipherable) suggested a German translation. In the 1909 German translation by Marie Durr of an abbreviated version of James's work, the term "specious present" is translated as *"die scheinbare Gegenwart"* (280). Husserl had, by 1909, already developed his analysis of time-consciousness and, judging from his underlining and marginal notes, he did not reread the chapter on time in the German translation. A recent commentator, Martin Wälde (1985, 25), uses the term *"Scheingegenwart,"* although he usually leaves the English term "specious present" untranslated in his German text. Although Miller (1984, 163) remarks that the "term 'specious present' came into prominence on the continent with the work of the 19th century psychologist Wundt and his followers," this is misleading. Mabbott, whom Miller cites as his source, does not make this claim, and Wundt did not use the term.

2. Husserl writes: "The same time, which belongs essentially to experience as such with the modes in which its intrinsic content is presented—and derived from these the modally determined now, before and after, simultaneity, succession

and so forth—is not to be measured by any state of the sun, by any clock, by any means, and generally cannot be measured at all" (1962, § 81).

3. I am adopting Plumer's (1985) equivocation on the word "see" here. In his analysis of our perception of the clock's second hand, Plumer claims that we only "see" at an instant and add memory in order to construct the image of movement. In the middle paragraph on 30, he remains consistent with this conception, claiming that we see one moment of the object and then experience after-images. But in the first paragraph on 30 he writes: "It is true that eventually we see something like a white streaky fan." Here his use of the term "see" is more consistent with Husserl's conception, i.e., we see (perceive, intend) more than just an instant. In this case seeing is an intentional act of consciousness that has a retentional-protentional structure and a corresponding specious present.

4. For a critical discussion of Edward Casey's (1977) suggestion that protentioning is a case of "primary-imagination," see Gallagher (1979).

Chapter 5

1. Concerning the concept of difference Hume states: "It might naturally be expected, that I should join *difference* to the other relations. But that I consider rather as a negation of relation, than as any thing real or positive" (1739, 15).

2. Voltaire wrote, in reference to Locke: "Such a multitude of reasoners having written the romance of the soul, a sage at last arose who gave, with an air of the greatest modesty, the history of it" (Voltaire, *Lettres philosophique*, 1734, trans. John Lockman, cited in Derrida 1980, 79).

3. See Husserl (1969, 255ff.; 1970a, 402–25; 1970b, 87–96). On Husserl's relation to Hume, see Berger (1939); Murphy (1980); and with specific reference to their concepts of time, see Bossert (1976).

4. As early as the *Logical Investigations* Husserl rejected the Humean concept of "bundle" which, he noted, is "never present in real fashion [*reell gegenwärtig*] in any human consciousness and never will be" (1970a, 546). See Findlay's "Introduction" (Husserl 1970a, 25; also see Husserl 1969, 225–26; Husserl 1991, 249 n. 6).

5. See Husserl (1977, 132). That the transcendental ego is, for Husserl as for Kant, formal, is clear from Husserl's claim that it is not "a *real part or phase* of the experiences themselves" (1962, § 156), and that "the experiencing Ego is still nothing that might be taken *for itself* and made into an object of inquiry on its *own* account . . . it is completely empty of essential components" (1962, § 214). See Husserl's warning about distinguishing the ego from the stream of experience (1962, §§ 214–15). "*One* pure Ego, *one* stream of experience filled with content along all three [temporal] dimensions, and in such filling holding essentially together and progressing through its continuity of content: these are necessary correlates" (1962, § 219).

6. The exclusion of signs from the intentional establishment of meaning is proposed in the first of the *Logical Investigations*. In the Second Investigation Husserl uses this logic to critique Hume's theory of abstraction which, interpreted

in its most radical way, amounted to nominalism (1970a, 402ff., esp. 422). The exclusion of signs from pure cognitive experience places Husserl in a very old, but still modern tradition that has its roots in Plato and is clearly inscribed in Augustine's thought. See, e.g., Augustine's *De Magistro*.

7. See Brough (1993) for an alternative view. Even Brough, however, agreeing with Wood (1989), recognizes that Derrida is to a certain extent explicating what one finds in Husserl's own analysis.

8. Again we must forego here any deeper analysis. We simply note that the passions reinforce the personal identity constituted by the imagination: "our identity with regard to the passions serves to corroborate that with regard to the imagination, by the making our distant perceptions influence each other, and by giving us a present concern for our past or future pains or pleasures" (Hume 1739, 261). Thus, in his examination of the passions, the self easily takes on an identity. It becomes the object of pride and humility (1739, 277) and is defined as "*that individual person, of whose actions and sentiments each of us is intimately conscious*" (1739, 286). Hume speaks of a "disposition of the mind" towards pride (1739, 287), and of "qualities of the mind" (1739, 291), and of a relative durability of the self (1739, 293). In the end, "Ourself is always present to us" (1739, 320; see 317, 339, 354). This presence to ourselves involves a temporal present which is momentary (1739, 427–28). We can be aware of only one now at a time (1739, 429) since the incompatibility of the parts of time make a specious present impossible. Still there is a persistent quality of mind: virtue "must depend upon durable principles of the mind, which extend over the whole conduct and enter into the personal character" (1739, 575). Although "the mind has the command over all its ideas, and can separate, unite, mix and vary them, as it pleases" (1739, 623–24), still, it is "almost impossible for the mind to change its character in any considerable article" (1739, 608).

9. A similar point is made by Prior (1968, chap. 1).

Chapter 6

1. Eugene Minkowski (1970) provides such an account. For the concept of the flow of consciousness as a "law," see Husserl (1966, 320).

2. For my purposes I need not explicate McTaggart's derivation which gives priority to the subjective and ideal A-series, or take a position with respect to the debate between A-theorists and B-theorists. I'm interested simply in using the definitions offered by McTaggart, insofar as they clarify traditional conceptions of time, as a conceptual tool rather than as a critical device. I do want to note, however, that McTaggart commits the "fallacy of the actual future" (Kline 1983) insofar as his description suggests that events have an existence in the future and simply slide into the present. This idea is actually inconsistent with his metaphysical beliefs about the unreality of time.

3. Dennett (1991, 214–21). Similar views are to be found in Dennett and Kinsbourne (1992); Baars (1988, 1987); and Newman and Baars (1993).

4. The similarities and differences between Merleau-Ponty and Derrida have been nicely clarified by Martin Dillon (1992, 1988) and Mark Yount (1992). Also see Gallagher (1997b). By focusing on Merleau-Ponty and Lyotard in the following considerations, I do not mean to ignore the fact that Derrida also develops a critique of seriality. He suggests, for example, that in *spacing,* "concatenations are possible which no longer obey the linearity of logical time, the time of consciousness or preconsciousness, the time of 'verbal representations' " (1978, 217). Like Merleau-Ponty and Lyotard, Derrida raises this issue with reference to Freud, and pursues a "discontinuist conception of time, as the periodicity and spacing of writing . . . [in which] we find neither the continuity of a line nor the homogeneity of a volume; only the differentiated duration and depth of a stage, and its spacing" (1981b, 225). This theme is pursued further in other essays; see, e.g., Derrida (1970; 1981b).

5. Merleau-Ponty suggests quite often and throughout his work that temporality is always linked in an intimate relationship with the body (e.g., 1962, 422). "In every focusing movement my body ties together a present, a past and a future, it secretes time" (1962, 239–40). This linkage continues throughout his last work *The Visible and the Invisible* (1968).

6. "Psychology has involved itself in endless difficulties by trying to base memory on the possession of certain contents or recollections, the present traces (in the body or the unconscious) of the abolished past, for from these traces we can never come to understand the recognition of the past as past" (Merleau-Ponty 1962, 265).

7. Sokolowski (1992) provides some useful descriptions of this systemic variation.

8. It's not difficult to identify pathological experiences that disrupt seriality. Because temporal experience depends on embodied existence, pathological and drug-related changes in body image or body schema are often accompanied by corresponding changes in temporal experience. See below, chapter 10.

9. Similar dissociation in reflective consciousness has been shown by Cumming (1972). Subjects were shown letters briefly and laterally masked, and were asked to indicate the presence of a specified target letter by pressing a key. Asked to respond quickly, subjects "tended to respond to the presence of a target letter with a fast press of the 'target-present' key, and then, a moment later, to verbally apologize for having made an error." See Allport (1988) for discussion.

10. See Marcel (1993) for further discussion. I'm grateful to Anthony Marcel for discussion and correspondence on these issues.

11. Glen Mazis succinctly describes this as a reversibility of time:

> When Cezanne points to a heightened sense of reversibility emerging between him, the painter, and Mount St. Victoire, the painted, in which he is now painting the mountain painting itself through him . . . there is a folding back on itself of an unfolding encounter within time. . . . Certainly, during ten years of painting that mountain, there are moments when Cezanne is lost to himself, become more mountain than man. . . . Such moments . . . become

part of a temporal thickness which alters both previous and later moments of experienced disconnection. (1992, 56)

12. Cited in Merleau-Ponty (1964, 164).

13. Lyotard (1990, 19). Michel Serres, in attempting to think of time as a "pure multiplicity," works his way toward similar conclusions. Thus, for example, he writes: "Time is a chaos, at first, it is first of all a disorder. The present, now, is this indiscernible jumble" (Serres 1995, 6, 97).

Chapter 7

1. Over the past fifteen years these results have been replicated and extended in a large number of studies. See Meltzoff and Moore (1994) for summary. Field et al. (1982), for instance, showed that two-day-old infants can imitate the smiling, frowning, or surprised expressions of adult models.

2. See, e.g., Schutz's review of Talcott Parsons's *Structure of Social Action* in Grathoff (1978, 134 n. 16). Schutz there cites Mead's publications of 1932 and 1938.

3. See Schutz (1962, 217 n. 10). Of course, Schutz would side with Husserl in maintaining that transcendental phenomenology operates on a different level than social psychology. Perhaps by 1957, however, Schutz had moved closer to Mead's theory. In his critique of Husserl he writes: "As long as man is born of woman, intersubjectivity and the we-relationship will be the foundation for all other categories of human existence" (1966, 82). Schutz never hesitates to adopt Mead's notions of the generalized other, the manipulatory area, and the I-Me distinction.

4. See Mead (1972, 38, 218; 1980, 190). "The whole process of thinking is the inner conversation going on between [a] generalized other and the individual. The perspective of the individual is, therefore, that of the social act. . . . the appearance of the self is antedated by the tendencies to take the attitudes of others, so that the existence of others is not a reflection of his self-experiences into other individuals" (1938, 152–53). The experiencing subject "enters his own experience as a self or individual, not directly or immediately, not by becoming a subject to himself, but only insofar as he first becomes an object to himself just as other individuals are objects to him or are in his experience, and he becomes an object to himself only by taking the attitudes of other individuals toward himself" (1972, 202–3).

5. Mead offers a more technical definition of the specious present: it is composed of a set of indications which we are able to make to ourselves and which mark "the limits of the immediate change" of our experience. The process of indication, however, is possible only as "a piece of behavior toward another individual which the human individual comes to use toward himself" (1938, 65). Even in this technical definition the specious present depends upon sociality and the social constitution of the self.

6. See Habermas (1987, 148, 137–38). "Heidegger's critical judgments on '*das Man*,' on the dictatorship of the public realm . . . are without any originality whatsoever, because they belong to a repertoire of opinions typical of a certain generation of German mandarins" (Habermas 1987, 140). Also see Habermas (1989).

7. At strategic locations in his analysis, Heidegger, without mentioning the name of his mentor, clearly distances himself from Husserl's approach (see Heidegger 1962, 151, 155, 161–62).

8. Heidegger uses the phrase "face-to-face" quite often (see, e.g. 1962, 310–11, 388–90, 393). Heidegger does say one time that Dasein's authentic existence does not isolate it from others and in fact allows for an authentic encounter with others (1962, 344). But this thought remains undeveloped throughout the remainder of *Being and Time*.

9. Levinas characterizes this past as "a past more ancient than any present, a past which was never present and whose anarchical antiquity was never given in the play of dissimulations and manifestations" (1981, 24). "Immemorial, unrepresentable, invisible, the past that bypasses the present, the pluperfect past, falls into a past that is a gratuitous lapse. It cannot be recuperated by reminiscence not because of its remoteness, but because of its incommensurability with the present. . . . Diachrony is the refusal of conjunction, the non-totalizable, and in this sense the infinite" (1981, 11). One can see here the influence of Levinas on Lyotard.

10. See Richard A. Cohen's excellent Introduction to Levinas (1987, 18–19). For Levinas's theological interpretation of this future, see 1982 (117ff.).

11. The idea of the infinite serves as another example of the inadequacy of intentionality. Levinas finds in Descartes an idea of the infinite that "would contain more than its *cogito*'s capacity" (1987, 134), and would thus remain beyond intentional fulfillment.

12. For a fascinating account of the importance of the face for intersubjective relations, see Cole (1997a, 1997b).

Chapter 8

1. John Drummond indicates that in the end the schema "is applicable only to the primal impression within perceptual acts" (1990, 125). I think Husserl remains ambiguous on this point.

2. One could, of course, interpret these things in a hierarchical fashion, and Husserl often speaks of a certain hierarchy in consciousness in which the temporality of the flux would be the most basic (see, e.g., 1962, § 85). In this case primal impression would be located on the very fundamental level; apprehension would be located in an intermediate position between primal impression and the full act. In some cases, however, Husserl makes hyletic elements the most basic. So Gerald Granel suggests: "It is therefore necessary to consider the *Lectures on Time-Consciousness* as an ensemble of investigations that depend on a 'hyletic phenomenology' and that, despite this, are conducted on a

deeper level . . . than the investigations of 'noetic phenomenology.' . . . And this evidently goes against the affirmation repeated many times by Husserl himself, concerning the 'normal' hierarchy between the hyletic and the transcendental" (1968, 29; see Husserl 1962, § 86).

3. Should we, for example, distinguish the meaning of the object from the object itself, the perceived *as such* from the thing perceived, that is, "the object *as* it is intended" from "the object that is intended"? Olafson notes, in contrast to most interpretations of noema as *Sinn*, that the conception of noema unites "within itself what has previously been distinguished as the object-that-is-intended and the object-as-it-is-intended" (1977, 164). Tugendhat agrees: "The object, together with its ways of being given, is now [in *Ideas*] characterized as 'noema' " (1977, 328). Gurwitsch (1982) is ambiguous on this point. On the one hand, he says that the thing perceived has noematic status, and is nothing other than the multiplicity of noemata through which it appears. On the other hand, he maintains that the particular noema is different, something less than the object, and equivalent to the object as it is intended. Føllesdal (1982a, 1982b), linking Husserl to Frege, maintains a clear distinction between noema, as *Sinn*, and object.

4. Still, the *Sinn-Bedeutung* distinction in Husserl does not entirely correspond to the one in Frege. For Husserl *Sinn* is equivalent to sense or meaning in general; *Bedeutung* is limited to linguistic meaning (see Langsdorf 1984).

5. I have in mind the distinction made by Emilio Betti (1980). E. D. Hirsch explains this distinction in the following way: "There is a difference between 'the meaning of a text' (which is unchanging) and 'the meaning of a text to us today' [its significance] (which changes)" (1967, 8).

6. This caution also pertains to reflection directed to the noema. Husserl states:

> It must be carefully noted, in the first place, that any transition from a phenomenon into a reflection which is itself an analysis of the *reell,* or of a completely different nature an analysis of its noema, generates new phenomena, and that we would fall into error were we to confuse the new phenomena—which in a certain sense are transformations of the old—with the old phenomena, and ascribe to the old what really or noematically is included in the new. Thus, for instance, it is not meant that the material contents . . . are present [*vorhanden*] in the perceptual experience in precisely the same way as they are present in the analyzing experience. . . . Obviously this distinction has an essential bearing on phenomenological method. (1962, § 98, trans. revised; also see 1973b, 255 n. 1; 1991, 132)

7. There is a great deal of disputation among phenomenologists and nonphenomenologists concerning the very existence of hyletic data (sensations), and, even if they do exist, whether it would be possible to locate them in consciousness. Merleau-Ponty, for instance, contests the existence of hyletic

data as described by Husserl. For Merleau-Ponty, the hyle-morphe distinction is the result of an abstraction from perceptual experience. "There is no *hyle*, no sensation which is not in communication with other sensations or the sensations of other people, and *for this very reason* there is no *morphe*, no apprehension or apperception, the office of which is to give significance to a matter that has none" (1962, 405). In effect, the most basic element of perceptual experience is already meaningful (see 1962, 4). For Merleau-Ponty, what Husserl had called "hyletic data," are not really in consciousness, but are properties of the object: "to make [hyle] into an element of consciousness, when in fact it is an object *for* consciousness, [is] to treat it as an incommunicable impression, whereas it always has a meaning" (1962, 5). Sartre (1956) had made similar objections against the concept of hyletic data. To be accurate, even Husserl was dissatisfied about the status of hyle (see Spiegelberg 1976). For further discussion, see Gallagher (1986a).

8. Ironically, the postmodern logic of spatiality that displaces temporality along with subjectivity, treats history in much the same way as Husserl does. Historicity, the anterior effect of the past, remains unacknowledged; the past remains a mere, unsaturated intentional object, without depth or its own significance. Jameson writes: "The past is thereby itself modified [in postmodern spatial logic. It becomes] a vast collection of images, a multitudinous photographic simulacrum." In "a society bereft of all historicity . . . the past as 'referent' finds itself gradually bracketed, and then effaced altogether, leaving us with nothing but texts" (Jameson 1992, 18).

9. See, e.g., David Carr's explication of the "historical reduction" (1974, 117ff.). Carr suggests that "the process of bracketing is identical with coming to awareness of [such] underlying presupposition[s] which otherwise remain hidden" (1974, 137). Also see Harvey (1989, 128–32).

10. McIntyre and Smith (1982, 87). It is noteworthy that their second proposition changes from "every noematic *Sinn* is a linguistic meaning" to, for them, the more accurate "every noematic *Sinn* is expressible as a linguistic meaning" (Smith and McIntyre 1982, 182). But they still claim that "noematic *Sinne* are 'intensional entities.' "

11. In some cases, following brain damage due to stroke, a subject may know the meaning of an object, but be unable to remember its name. It would seem that in such cases meaning and language are dissociated. But that's not correct. The subject knows the meaning of the object in the sense that he can place it in a linguistic context. The subject is usually able to provide a set of signifiers associated with the object. He may not be able to say "pogo stick," but he will be able to say "person," "ground," "spring," "jump," "play," and so forth. He may even be able to put the object to use. The problem is simply that he cannot remember the correct name.

12. Merleau-Ponty indicates that "the whole of the spoken language surrounding the child snaps him up like a whirlwind, tempts him by its internal articulations, and brings him *almost* up to the moment when all this noise begins to mean something" (1964b, 40). Certain elements essential to language

development, however, may actually be innate, and closely linked to the capabilities of the human body (see, e.g., Kuhl and Meltzoff 1982).

13. For a summary of this research and its relevance to Husserl and Merleau-Ponty, see chapter 7, and Gallagher and Meltzoff (1996).

14. Language acquisition is more like acquiring a habitual way of interacting with other persons than like an intellectual process. Merleau-Ponty contends that "to learn to speak is to learn to play a series of *roles*, to assume a series of conducts or linguistic gestures" (1964a, 109). To the extent that language constrains intentionality, intentionality is also constrained by those others (and the generalized other) to whom we owe our language. But in this case, the language that is important is not language as a cultural *object* (as Merleau-Ponty contends, 1962, 354), but language in its anterior relation to us (see Gallagher 1992a).

15. Evidence for this view can be found in psychology. For example, personality traits that originate in our relations with others can affect our perceptual experience. Studies of psychological rigidity, originating within childhood relations with others, indicate that it is usually accompanied by either "perceptual rigidity" or a greater perceptual flexibility that compensates for the rigidity in personality. For example, many psychologically rigid subjects have difficulty in perceiving instances of physical change or transformation. Merleau-Ponty (1964a, 100ff.) cites a number of psychological studies that attest to this conclusion. The phenomenon of echopraxis (unconsciously mimicking another person's movements, taking on their postures and facial expressions unintentionally) also provides evidence for this point.

16. We need not take up the Marxist critique of Husserl's phenomenology to see that for a less abstract account of perception and understanding, the concept of intentionality must be opened up to take into account the effects of economic, cultural, and social factors that condition our perception and understanding. Intentionality is an engagement in the real world because both superstructural and substructural aspects of the real world already condition and constrain intentionality (see, e.g., Thao 1986; Lyotard 1991b, 123ff.). Edward T. Hall (1983) makes it clear how many of these social and economic determinations affect the experience of time.

17. Smith and McIntyre want to extend Husserl's concept of intentionality in the direction of a "pragmatics" and thereby introduce "contextual influences" (1982, 219ff.). These contextual influences include the background belief-systems that are presupposed by the intentional act. Smith and McIntyre follow Husserl in classifying this "immanent context" as belonging to mental life, "though not events in the stream of consciousness *per se*." Still, they admit that background knowledge is "not a part of the act's noematic Sinn," but is "presupposed by the act or its Sinn." This background is a presupposition that escapes the phenomenological *epoché*, however (1982, 221). Much of this is developed by Husserl in his concept of "horizon" (see 1970c, 44ff.), which is a forerunner of Heidegger's concept of the hermeneutical circle.

18. Schutz (1967, 78–86) explicates the notion of an "interpretive scheme" that he finds in Husserl. For the development of this concept in psychology,

see Bartlett (1932); and Anderson and Pearson (1984, 255–91). For the related concept of theory-laden perception as it is developed in cognitive science, see Churchland (1984, 79–80).

Chapter 9

1. See, e.g., Husserl's notions of the horizon as "predelineated" (1970c, § 19) and the "frame of indeterminateness" (1973b, § 21c; also Smith and McIntyre 1982, 246ff.). Hans-Georg Gadamer, in contrast, rightly contends that with the concept of the lifeworld Husserl attempts to clarify and resolve the problem of historicism. For Husserl, "*the doctrine of the life-world is intended to make the transcendental reduction flawless. *The point where problems that form the real object of controversy lie is the level of the fundamental question of constitution, that of the primal ego itself, that is, of the self-constitution of temporality" (Gadamer 1976, 164).

2. Smith and McIntyre (1982, 19). They suggest that "the complete 'meaning' of an individuate act, as we have described it, typically includes not only the *Sinn* that is actually and 'explicitly' present in the act, that which we properly call the *Sinn* of the act, but also the system of *Sinne* correlated with certain related background beliefs" (390). This clearly puts the adequacy of phenomenological reflection into question.

3. James offers an equally ambiguous conception of continuity. Radical empiricism maintains "the continuity of experience," the "continuous structure" of the universe (see the final chapter of *A Pluralistic Universe* in James 1942, and 1909b, 7). Yet, taken as it appears, "our universe is to a large extent chaotic. No one single type of connexion runs through all the experiences that compose it" (1976, 24).

4. This is not what Derek Parfit (1984) would call a reductionist account of the person. The person is something more than the network; although produced by the network, it also helps to transform the network.

5. The concept of network might seem the product of an overly technological metaphor. But a similar conception is to be found in nontechnological societies. As David LeBreton notes, in contrast to the Western notion of the human body fixed in the laws of substance, for example, "in traditional societies where the individual is subordinate to the collective, the body is a *connector,* it binds the individual to the group and the cosmos through a network of interchanges. [Such] cultural concepts . . . regard the substance of one man and the substance of the world as the same matter" (LeBreton 1991, 89).

6. See Balaban (1990, chap. 1). Sartre is famous for rejecting the hypothesis of the unconscious; he equates the psychic entirely with conscious acts (see Sartre 1956, 570).

7. Thus, as Heidegger indicates, "the meaning of phenomenological description as a method lies in *interpretation* [*Auslegung*]" (1965, 61). This is also one of the issues of the Habermas-Gadamer debate. For discussion, see

Gallagher (1992b). For a critical discussion of the hermeneutical critique of phenomenology, see Hopkins (1991).

8. Although Pöppel cites a good bit of psychological evidence for this thesis, he admits that the precise nature of the neural mechanism is a matter of speculation.

9. The idea that the content of experience can determine the magnitude of W can be seen in studies of the perception of ambiguous figures. As part of the evidence that W is approximately, but consistently 3 seconds in duration, Pöppel cites the example of the Necker cube. When looking at a Necker cube and when the two perspectives have been recognized, "it is impossible while looking at the cube to see only one perspective continuously. Automatically after some time there is an automatic reversal to the other perspective. The spontaneous reversal rate of the Necker cube and other ambiguous figures shows values close to 3 seconds for each discrete precept" (1994, 195). Kelso, et al. (1994), however, demonstrated that if the semantic features of the cube are changed, that is, if varient perspectives from the classical Necker cube are presented, reversal intervals are more sporadic or subjects tend to get fixed on one perspective for a longer time (see Varela 1998 for a summary of the Kelso experiment). Marcel (1983) points out that both perspectives of the Necker cube must be represented nonconsciously, even if only one at a time can be effected consciously.

10. For an interesting and detailed dynamical model of retention on the subpersonal (neuronal) level and its relation to Husserl's concept of retention, see Varela (1998). Although Varela draws from Pöppel's work, he allows for a wider variation in the magnitude of system states and greater flexibility in the length of temporal windows, citing such variables as context, fatigue, sense modality, and age of subject. Like Pöppel, however, Varela also maintains that the microgenesis of time-consciousness is presemantic. I am arguing here that semantic factors sometimes interfere with or shape this process.

11. It's also possible to find instances of events from the past, of which the subject has no knowledge, influencing present behavior. Research on amnesia, for example, suggests that a past experience can change present behavior even when that stimulus is not remembered. Claparède cites the case of a patient who, although unable to explain his behavior, refused to shake hands. Unremembered by the patient, he had been pricked by a pin hidden in the hand (Claparède 1911). Patients under anesthesia can learn and retain knowledge, yet not remember the learning event. As a result, it's possible for patients who have learned certain facts while under the effect of anesthesia, but who do not remember learning them, and do not realize that they know the facts, to use those facts in solving a problem at a later time (Andrade 1995; Andrade, et al. 1994).

12. Translators often come to realize that certain things said in one language are unsayable in another language. This suggests the possibility that there are things that cannot be said in any language. Marcel (1983) cites several studies that indicate that children do not experience the typical adult feelings of euphoria following the administration of d-amphetamine. Following

a suggestion made by Robbins and Sahakian (1979), that this lack of specific effect may be due to a lack of a cognitive model for the feeling, Marcel writes: "it is a real possibility that autonomic processes can have no issue in phenomenal experience or in modulating even the tone of behavior unless an appropriate cognitive, phenomenological category has been acquired" (1983, 291). It seems possible that even adults, unable to construct the proper categories, or lacking the required vocabulary, simply have no access to certain aspects of their embodiment that nonetheless constantly condition their experience.

13. Williams (1992), cited in Cole (1997b, 90). Williams, in correspondence with Cole, wrote:

> I did not empathise with what the face was expressing but with the system that the facial disconnections spoke of. When I searched in my own eyes, [when looking in a mirror for hours on end] I did not look at my face, I searched for connectedness between soul and expression through body—most of the time I found none, except in my eyes. Sometimes I saw dead eyes in an animated face, sometimes I saw alive eyes in a disconnected face. I also avoided looking at faces because of the meaningless of their component parts, [which] led to non-interpretable sensory-based behaviours and curiosity which were generally not welcomed. (Cole 1997b, 94)

Cole also cites Asperger who wrote: "autistic children have a paucity of facial and gestural expression. In ordinary two-way interaction they are unable to act as a proper counterpart to their opposite number, and hence they have no use for facial expression as a contact-creating device" (1997b, 79).

14. See Caputo (1987, 289ff.) for suggestions concerning the word "persona."

15. When all is said and done, Husserl's constant appeal to a transcendental ego remains nonphenomenological. His attempts to describe the identity of this ego always end up in one of two ways: either the ego is characterized as a "pole" with rays of intention emanating from its center (see 1970c, § 31–32), or it is reduced to the "concrete subjective processes" of intentional life (see 1962, 214–16; 1970c, §§ 16, 37). In the first case, reflection reifies and thereby falsifies the ego which is precisely not a thing. In the second case, Husserl is more honest, but also more Humean, for when the phenomenologist enters most intimately into what is called the ego, reflection can only stumble on some particular perception or other: "We are nothing but . . . a perpetual flux and movement," as Hume says. That is, the transcendental ego appears to be nothing but a system of differences.

16. This in opposition to Levinas's statement: "The ancient adage designed to dissipate the fear of death—'If you are, it is not; if it is, you are not'—without doubt misunderstands the entire paradox of death, which is a unique relationship with the future" (1987, 71).

17. "Space and time, Einstein once said, are modes by which we think and not conditions under which we live" (Michon and Jackson 1985, 54). "For us

who are convinced physicists, the distinction between past, present, and future is only an illusion, however persistent" (Einstein and Besso 1972; cited in Michon and Jackson 1985, 54).

18. In *Signs* Merleau-Ponty writes: "It is asked '*Where* is history made? Who makes it? What is this movement which traces out and leaves behind the figures of the wake?' . . . Everywhere there are meanings, dimensions, and forms in excess of what each consciousness could have produced; and yet it is men who speak and think and see. We are in the field of history as we are in the field of language or existence" (1964b, 20).

19. Farmer (1990) summarizes some of this discussion. Kant, for example, in his *Inaugural Dissertation* (1929) had noted that the principle of noncontradiction presupposes time and that this puts it beyond the pale of rational explanation. But even earlier than Kant, Leibniz had translated this principle into a formulation that avoided the appeal to time.

Chapter 10

1. Friedman (1990) reviews the psychological evidence for a number of such phenomena.

2. Paul Natorp, *Einleitung in die Psychologie nach kritischer Methode,* cited by Husserl (1970a, 564).

3. Friedman captures the essence of this approach: "The only possible answers I can imagine involve 'quantities' of mental events, perceptions, and memories. . . . The contents of an interval can be thought of in part as the number of stimuli that occur within it" (1990, 23–24). He cites the psychologist Marianne Frankenhaeuser: "We may assume that the experience of a certain duration is related to the total amount of experience (sensations, perceptions, cognitive and emotional processes, etc.) which takes place within this time period, in short, the *amount of mental content*" (1990, 24). Friedman himself offers a qualification of this view by considering the effects of attention and memory (1990, 25–26).

4. David Wood alludes to these biological temporalities:

> The subjectivity of a temporally conscious being is an embodied subjectivity. One consequence of this fact is that even if there are clearly isolable sequences of experience such as phenomenological temporality describes, they are still the experiences of a being already occupied by and with a multiplicity of somatic temporalities. For example, when listening to music, one may get distracted, or get tired and fall asleep, or even die. These fracturings of the isolable calm of a particular series of conscious acts are the predictable consequences of the periodicities that inhabit the embodied subject. (1989, 325–26)

5. For example, on Lacan's account, schizophrenia involves the breakdown of the ordinal series of experience—the narrative stream. Lacan's description

assumes what Jameson identifies as a twofold proposition: "first, that personal identity is itself the effect of a certain temporal unification of past and future with one's present; and second, that such active temporal unification is itself a function of language" (Jameson 1992, 26–27).

6. On this issue, also see Paul Connerton. He notes "the difficulty of extracting our past from our present: not simply because present factors tend to influence—some might want to say distort—our recollections of the past, but also because past factors tend to influence, or distort, our experience of the present" (1989, 20). In this regard he analyzes bodily practices and postures that incorporate pasts that continue to operate on present practices (1989, 72ff.).

7. See Gallagher and Meltzoff (1996) on the innateness of the body schema; and Sheets-Johnstone (1990) concerning evolution and the body's role in cognition. Connerton (1989) provides a detailed examination of bodily and social practices in this regard.

8. See Casey (1983) and Connerton (1989), who cites the work of Maurice Halbwachs —*Les cadres sociaux de la mémoire* (Paris: 1925), and *La mémoire collective* (Paris: 1950).

9. The selectivity involved in the constructive inferences of memory can account for the systematic distortions that sometime occur when a more plausible time is substituted for the objective time of a past event. See the experiments conducted by Friedman and Wilkins (1985).

10. In the spirit of the criticisms made by Merleau-Ponty and Lyotard, outlined above (see chapter 6), David Wood writes: "Proof that Husserl is still committed to a view that lies confortably within the tradition can be seen in the impossibility of Husserl's accommodating, say, Freud's concept of the delayed effect, become conscious of a content that was never conscious" (1989, 124).

11. For the preliterate mind, language and consciousness may be more juxtaposed than flowing. Olson (1994), arguing that for prereading children signs are understood as emblems rather than as words, cites studies (including Berthoud-Papandropoulou 1978; Ferreiro 1985; and Serra 1992) of preliterate children who are shown a text which reads: "Three little pigs." If "the text is then read to them while the words are pointed out they tend to take each of the words as a representation, an emblem, of a pig. Consequently, if the final word is erased and children are asked, 'Now what does it say' they may reply 'Two little pigs.' Alternatively, if each of the three words is pointed to in turn and the child is asked what each says, they reply, 'One little pig; another little pig; and another little pig' " (Olson 1994, 76). These results also suggest that the children perceive the emblems as constituting a juxtapositional representation rather than a flowing sense.

12. This is a generalized philosophical version of a consensus that has recently been developing in cognitive psychology. Thus, Friedman suggests that it is more productive for psychology "to consider the many things that time is in the world and the many ways in which humans experience it. . . . To define time as some unitary dimension that cuts across all of these features is to lose sight of the special challenges they pose for perception and cognition." He concludes

that "we are more likely to understand the nature of temporal experience by examining its different facets than by searching for a common core" (1990, 5–6). Richard Block reaches a similar conclusion: "No simple model can purport to explain the variety of temporal behaviors and phenomena that are experienced by individuals" (1990, xiii). He suggests that the fact that psychologists continue to assume a single model has limited the progress of cognitive science (1990, vxiii). Ulric Neisser, citing the fact that behavior and cognition are more innate than we thought, and more socially and culturally determined, and more context dependent than we thought, makes the more general claim that such complexities "make it less and less likely that any single principle can explain all of cognition. . . . Grand theories based on single global explanatory principles have had their day in psychology, but that day is drawing to a close" (1994, 227, 239).

13. Stephen Kern writes: "the metaphor of 'stream' is not entirely appropriate to describe this mental activity, because it suggests a steady flow in a fixed course, while Molly's mind revolves about her universe in defiance of conventional calculations of its pace or direction" (1983, 28).

Works Cited

Allport, A. 1988. "What Concept of Consciousness?" In *Consciousness in Contemporary Science,* ed. A. J. Marcel and E. Bisiach, 159–81. Oxford: Clarendon Press.

Anderson, R. C. 1984. "The Notion of Schemata and the Educational Enterprise." In *Schooling and the Acquisition of Knowledge,* ed. R. C. Anderson, R. J. Spiro, and W. E. Montague. Hillsdale, N.J.: Lawrence Erlbaum.

———, and Pearson, P. D. 1984. "A Schema-Theoretic View of Basic Processes in Reading Comprehension." In *Handbook of Reading Research,* ed. P. D. Pearson. New York: Longman, 1984.

Andrade, J. 1995. "Learning during Anesthesia: A Review." *British Journal of Psychology* 86: 479–506.

———, et al. 1994. "Cognitive Performance during Anesthesia." *Consciousness and Cognition* 3: 148–65.

Aquinas, T. 1951. *Summa Theologiae.* Matriti: Biblioteca de Autores Christianus.

Atwood, M. 1976. *Surfacing.* New York: Popular Library.

Baars, B. J. 1987. "Biological Implications of a Global Work Space Theory of Consciousness: Evidence, Theory, and Some Phylogenetic Speculations." In *Cognition, Language, and Consciousness: Integrative Levels,* ed. Gary Greenberg and Ethel Tobach, 209–36. Hillsdale, N.J.: Lawrence Erlbaum.

———. 1988. *A Cognitive Theory of Consciousness.* Cambridge: Cambridge University Press.

———. 1994. "A Thoroughly Empirical Approach to Consciousness." *Psyche: An Interdisciplinary Journal of Research on Consciousness* 1 (6): electronic journal.

Balaban, O. 1990. *Subject and Consciousness: A Philosophical Inquiry into Self-Consciousness.* Savage, Md.: Rowman and Littlefield.

Barlow, H. 1975. "Visual Experience and Cortical Development." *Nature* 258: 199–204.

Barr, H. L., et al. 1972. *LSD: Personality and Experience.* New York: Wiley-Interscience.

Bartlett, F. C. 1932. *Remembering: A Study in Experimental and Social Psychology.* Cambridge: Cambridge University Press.

Bech, P., L. Rafaelsen, and O. Rafaelsen 1973. "Cannabis and Alcohol: Effects on Estimation of Time and Distance." *Psychopharmacologia* (Berlin) 32: 373–81.

Bell, J. L. 1995. "Infinitesimals and the Continuum." *The Mathematical Intelligencer* 17: 55–57.

Berger, G. 1939. "Husserl et Hume." *Revue internationale de philosophie* 2: 342–53.

Bergson, H. 1965. *Duration and Simultaneity: With Reference to Einstein's Theory*, trans. L. Jacobson. Indianapolis: Bobbs-Merrill.

Bernet, R. 1985. "Einleitung" to Edmund Husserl, *Texte zur Phänomenologie des inneren Zeitbewusstseins (1893–1917)*. Hamburg: Felix Meiner.

Bernstein, B. 1961. "Aspects of Language and Learning in the Genesis of the Social Process." *Journal of Child Psychology* 1: 313–24.

———. 1977. *Class, Codes, and Control: Towards a Theory of Educational Transmission*. London: Routledge and Kegan Paul.

Berthoud-Papandropoulou, I. 1978. "An Experimental Study of Children's Ideas about Language." In *The Child's Conception of Language*, ed. A. Sinclair, J. Jarvella, and W. Levelt, 55–64. Berlin: Springer-Verlag.

Betti, E. 1980. "Hermeneutics as the General Methodology of the Geisteswissenschaften." In *Contemporary Hermeneutics: Hermeneutics as Method, Philosophy, and Critique*, ed. and trans. J. Bleicher. London: Routledge and Kegan Paul.

Bisiach, E., A. Berti, and G. Vallar. 1985. "Analogical and Logical Disorders Underlying Unilateral Neglect of Space." In *Attention and Performance*, vol. 11, ed. M. I. Posner and O. S. M. Marin, 238–49. Hillsdale N.J.: Lawrence Erlbaum.

Block, R. A. 1990. "Editor's Introduction." *Cognitive Models of Psychological Time.* Hillsdale, N.J.: Lawrence Erlbaum.

Blumenberg, H. 1986. *Lebenszeit und Weltzeit.* Frankfurt am Main : Suhrkamp.

Boring, E. G. 1933. *The Physical Dimensions of Consciousness.* New York: Dover, 1963 reprint.

———. 1936. "Temporal Perception and Operationalism." *American Journal of Psychology* 48: 519–21.

———. 1942. *Sensation and Perception in the History of Experimental Psychology.* New York: Appleton-Century-Crofts.

Bossert, P. J. 1976. "Hume and Husserl on Time and Time-Consciousness." *Journal of the British Society for Phenomenology* 7: 44–52.

Bregman, A. S., and A. I. Rudnicky. 1975. "Auditory Segregation: Stream or Streams?" *Journal of Experimental Psychology: Human Perception and Performance* 1: 263–67.

Brentano, F. 1966. *The True and the Evident*, trans. R. M. Chisholm and E. Politzer. London: Routledge and Kegan Paul.

———. 1975. *On the Several Senses of Being in Aristotle*, ed. and trans. R. George. Berkeley: University of California Press.

Broad, C. D. 1923. *Scientific Thought.* Paterson, N.J.: Littlefield, Adams, 1959.

———. 1938. *An Examination of McTaggart's Philosophy.* Cambridge: Cambridge University Press.

Broekman, J. W. 1963. *Phänomenologie und Egologie.* The Hague: Nijhoff.

Brough, J. 1970. *A Study of the Logic and Evolution of Edmund Husserl's Theory of the Constitution of Time-Consciousness, 1893–1917.* Dissertation, Georgetown University.

———. 1972. "The Emergence of an Absolute Consciousness in Husserl's Early Writings on Time-Consciousness." *Man and World* 5: 298–326.

———. 1993. "Husserl and the Deconstruction of Time." *Review of Metaphysics* 46: 503–36.

Buytendijk, J. F. J. 1974. *Prolegomena to an Anthropological Physiology,* trans. A. I. Orr, et al. Pittsburgh: Duquesne University Press.

Caputo, J. D. 1987. *Radical Hermeneutics.* Bloomington: Indiana University Press.

Carr, D. 1974. *Phenomenology and the Problem of History.* Evanston: Northwestern University Press.

———. 1987. *Interpreting Husserl.* Dordrecht: Kluwer/Nijhoff.

Casey, E. 1977. "Imagining and Remembering." *Review of Metaphysics* 31: 187–209.

———. 1983. "Keeping the Past in Mind." *Review of Metaphysics* 37: 77–95.

Chisholm, R., ed. 1960. *Realism and the Background of Phenomenology.* Glencoe: Free Press.

Churchland, P. M. 1984. *Matter and Consciousness: A Contemporary Introduction to the Philosophy of Mind.* Cambridge: MIT Press.

Claparède, E. 1911. "Récognition et moiité." *Archives de Psychologie* 11: 75–90.

Clay, E. R. 1882. *The Alternative: A Study in Psychology.* London: Macmillan.

Cobb-Stevens, R. 1982. "A Fresh Look at James's Radical Empiricism." In *Phenomenology: Dialogue and Bridges,* ed. R. Bruzina and B. Wilshire, 109–21. Albany: SUNY Press.

Cole, J. 1997a. *About Face.* Cambridge: MIT Press.

———. 1997b. "On 'Being Faceless': Selfhood and Facial Embodiment." In *Models of the Self,* ed. S. Gallagher and J. Shear, *Journal of Consciousness Studies* 4: 467–84.

Connerton, P. 1989. *How Societies Remember.* Cambridge: Cambridge University Press.

Cooper, E. D. 1995. "Searle's Room." *PSYCHE Electronic Discussion Forum* (psyche-d%nki.bitnet@uga.cc.uga.edu), 6 February 1995.

Corteen, R. J., and D. Dunn. 1974. "Shock-Associated Words in a Non-Attended Message: A Test for Momentary Awareness." *Journal of Experimental Psychology* 102: 1143–44.

Crain, P., S. Goldstone, and W. Lhamon. 1975. "Temporal Information Processing and Psychopathology." *Perceptual and Motor Skills* 41: 219–24.

Crick, F., and C. Koch. 1992. "The Problem of Consciousness." *Scientific American* (U.K.) 267: 111–17.

Cumming, G. D. 1972. Visual Perception and Metacontrast at Rapid Input Rates. Unpublished D. Phil. thesis, University of Oxford.

Deleuze, G. 1953. *Empirisme et subjectivité: Essai sur la nature humaine selon Hume.* Paris: Presses universitaires de France.

Dennett, D. C. 1991. *Consciousness Explained.* Boston: Little, Brown and Company.

————, and M. Kinsbourne. 1992. "Time and the Observer: The Where and When of Consciousness in the Brain." *Behavioral and Brain Sciences* 15: 183–247.

Derrida, J. 1970. "Ousia and Gramme: A Note to a Footnote in *Being and Time*," trans. E. S. Casey. In *Phenomenology in Perspective,* ed. F. J. Smith. The Hague: Martinus Nijhoff.

————. 1973. *Speech and Phenomena and Other Essays on Husserl's Theory of Signs,* trans. D. B. Allison. Evanston: Northwestern University Press.

————. 1976. *Of Grammatology,* trans. G. C. Spivak. Baltimore: Johns Hopkins University Press.

————. 1978. *Writing and Difference,* trans. A. Bass. Chicago: University of Chicago Press.

————. 1980. *The Archeology of the Frivolous: Reading Condillac,* trans. J. P. Leavey, Jr. Pittsburgh: Duquesne University Press.

————. 1981a. *Positions,* trans. A. Bass. Chicago: University of Chicago Press.

————. 1981b. *Dissemination,* trans. B. Johnson. Chicago: University of Chicago Press.

Dewey, J. 1977. "Meaning and Existence." In *Dewey and his Critics: Essays from the Journal of Philosophy,* ed. S. Morgenbesser. New York: Journal of Philosophy, Inc.

Dillon, M. 1988. *Merleau-Ponty's Ontology.* Bloomington: Indiana University Press.

————. 1992. "Temporality: Merleau-Ponty and Derrida." In *Merleau-Ponty, Hermeneutics, and Postmodernism,* ed. T. W. Busch and S. Gallagher, 189–212. Albany: SUNY Press.

Dreyfus, H. L. 1982. *Husserl, Intentionality, and Cognitive Science.* Cambridge: MIT Press.

Drummond, J. J. 1990. *Husserlian Intentionality and Non-Foundational Realism: Noema and Object.* Dordrecht: Kluwer Academic Publishers.

Dummett, M. 1960. "A Defense of McTaggart's Proof of the Unreality of Time." *Philosophical Review* 69. Reprinted in *Time,* ed. J. Westphal and C. Levenson, 112–18. Indianapolis: Hackett, 1993.

Einstein, A., and M. Besso. 1972. *Correspondence 1903–1955.* Paris: Hermann.

Evans, J. C. 1990. "The Myth of Absolute Consciousness." In *Crises in Continental Philosophy,* ed. A. B. Dallery and C. Scott. Albany: SUNY Press.

Farmer, D. J. 1990. *Being in Time: The Nature of Time in Light of McTaggart's Paradox.* Lanham: University Press of America.

Ferreiro, E. 1985. "Literacy Development: A Psychogenetic Perspective." In *Literacy, Language, and Learning: The Nature and Consequences of Reading and Writing,* ed. D. R. Olson, N. Torrance, and A. Hildyard, 217–28. Cambridge: Cambridge University Press.

Field, T. M., et al. 1982. "Discrimination and Imitation of Facial Expression by Neonates." *Science* 218: 179–81.

Findlay, J. N. 1975. "Husserl's Analysis of the Inner Time-Consciousness." *The Monist* 59: 3–20.

Fink, M. 1978. "Psychoactive Drugs and the Waking EEG: 1966–1976." In *Psychopharmacology: A Generation of Progress*, ed. M. A. Lipton, A. Dimascio, and K. F. Killam. New York: Raven Press.

Flynn, T. R. 1991. "Foucault and the Spaces of History." *The Monist* 74: 165–86.

Føllesdal, D. 1982a. "Brentano and Husserl on Intentional Objects and Perception." In *Husserl, Intentionality, and Cognitive Science*, ed. H. L. Dreyfus, 31–41. Cambridge: MIT Press.

———. 1982b. "Husserl's Notion of Noema." In *Husserl, Intentionality, and Cognitive Science*, ed. H. L. Dreyfus, 73–80. Cambridge: MIT Press.

Forster, P. M., and E. Gouvier. 1978. "Discrimination without Awareness?" *Quarterly Journal of Experimental Psychology* 30: 289–95.

Fraisse, P. 1963. *The Psychology of Time*, trans. J. Leith. New York: Harper and Row.

Freud, S. 1965. *The Interpretation of Dreams*, trans. J. Strachey. New York: Avon.

Friedman, W. 1990. *About Time: Inventing the Fourth Dimension*. Cambridge: MIT Press.

———, and A. Wilkins. 1985. "Scale Effects in Memory for the Time of Events." *Memory and Cognition* 13: 168–75.

Gadamer, H.-G. 1976. *Philosophical Hermeneutics*, trans. D. E. Linge. Berkeley: University of California Press.

———. 1989. *Truth and Method*, trans. J. Weinsheimer and D. G. Marshall. New York: Crossroad.

Gallagher, S. 1979. "Suggestions towards a Revision of Husserl's Phenomenology of Time-Consciousness." *Man and World* 12: 445–64.

———. 1986a. "Hyletic Experience and the Lived Body." *Husserl Studies* 3: 131–66.

———. 1986b. "Body Image and Body Schema: A Conceptual Clarification." *The Journal of Mind and Behavior* 7: 541–54.

———. 1992a. *Hermeneutics and Education*. Albany: SUNY Press.

———. 1992b. "Language and Imperfect Consensus: Merleau-Ponty's Contribution to the Habermas-Gadamer Debate." In *Merleau-Ponty, Hermeneutics, and Postmodernism*, ed. T. Busch and S. Gallagher, 69–82. Albany: SUNY Press.

———. 1995. "Body Schema and Intentionality." In *The Body and the Self*, ed. J. Bermúdez, A. Marcel, and N. Eilan, 225–44. Cambridge: MIT/Bradford Press.

———. 1996. "The Moral Significance of Primitive Self-Consciousness." *Ethics* 107 (1): 129–40.

———. 1997a. "Mutual Enlightenment: Recent Phenomenology in Cognitive Science." *Journal of Consciousness Studies* 4 (3): 195–214.

———. 1997b. "On the Pre-Noetic Reality of Time," in *Écart and Différance: Merleau-Ponty and Derrida on Seeing and Writing*, ed. M. Dillon, 134–48. Atlantic Highlands: Humanities Press.

———, and A. N. Meltzoff. 1996. "The Earliest Sense of Self and Others: Merleau-Ponty and Recent Developmental Studies." *Philosophical Psychology* 9 (2): 213–36.

Goethe, J. W. von. 1963. *Goethe's World View Presented in his Reflections and Maxims,* ed. R. Ungar, trans. H. Norden. New York: Frederick Ungar.

Goldstone, S., and J. Goldfarb. 1962. "Time Estimation and Psychopathology." *Perceptual and Motor Skills* 15: 28–30.

Granel, G. 1968. *Le Sens du temps et de la perception chez E. Husserl.* Paris: Gallimard.

Grathoff, R., ed. 1978. *The Theory of Social Action: The Correspondence of Alfred Schutz and Talcott Parsons.* Bloomington: Indiana University Press.

Gurwitsch, A. 1943. "William James's Theory of the 'Transitive Parts' of the Stream of Consciousness," reprinted in *Studies in Phenomenology and Psychology.* Evanston: Northwestern University Press, 1966.

———. 1966. *Studies in Phenomenology and Psychology.* Evanston: Northwestern University Press.

———. 1982. "Husserl's Theory of the Intentionality of Consciousness." In *Husserl, Intentionality, and Cognitive Science,* ed. H. L. Dreyfus. Cambridge: MIT Press.

Haaparanta, L. 1994. "Intentionality, Intuition, and the Computational Theory of Mind." In *Mind, Meaning, and Mathematics,* ed. L. Haaparanta, 211–13. Dordrecht: Kluwer.

Habermas, J. 1987. *The Philosophical Discourse of Modernity,* trans. F. G. Lawrence. Cambridge: MIT Press.

———. 1989. "Work and *Weltanschauung:* The Heidegger Controversy from a German Perspective," trans. J. McCumber. *Critical Inquiry* 15: 431–56.

Hall, E. T. 1983. *The Dance of Life: The Other Dimension of Time.* Garden City: Anchor/Doubleday.

Harris, E. 1988. *The Reality of Time.* Albany: SUNY Press.

Harvey, C. W. 1989. *Husserl's Phenomenology and the Foundations of Natural Science.* Athens: Ohio University Press.

Heidegger, M. 1962. *Being and Time (Sein und Zeit,* 1927), trans. J. Macquarrie and E. Robinson. New York: Harper and Row.

———. 1971. *Poetry, Language, Thought,* trans. A. Hofstadter. New York: Harper and Row.

———. 1972. *On Time and Being,* trans. J. Stambaugh. New York: Harper and Row.

———. 1982. *The Basic Problems of Phenomenology,* trans. A. Hofstadter. Bloomington: Indiana University Press.

Heuer, F. 1994. "Remembering Emotional Events," Medical Research Council, Applied Psychology Unit Seminar, Cambridge, England, 2 June 1994.

Hirsch, E. D. 1967. *Validity in Interpretation.* New Haven: Yale University Press.

Hollister, L. E. 1978. "Psychotomimetic Drugs in Man." In *Handbook of Psychopharmacology,* vol. 11, ed. L. Iverson, S. Iverson, and S. Snyder, 389–424. New York: Plenum Press.

Hopkins, B. C. 1991. "Phenomenological Self-Critique of its Descriptive Method." *Husserl Studies* 8: 129–50.

Hubel, D. H., and T. N. Wiesel. 1963. "Receptive Fields of Cells in Striate Cortex of Very Young, Visually Inexperienced Kittens." *Journal of Neurophysiology* 26: 994–1002.

Hume, D. 1739. *A Treatise of Human Nature*, ed. L. A. Selby-Bigge. Oxford: Clarendon Press, 1975.

Husserl, E. 1928. *Vorlesungen zur Phänomenologie des inneren Zeitbewusstseins*, ed. Martin Heidegger. In *Jahrbuch für Philosophie und phänomenologische Forschung*, 1928.

————. 1962. *Ideas: General Introduction to Pure Phenomenology*, trans. W. R. Boyce Gibson. New York: Collier Books, original ed. 1931.

————. 1964. *The Phenomenology of Internal Time-Consciousness*, trans. J. S. Churchill. Bloomington: Indiana University Press. Translation of Husserl 1928.

————. 1966a. *Zur Phänomenologie des inneren Zeitbewusstseins (1893–1917)*, ed. R. Boehm. *Husserliana* X. The Hague: Nijhoff, 1966.

————. 1966b. *Analysen zur Passiven Synthesis (1918–1926)*, ed. M. Fleisher. *Husserliana* XI. The Hague: Nijhoff.

————. 1969. *Formal and Transcendental Logic*, trans. D. Cairns. The Hague: Nijhoff.

————. 1970a. *Logical Investigations*, trans. J. Findlay. London: Routledge and Kegan Paul.

————. 1970b. *The Crisis of European Sciences and Transcendental Phenomenology*, trans. D. Carr. Evanston: Northwestern University Press.

————. 1970c. *Cartesian Meditations*, trans. D. Cairns. The Hague: Nijhoff.

————. 1973a. *Ding und Raum*, ed. U. Claesges, *Husserliana* XVI. The Hague: Nijhoff.

————. 1973b. *Experience and Judgment*, rev. and ed. L. Landgrebe; trans. J. S. Churchill and K. Ameriks. Evanston: Northwestern University Press.

————. 1977. *Phenomenological Psychology*, trans. J. Scanlon. The Hague: Nijhoff.

————. 1991. *Collected Works*. Vol. 4: *On the Phenomenology of the Consciousness of Internal Time (1893–1917)*, trans. J. Brough. Dordrecht: Kluwer Academic. Translation of Husserl 1966a.

James, W. 1890. *The Principles of Psychology*. New York: Dover, 1950.

————. 1894. "The Knowing of Things Together." In *Essays in Philosophy*. Cambridge: Harvard University Press, 1978.

————. 1909a. *Psychologie*, trans. M. Durr. Leipzig: Quelle und Meyer.

————. 1909b. *The Meaning of Truth*. New York: Longmans, Green.

————. 1912. *The Works of William James: Essays in Radical Empiricism*, ed. R. B. Perry. Cambridge: Harvard University Press, 1976.

————. 1942. *Essays in Radical Empiricism and a Pluralistic Universe*. New York: Longmans, Green.

Jameson, F. 1992. *Postmodernism or, the Cultural Logic of Late Capitalism*. Durham: Duke University Press.

Johnsen, B. C. 1994. "A Model Devoid of Consciousness." *Behavioral and Brain Sciences* 17: 176–77.

Johnson-Laird, P. 1983. *Mental Models*. Cambridge: Cambridge University Press.

Jones, R. T. 1978. "Marihuana: Human Effects." *Handbook of Psychopharmacology*, vol. 12 ed. L. Iverson, S. Iverson and S. Snyder, 373–412. New York: Plenum Press.

Joyce, J. 1914. *Ulysses*. New York: Random House, 1961.

Kant, I. 1929. *Kant's Inaugural Dissertation and Early Writings on Space,* trans. J. Handyside. London: Open Court.

Kelso, J. A. S., et al. 1994. "Multistability and Metastability in Perceptual and Brain Dynamics." in *Multistability in Cognition,* ed. M. Staedler and P. Kruse. Berlin: Springer.

Kern, S. 1983. *The Culture of Time and Space: 1880–1918.* Cambridge: Harvard University Press.

Khersonsky, N. 1935/36. "La notion du temps." *Recherches Philosophiques* 5: 41–51.

Kline, G. L. 1983. "Form, Concrescence, and Concretum." In *Explorations in Whitehead's Philosophy,* ed. L. S. Ford and G. L. Kline, 104–46. New York: Fordham University Press.

Kolb, L. C. 1959. "The Body Image in the Schizophrenic Reaction." In *Schizophrenia: An Integrated Approach,* ed. A. Auerbach, 87–97. New York: Ronald Press.

Kuhl, P. K., and A. N. Meltzoff. 1982. "The Bimodal Perception of Speech in Infancy." *Science* 218: 1138–41.

Langsdorf, L. 1984. "The Noema as Intentional Entity: A Critique of Føllesdal." *Review of Metaphysics* 37: 757–84.

Laurie, P. 1971. *Drugs: Medical, Psychological, and Social Factors.* Baltimore: Penguin.

LeBreton, D. 1991. "Body and Anthropology: Symbolic Effectiveness." *Diogenes* 153: 85–100.

Legerstee, M. 1991. "The Role of Person and Object in Eliciting Early Imitation." *Journal of Experimental Child Psychology* 51: 423–33.

Levinas, E. 1969. *Totality and Infinity,* trans. A. Lingis. Pittsburgh: Duquesne University Press.

———. 1973. *The Theory of Intuition in Husserl's Phenomenology,* trans. A. Orianne. Evanston: Northwestern University Press.

———. 1978. *Existence and Existents,* trans. A. Lingis. The Hague: Nijhoff.

———. 1981. *Otherwise than Being or Beyond Essence,* trans. A. Lingis. The Hague: Nijhoff.

———. 1987. *Time and the Other,* trans. R. A. Cohen. Pittsburgh: Duquesne University Press.

Libet, B. 1985. "Subjective Antedating of a Sensory Experience and Mind-Brain Theories." *Journal of Theoretical Biology* 114: 563–70.

———. 1992. "The Neural Time-Factor in Perception, Volition and Free Will." *Revue de Métaphysique et de Morale* 2: 255–72.

———, et al. 1979. "Subjective Referral of the Timing for a Conscious Sensory Experience." *Brain* 102: 193–224.

Locke, J. 1694. *An Essay Concerning Human Understanding.* New York: Dover, 1959.

Lotze, R. H. 1887. *Metaphysic in Three Books : Ontology, Cosmology, and Psychology,* 2d ed., trans. B. Bosanquet. Oxford: Clarendon Press.

Lyotard, J.-F. 1988. *The Differend: Phrases in Dispute,* trans. G. Van Den Abbeele. Minneapolis: University of Minnesota Press.

————. 1989. *The Lyotard Reader,* ed. A. Benjamin. Oxford: Basil Blackwell.

————. 1990. *Heidegger and the Jews,* trans. A. Michel and M. Roberts. Minneapolis: University of Minnesota Press.

————. 1991a. *The Inhuman,* trans. G. Bennington and R. Bowlby. Stanford: Stanford University Press.

————. 1991b. *Phenomenology,* trans. B. Beakley. Albany: SUNY Press.

Mabbott, J. D. 1951. "Our Direct Experience of Time." *Mind* 60: 153–67.

Madison, G. 1981. *The Phenomenology of Merleau-Ponty.* Athens: Ohio University Press.

Mansky, P. A. 1978. "Opiates: Human Psychopharmacology." In *Handbook of Psychopharmacology,* vol. 12, ed. L. Iverson, S. Iverson, and S. Snyder, 95–185. New York: Plenum Press.

Marcel, A. J. 1980. "Conscious and Preconscious Recognition of Polysemous Words: Locating the Selective Effects of Prior Verbal Context." In *Attention and Performance,* vol. 8, ed. R. S. Nickerson. Hillsdale, N.J.: Erlbaum.

————. 1983. "Conscious and Unconscious Perception: An Approach to the Relations between Phenomenal Experience and Perceptual Processes." *Cognitive Psychology* 15: 238–300.

————. 1988. "Phenomenal Experience and Functionalism." In *Consciousness in Contemporary Science,* ed. A. J. Marcel and E. Bisiach, 121–58. Oxford: Clarendon Press, 1988.

————. 1993. "Slippage in the Unity of Consciousness." In *Experimental and Theoretical Studies of Consciousness,* Ciba Foundation Symposium no. 174. Chichester: John Wiley and Sons.

————, and E. Bisiach. 1988. *Consciousness in Contemporary Science.* Oxford: Clarendon Press.

Marx, W. 1987. *Is There a Measure on Earth?* trans. T. J. Nenon and R. Lilly. Chicago: University of Chicago Press.

Mayer-Gross, W. 1964. "Problems of the Depressive Cycle." In *Depression: Proceedings of Symposium at Cambridge,* ed. E. B. Davies, 37–40. Cambridge: Cambridge University Press.

Mazis, G. 1992. "Merleau-Ponty and the 'Backward Flow' of Time." In *Merleau-Ponty, Hermeneutics, and Postmodernism,* ed. T. W. Busch and S. Gallagher, 53–68. Albany: SUNY Press.

McIntyre, R., and D. W. Smith. 1982. "Husserl's Identification of Meaning and Noema." In *Husserl, Intentionality, and Cognitive Science,* ed. H. L. Dreyfus, 81–92. Cambridge: MIT Press.

McTaggart, J. M. E. 1908. "The Unreality of Time." *Mind* 17 (New Series, no. 68): 457–74.

Mead, G. H. 1938. *The Philosophy of the Act.* Chicago: University of Chicago Press.

————. 1972. *On Social Psychology.* Chicago: University of Chicago Press.

————. 1980. *The Philosophy of the Present.* Chicago: University of Chicago Press; original: 1932.

Melges, F. T., and A. M. Freeman. 1977. "Temporal Disorganization and Inner-

Outer Confusion in Acute Mental Illness." *American Journal of Psychiatry* 134: 874–77.

Mellor, D. H. 1981. *Real Time.* Cambridge: Cambridge University Press.

Meltzoff, A. N., and M. K. Moore. 1977. "Imitation of Facial and Manual Gestures by Human Neonates." *Science* 198: 75–78.

———. 1983. "Newborn Infants Imitate Adult Facial Gestures." *Child Development* 54: 702–9.

———. 1989. "Imitation in Newborn Infants: Exploring the Range of Gestures Imitated and the Underlying Mechanisms." *Developmental Psychology* 25: 954–62.

———. 1994. "Imitation, Memory, and the Representation of Persons." *Infant Behavior and Development* 17: 83–99.

Merleau-Ponty, M. 1962. *Phenomenology of Perception* (*Phénoménologie de la Perception,* 1945), trans. C. Smith. London: Routledge and Kegan Paul.

———. 1964a. *The Primacy of Perception,* ed. J. M. Edie. Evanston: Northwestern University Press.

———. 1964b. *Signs,* trans. R. McCleary. Evanston: Northwestern University Press.

———. 1968. *The Visible and the Invisible,* trans. A. Lingis. Evanston: Northwestern University Press.

Meyer, R. E. 1978. "Behavioral Pharmacology of Marihuana." In *Psychopharmacology: A Generation of Progress,* ed. M. A. Lipton, A. Dimascio, and K. F. Killam. New York: Raven Press.

Michon, J. A., and J. L. Jackson, eds. 1985. *Time, Mind, and Behavior.* Berlin: Springer.

Miller, I. 1982. "Husserl's Account of our Temporal Awareness." In *Husserl, Intentionality, and Cognitive Science,* ed. H. L. Dreyfus, 125–46. Cambridge: MIT Press.

———. 1984. *Husserl, Perception, and Temporal Awareness.* Cambridge: MIT Press.

Minkowski, E. 1970. *Lived Time: Phenomenological and Psychopathological Studies,* trans. Nancy Metzel. Evanston: Northwestern University Press.

Mohanty, J. N. 1971. "Husserl's Concept of Intentionality." In *Analecta Husserliana,* vol. 1, ed. A-T. Tymieniecka. New York: Humanities Press.

———. 1982. *Husserl and Frege.* Bloomington: Indiana University Press.

Mundle, C. W. K. 1954. "How Specious is the 'Specious Present'?" *Mind* 63: 26–48.

Murphy, R. T. 1980. *Hume and Husserl: Towards Radical Subjectivism.* The Hague: Nijhoff.

Myers, G. 1971. "William James on Time Perception." *Philosophy of Science* 38: 353–60.

Neisser, U. 1994. "Multiple Systems: A New Approach to Cognitive Theory." *European Journal of Cognitive Psychology* 6: 225–42.

Newman, J., and B. J. Baars. 1993. "A Neural Attentional Model for Access to Consciousness: A Global Workspace Perspective." *Concepts in Neuroscience* 4: 255–90.

Oatley, K. 1988. "On Changing One's Mind: A Possible Function of

Consciousness." In *Consciousness in Contemporary Science*, ed. A. J. Marcel and E. Bisiach, 369–89. Oxford: Clarendon Press.

Olafson, F. A. 1977. "Husserl's Theory of Intentionality in Contemporary Perspective." In *Husserl: Expositions and Appraisals*, ed. F. Elliston and P. McCormick. Notre Dame: University of Notre Dame Press.

Olson, D. R. 1994. *The World on Paper.* Cambridge: Cambridge University Press.

Ornstein, R. E. 1969. *On the Experience of Time.* Baltimore: Penguin.

Parfit, D. 1984. *Reasons and Persons.* Oxford: Clarendon Press.

Penrose, R. 1989. *The Emperor's New Mind.* Oxford: Oxford University Press.

———. 1994. *Shadows of the Mind: A Search for the Missing Science of Consciousness.* Oxford: Oxford University Press.

Petitot, J., et al. 1998. *Naturalizing Phenomenology: Issues in Contemporary Phenomenology and Cognitive Science.* Stanford: Stanford University Press.

Plumer, G. 1985. "The Myth of the Specious Present." *Mind* 94: 19–35.

Pontius, A. 1977. "Somesthetic Hallucinations and Motility in Schizophrenia: Neurophysiological Views and Information Flow Model." *Perceptual and Motor Skills* 44: 79–95.

Pope, K. S. 1978. "How Gender, Solitude, and Posture Influence the Stream of Consciousness." In *The Stream of Consciousness: Scientific Investigations into the Flow of Human Experience*, ed. K. S. Pope and J. L. Singer, 259–99. New York: Plenum Press.

———, and J. L. Singer. 1978. *The Stream of Consciousness: Scientific Investigations into the Flow of Human Experience.* New York: Plenum Press.

Pöppel, E. 1978. "Time Perception." In *Handbook of Sensory Physiology*, ed. R. Held, H. W. Leibowitz, and H.-L. Teuber, 713–29. Heidelberg: Springer-Verlag.

———. 1988. *Mindworks: Time and Conscious Experience.* Boston: Harcourt Brace Jovanovich.

———. 1994. "Temporal Mechanisms in Perception." *International Review of Neurobiology* 37: 185–202.

———, K. Schill, and N. von Steinbüchel. 1990. "Sensory Integration within Temporally Neutral System States: A Hypothesis." *Naturwissenschaften* 77: 89–91.

Prior, A. N. 1968. *Papers on Time and Tense.* Oxford: Oxford University Press.

Quinton, A. 1975. "The Soul." In *Personal Identity*, ed. J. Perry. Berkeley: University of California Press.

Reisberg, D., and F. Heuer. 1992. "Remembering the Details of Emotional Events." In *Affect and Accuracy in Recall: The Problem of "Flashbulb" Memories*, ed. E. Winograd and U. Neisser. Cambridge: Cambridge University Press.

Ricoeur, P. 1984. *Time and Narrative,* vol. 1, trans. K. McLaughlin and D. Pellauer. Chicago: University of Chicago Press.

Robbins, T. W., and B. J. Sahakian. 1979. " 'Paradoxical' Effects of Psychomotor Stimulant Drugs in Hyperactive Children from the Standpoint of Behavioural Pharmacology." *Neuropharmacology* 18: 931–50.

Rosenfield, I. 1992. *The Strange, Familiar, and Forgotten: An Anatomy of Consciousness.* New York: Alfred A. Knopf.

Ruhnau, E. 1995. "Time Gestalt and the Observer: Reflections on the 'Tertium

Datur' of Consciousness." In *Conscious Experience,* ed. T. Metzinger, 165–84. Thorverton: Imprint Academic.

Rutschmann, J. 1973. "Time Judgments by Magnitude Estimation and Magnitude Production and Anxiety: A Problem of Comparison between Normals and Certain Schizophrenic Patients." *Journal of Psychology* 85: 187–223.

Sartre, J-P. 1956. *Being and Nothingness,* trans. H. Barnes. New York: Philosophical Library.

Sartre, J-P. 1970. "Intentionality: A Fundamental Idea of Husserl's Phenomenology," trans. Joseph P. Fell. *Journal of the British Society for Phenomenology* 1: 4–5.

Scheler, M. 1973. *Formalism in Ethics and Non-Formal Ethics of Values,* trans. M. Frings and R. Funk. Evanston: Northwestern University Press.

Schutz, A. 1932. *Der sinnhafte Aufbau der sozialen Welt.* Frankfurt: Suhrkamp, 1974. English translation: *The Phenomenology of the Social World,* trans. G. Walsh and F. Lehnert. Evanston: Northwestern University Press, 1967.

———. 1962. *Collected Papers,* vol. 1. The Hague: Nijhoff.

———. 1966. *Collected Papers,* vol. 3. The Hague: Nijhoff.

Searle, J. 1982. "What is an Intentional State?" In *Husserl, Intentionality, and Cognitive Science,* ed. H. L. Dreyfus, 259–76. Cambridge: MIT Press.

———. 1983. *Intentionality: An Essay in the Philosophy of Mind.* Cambridge: Cambridge University Press.

———. 1992. *The Rediscovery of the Mind.* Cambridge: MIT/Bradford Press.

Serra, E. 1992. "Children's Understanding of How Writing Reflects Speech." Unpublished paper, Centre for Applied Cognitive Science, Ontario Institute for Studies in Education, Toronto.

Serres, M. 1995. *Genesis,* trans. G. James and James Nielson. Ann Arbor: University of Michigan Press.

Shatz, C. J. 1990. "Impulse Activity and the Patterning of Connections during CNS Development." *Neuron* 5: 745–56.

———. 1992. "The Developing Brain." *Scientific American* (UK) 267 (3): 35–41.

Sheets-Johnstone, M. 1990. *The Roots of Thinking.* Philadelphia: Temple University Press.

Sillito, A. M. 1987. "Visual System: Environmental Influences." In *The Oxford Companion to the Mind,* ed. R. L. Gregory. Oxford: Oxford University Press.

Slife, B. D. 1993. *Time and Psychological Explanation.* Albany: SUNY Press.

Smith, D. W., and R. McIntyre. 1982. *Husserl and Intentionality: A Study of Mind, Meaning, and Language.* Dordrecht: D. Reidel.

Sokolowski, R. 1992. "Parallelism in Conscious Experience." *Daedalus* 121 (1): 87–103.

Solomon, R. 1977. "Husserl's Concept of the Noema." In *Husserl: Expositions and Appraisals,* ed. F. Elliston and P. McCormick, 168–81. Notre Dame: University of Notre Dame Press.

Spiegelberg, H. 1976. *The Phenomenological Movement.* The Hague: Nijhoff.

Stern, W. 1897. "Psychische Präsenzzeit." *Zeitschrift für Psychologie* 13.

————. 1898. *Psychologie der Veränderungsauffassung*. Breslau: Preuss und Junger.

Stevens, R. 1974. *James and Husserl: The Foundations of Meaning*. The Hague: Nijhoff.

Strange, J. R. 1978. "A Search for the Sources of the Stream of Consciousness." In *The Stream of Consciousness: Scientific Investigations into the Flow of Human Experience*, ed. K. S. Pope and J. L. Singer, 9–29. New York: Plenum Press.

Straus, E. 1966. *Phenomenological Psychology*, trans. E. Eng. New York: Basic Books.

Strawson, G. 1994. *Mental Reality*. Cambridge: MIT Press.

Thao, T. D. 1986. *Phenomenology and Dialectical Materialism*, trans. D. J. Herman and D. V. Morano. Dordrecht: D. Reidel.

Tinklenberg, W. J., et al. 1972. "Marihuana and Alcohol: Time Production and Memory Functions." *Archives of General Psychiatry* 27: 812–15.

Tugendhat, E. 1977. "Phenomenology and Linguistic Analysis." In *Husserl: Expositions and Appraisals*, ed. Frederick Elliston and Peter McCormick. Notre Dame: University of Notre Dame Press.

van Gelder, T. 1998. "Wooden Iron? Husserlian Phenomenology Meets Cognitive Science." In *Naturalizing Phenomenology: Issues in Contemporary Phenomenology and Cognitive Science*, ed. J. Petitot, et al. Stanford: Stanford University Press. In press.

Varela, Francisco, J. 1998. "The Specious Present: A Neurophenomenology of Time Consciousness." In *Naturalizing Phenomenology: Issues in Contemporary Phenomenology and Cognitive Science*, ed. J. Petitot, et al. Stanford: Stanford University Press. In press.

Wälde, M. 1985. *Husserl und Schapp: Von der Phänomenologie des inneren Zeitbewusstseins zur Philosophie der Geschichten*. Basel: Schwabe and Co.

Ward, J. 1878–89. "Psychology." *Encyclopaedia Britannica*, 9th ed. New York: Scribners.

Weiskrantz, L. 1986. *Blindsight: A Case Study and Its Implications*. New York: Oxford University Press.

Whitrow, G. J. 1963. *The Natural Philosophy of Time*. London: Thomas Nelson.

Wiesel, T. N., and D. H. Hubel. 1963. "Effects of Visual Deprivation on Morphology and Physiology of Cells in the Cat's Lateral Geniculate Body," and "Single-Cell Responses in Striate Cortex of Kittens Deprived of Vision in One Eye." *Journal of Neurophysiology* 26: 978–93; 1003–17.

Williams, D. 1992. *Nobody Nowhere*. London: Corgi Books; New York: Random House.

Wilshire, B. 1968. *William James and Phenomenology: A Study of the Principles of Psychology*. Bloomington: Indiana University Press.

Wittgenstein, L. 1953. *Philosophical Investigations*, trans. G. E. M. Anscombe. New York: Macmillan.

Wood, D. 1989. *The Deconstruction of Time*. Atlantic Highlands: Humanities Press.

Woolf, V. 1925. *The Common Reader*. New York: Harcourt, Brace, 1953.

Wyschogrod, E. 1990. *Saints and Postmodernism: Revisioning Moral Philosophy.*
    Chicago: University of Chicago Press.
Yount, M. 1992. "Two Reversibilities: Merleau-Ponty and Derrida." In *Merleau-
    Ponty, Hermeneutics, and Postmodernism,* ed. T. W. Busch and S. Gallagher,
    213–26. Albany: SUNY Press.
Zihl, J., and D. vonCramon. 1980. "Registration of Light Stimuli in the Cortically
    Blind Hemifield and its Effect on Localization." *Behavior and Brain
    Research* 1: 287–98.

Index

A-Series (McTaggart), 86–87, 89, 174–76
absolute subjectivity, 78, 174
act-intentionality, 131
action, 114, 145, 193
aesthetic experience, 95, 98
agency, 156
Allport, G., 94, 137
alter ego, 110, 116, 121
alterity, 13, 145ff., 167–68, 174; in
    Heidegger, 115–17; in Levinas,
    121–26; in retention, 81, 108–9; in
    time-consciousness, 79
amnesia, 215n11
Anderson, R., 149
analogical appresentation (Husserl), 111,
    114
anesthesia, 215n11
anteriority, 174, 181, 190, 196
anterior functioning of language, 141,
    144, 182, 196–97
apprehension (*Auffasung*), 46, 63,
    110–11, 131, 135, 139, 144; as
    sense-bestowing, 44; *see* noetic schema
Aquinas, Thomas, 42, 44, 134
arche-writing (Derrida), 81, 84, 201
Aristotle, 6, 8, 42, 100, 122, 166, 173
art, 95–96, 101–2, 169, 199
Atwood, M., 95
auditory fusion, 164
auditory hallucinations, 185
Augustine, 6, 100, 103, 140, 173, 175, 177;
    Confessions, 6; *distentio*, 6- 7, 198; on
    language, 207n6
authentic temporality, 118, 123
authenticity, 117–19, 120–21
autism, 169
autobiography, 174, 191
autonomic nervous system, 136–37, 185

avant-garde, 95

B-Series (McTaggart), 86–87, 89, 100–101,
    174, 176
Baars, B., 2
background knowledge, 149–50, 153, 190
backwards projection (referral) in time
    (Libet), 3, 187, 201
Bartlett, F., 192
Beckett, S., 101
Bedeutung; see reference
being-towards-death, 118, 120–21, 125,
    160, 171–72
being-with (*Mitsein*), 116, 121
Bergson, H., 66, 89, 92
binding problem, 162
biological clock, 181, 184
Bisiach, E., 94
blindsight, 92–93, 99
Block, R., 219n12
body; *see* embodiment
body image, 114, 185
body schema, 174, 182, 188–89, 191
boredom, 185
Boring, E. G., 18, 27, 28
brain, 3, 22–23, 88, 92, 98, 106, 186–88
Brentano, F., 7, 33, 54, 59, 122, 130;
    Husserl's criticism of, 39–41, 45, 51,
    76; on intentionality, 14, 44–45, 205n8;
    on original association, 39, 41–42; and
    PSA, 61–62; on temporal content, 46,
    180; on time-consciousness, 35–36
Broad, C. D., 4, 17, 51, 57, 59, 60; diagram
    of time-consciousness, 23–24, 38,
    48–49, 52, 204n3; and Husserl, 34–36,
    65; and LA1, 23ff., 37–39; and PSA, 63;
    and specious present, 18, 23–28
Broekman, J. W., 33

Brough, John, 33, 49
Burke, J., 165
Buytendijk, 137

Carr, D., 140, 212n9
Casey, E., 189
Cézanne, P., 95, 101
Churchill, James, 34
Clay, E. R., 17, 27, 32, 52
cogito, 81, 84, 100
cognitive interpretation of time
   distortions, 181
cognitive paradox, 12, 122, 176; in
   Augustine, 6–7; in Brentano, 41;
   in Husserl, 42, 46–47; and Lotzean
   assumptions, 4, 21–23; and personal
   identity, 73–74; and specious present,
   10, 21–23
cognitive psychology, 1, 3, 14, 149, 192
cognitive representation of time, 7
cognitive schema, 149–50, 153
cognitive science, 2–4, 12, 14, 60, 88, 104
Cole, J., 168
communication, 142, 168
community, 110, 145
complexity, 88
computer memory, 191
conception-dependence, 148–50
connectionism, 88
Connerton, P., 218n6
consciousness, 1–3, 7, 20, 25, 35, 44,
   74, 101, 156; enduring/extended, 62,
   64–65, 76; formal structure of, 12, 55,
   66, 80, 90, 104, 114, 153, 180–81; as an
   interpretive process, 181; maximum
   and minimum durations, 27–28;
   momentary, 22–25, 31, 35–36, 39,
   50–51, 59, 62–65; phase of, 38, 47, 50,
   61, 64–66, 68, 80, 87, 90, 105; unity of,
   3, 13, 35, 66, 73, 75–77, 108; see noetic
   act, retentional-protentional structure,
   stream of consciousness
constitution, 75, 81, 86, 105, 140
content, 44–45, 67–68, 96, 98, 104–5,
   111, 145, 153–54, 161; hyletic, 135;
   intentional, 94, 163; intentional versus
   real, 44, 47–48; as temporal, 179–82,
   186, 190, 200
conversation, 146
Crick, Francis, 2

culture, 95, 139, 166, 182, 189; cultural
   practices, 174

das Man (the They), 115–21
Dasein (Heidegger), 115–21
death, 108, 117–18, 123, 170–72; as
   intentional object, 170
deconstruction, 2, 74, 81, 85, 101
deferral, 79
Deleuze, G., 83
Dennett, D., 2–3, 88, 96, 99, 143, 185–88,
   199–201
depersonalization, 185
depression, 185
Derrida, J., 106, 151, 201–2; Hume,
   83–85; on Husserl's concept of time-
   consciousness, 2, 13, 74, 79ff., 81; and
   Merleau-Ponty, 208n4
Descartes, 115, 140
descriptive abstraction, 65
desire, 123, 134
Dewey, J., 142
diacritical difference, 88, 91
diagram(s), 19, 20, 24, 76–77, 188, 203n1,
   204n3
Dietze, I., 18
différance (Derrida), 79, 81, 83–85, 88,
   124
differend (Lyotard), 102
differential access to experience, 94
Dilthey, W., 133
discontinuity, 124
dispersed identity; see identity, dispersed
disposition (Befindlichkeit), 118–20
double intentionality; see intentionality
dream, 192–93, 195
Drummond, J., 210n1
Dreyfus, H., 2, 12, 133
Duchamp, M., 101
Dummett, M., 177
duration: of conscous act, 25, 35, 38, 51,
   62, 64–65; Locke's conception of, 9;
   and specious present, 18, 28, 35, 51, 55,
   59
durée (Bergson), 92

earlier/later, 55, 87, 100, 118; see B-Series
écart (Merleau-Ponty), 97, 124
education, 146
effective history; see historical effect

ego, 130, 142, 145, 172; transcendental, 78, 110, 121, 125, 134, 156, 169–70, 206n5, 216n15
eidetic reduction, 90–91, 151
eidos, 90
Einstein, A., 3, 173, 204n4, 216n17
ek-static structure of living present, 80
embodied perspective, 89
embodiment, 5, 14, 97; facial, 124; in Husserl's analysis of intersubjectivity, 111, 114; and hyle, 134–37, 182–84; as keeping the past, 189; and personal identity, 10, 73; as prenoetic constraint, 174, 182–84; and reversibility, 95
emotional schemas, 150
Empedocles, 42, 122
Epicurus, 170, 172
epoche (phenomenological reduction), 54, 84, 110, 115, 120, 135ff., 149, 201; see phenomenological method
Ereignis (Heidegger), 101
esse intentionale, 45–46
ethical relations, 122–23, 125, 168, 172
Evans, J. C., 33
evidence, 82
excogito, 83, 106; see imagination
existential temporality, 119
expectation, 6–7, 40, 67, 168, 173, 176, 193
expressibility, 141, 196
exteriority, 121
extra-intentional, 14, 79, 83, 85, 101, 122, 124, 136, 152–54; see prenoetic
eyestrain, 137

face (face-to-face), 120–24, 160, 167–70; in Heidegger 210n8
fallacy of the actual future, 203n1, 207n2
fatigue, 18, 137, 164
Findlay, J., 34, 37
finitude, 80, 134, 150, 166
first-person identity, 73
flesh (Merleau-Ponty), 98, 106
flow of consciousness; see stream of consciousness
flux of consciousness; see stream of consciousness
folk psychology, 88
forgetting, 97, 101–3, 160
Føllesdal, D., 132–33, 140–41, 149, 151

foundationalism, 82
Fraser, A. C., 9
Frege, G., 133
Freud, S., 97, 102–3, 106, 157, 159, 192–93, 218n10
Friedman, W., 203n2, 217n3, 218n12
future: in the A-Series, 87; beyond intentional control, 175; and death, 117–18, 122–23; indeterminacy of, 52, 193; and possibilities, 113, 117–18; and protention, 52, 57, 67- 68; real versus intentional, 54; in specious present, 17, 20, 23, 57

Gadamer, H.-G., 142–43, 164, 166, 196; on life-world, 214n1
generalized other, 112, 115–16, 118–21
genetic analysis, 139
gesture, 145, 168
Goethe, J. W. von, 167
grammar, 196
Gurwitsch, A., 33, 37, 75, 132–33, 147, 150–51

Habermas, J., 115, 120, 210n6
Harris, E., 33
Hegel, G. W. F., 112
Heidegger, M., 108, 145, 160; on authentic time, 115–20; Being and Time, 134; in contrast to Levinas, 123; on death, 115–20, 170–72; and Merleau-Ponty, 89
Herbart, J. F., 7, 21, 33, 35 , 54, 61
hermeneutical as, 105, 148, 153, 181
hermeneutical aspects of language, 141
hermeneutical circle, 149
hermeneutical concept of intentionality, 134, 147–48
hermeneutical dimensions, 14, 133, 138, 150–51
hermeneutical effect, 139
hermeneutics, 160–61, 164–65, 181, 190
historical effect (Wirkungsgeschichte), 5, 14, 104–5 139–40, 153, 165–66, 177, 190
historicism, 133
historicity, 120, 138–40, 166
holocaust, 102
horizon (Husserl), 149, 152–53, 158
horizontal intentionality (Längsintentionalität), 50–51, 77, 154

Hume, D., 8–9, 11, 59, 65, 88, 154, 180;
on difference, 206n1; and Husserl
206n3; on passions 207n8; on personal
identity, 73–85

Husserl, E., 168, 173, 186, 190, 198, 201;
and cognitive science, 2; on content,
180ff.; Derrida's deconstruction of,
79–81; distinction between real and
intentional, 11; and Heidegger, 115ff.;
on historical effect, 139ff.; on Hume,
74ff.; on hyle, 135ff., 183; on identity,
152; on intentionality, 43ff., 105, 130ff.,
141–42, 150–51; on intersubjectivity,
110ff., 145; and James, 32ff.; on
language, 140ff.; and Levinas, 120–21;
limitations of his analysis, 12–14; and
Merleau-Ponty, 89ff.; on the noema,
45–46, 132ff.; and personal identity,
74ff.; on protention, 67–69; and PSA,
60–64; on reflection, 64–67, 89ff.,
159–60; on remembering, 192; on
self-constitution, 78; on seriality, 87;
and specious present, 32ff., 53–60; on
time-consciousness, 4–5, 39–42, 46–52,
53–60, 153

Husserl Archives, 33

hyle (hyletic content, hyletic data), 42,
44–46, 131, 134ff., 150, 168, 182–83,
185; disputed status of, 211n7; as most
basic level of consciousness, 210n2; as
reflective abstraction, 135; see sensation

hypochondria, 185

I-Thou relation, 146

identity, 73, 75, 77–83, 84, 124–25, 148,
151; as intentional, 78; dispersed,
153–54, 156, 158

imagination, 75–77, 83–84, 154

immanent object, 45

immediate experience, 28, 55, 79

inauthenticity, 117, 119–21; inauthentic
temporality, 118

incompleteness of intentionality, 134,
150, 153

information processing, 181, 187

integration, 67–68, 161

intellectual synthesis, 89; see judgment

intentional content, 11, 181–82, 188

intentional object, 44

intentionality, 2, 41, 91–92, 119, 150, 153,
183; act- versus operative, 131; and
alterity, 121–23; and the body, 136; and
death, 170–71; distinction between real
(reell) and intentional, 44; as double,
48, 76, 77, 105, 180; and forgetting,
97–98; Gurwitsch on, 147; Husserl's
concept of, 11–12, 41ff., 104–5;
inadequacy of, 166; as incomplete, 134,
153; as interpretive/hermeneutical,
106, 148, 181; and intersubjectivity, 145;
in James, 156; and language, 140–42;
narrow view of, 129ff.; prenoetic
constraints on, 133ff., 174, 189; as
relation, 42–43, 129, 130; Sartre's
concept of, 105; and the unconscious,
159

intermodal differences; see intersensory
differences

interpretation, 131, 134, 141, 148, 165

intersensory differences, 30, 58, 161,
204n5

intersubjectivity, 5, 14, 108–9, 111,
114–15, 140, 145

introspection, 13

James, W., 53–54, 89, 125, 144; and
cognitive paradox 7; on content,
179–80; and Husserl, 2, 32ff.; on
identity, 155–56; inconsistency of his
analysis, 52; and Locke, 9; and Lotzean
assumptions, 22–23; and personal
identity, 10–11, 73; radical empiricism,
99, 155–56, 214n3; and specious
present, 4, 17ff., 26ff.; and stream of
consciousness, 10; see specious present

Johnson-Laird, P., 91

Joyce, J., 96, 104, 199–202

Joycean machine, 3, 88, 96, 104, 199–201

Joycean theory, 202

judgment, 132; comparative, 7, 11, 63, 73,
89

justice, 125, 168

Kant, I., 13, 67, 75, 77, 81, 104, 106, 169 ,
179, 217n19

Kline, G. L., 203n1, 207n2

Koch, C., 2

Korsakoff's syndrome, 185

LA1 (first Lotzean assumption), 31, 36,
39, 41–42, 51–52, 53, 155; in Broad's

analysis, 23ff.; defined, 22; and PSA, 60–64
LA2 (second Lotzean assumption), 77, 89, 130; in Broad's analysis, 24–26; defined, 22; and perplexities, 30–31, 53–54, 57–60; and PSA, 60ff.; rejection by Husserl, 37–39, 41–42, 47–48, 51–52
Lacan, J., 217n5
Langsdorf, L., 2
Längsintentionalität; see horizontal intentionality
language, 91, 99, 157, 165, 167; anterior functioning of, 141, 144, 146–50, 182, 196–97; hermeneutical aspects of, 140ff.; in Husserl, 79, 140; and meaning, 142ff.; as prenoetic force, 196–97; as superpersonal, 189; temporality of, 193; *see* expressibility, textuality
language acquisition, 213n14
Legerstee, M., 124
Leibniz, G. W. F., 173, 217n19
Levinas, E., 5, 108, 120–26, 142–43, 145, 160, 167–68, 171–72; on the infinite, 210n11; on the past, 210n9
Libet, B., 3, 23
life-world, 138–39, 152–53, 158, 164, 190
linearity (linear order), 3 , 88, 90, 193
linguistic expression, 132
linguistic meaning, 133, 141, 145
linguistic practices, 99, 143, 158
linguistic signs, 79
linguisticality, 81, 85, 112
literacy, 197
living present (Husserl), 13, 78, 80, 91, 100–101, 123–24, 160
Locke, John, 2, 4–9, 13, 73, 75, 77, 83, 88, 108, 180, 198
longitudinal intentionality; *see* horizontal intentionality
Lotze, R. H., 7, 11, 21, 23, 33, 37, 54, 61, 63, 66; theory of temporal signs, 23
Lotzean assumptions, 22–23, 30–31, 38, 41, 48, 51–52, 53, 57–59, 61–62, 64; *see* LA1, LA2
Lyotard, Jean-François, 5, 86, 88, 99, 100–105, 146, 160, 167, 169; critique of phenomenology, 100

Mabbott, J. D., 17–18, 23–26, 28, 30, 37, 54–55, 60, 63
Madison, G., 95
Mallarmé, S., 85
Marcel, A. J., 1, 93, 162–64, 208n10, 215n12
Marcel, G., 117
Marx, W., 172
masking; *see* perceptual masking
maximum and minimum durations, 54
Mazis, G., 95, 208n11
McIntyre, R., 140–42, 148, 150, 153
McTaggart, J. M. E., 29, 55–58, 86–87, 89, 100, 172–73, 175–77
Mead, G. H., 108, 111–12, 115–17, 122, 125–26, 142–43, 145, 209nn4, 5
meaning, 45–46, 48, 51, 54, 132ff., 140; also see *Sinn*
Meinong, A., 7, 35–36, 39, 54, 192
Mellor, H., 175, 178
Meltzoff, A., 109, 115, 144, 213n13
meme, 88
memory , 59–60, 123, 190; accuracy of, 192; in Augustine, 6–7, 59; in Brentano, 40–41, 59; distinguished from retention, 51; and embodiment, 188–89; and emotion, 192; and forgetting, 102; in Hume, 83; in McTaggart, 176; in neonate imitation, 110; screen memory, 97ff.; short-term, 94; *also see* recollection, re-presentation
memory images, 4, 11, 26, 30, 37–38, 48, 51, 57
memory storage, 191
mental contents, 43
Merleau-Ponty, M., 86, 88ff., 95–101, 123, 138, 140, 145; and alterity, 108, 114; on content, 97, 104ff.; and Derrida, 208n4; on LA2, 89; on language, 142–44; *Phenomenology of Perception*, 89; on reflection, 89ff., 173; on the reversibility of temporal experience, 95ff., 99; on screen memory, 97ff.; on syncretism, 125; *The Visible and the Invisible*, 89
metaphor, 14, 66, 99, 104, 106, 152, 154–56, 160, 167, 186, 196, 199, 202, 219n13
metapsychology, 106
Mill, J. S., 117

Miller, I., 34, 37, 53, 60–62, 64, 67
Minkowski, E., 207n6
Möbius, P., 167
Möbius Syndrome, 167–68
Mohanty, J. N., 133
momentary act of awareness, 18; *see*
    consciousness: momentary
mood (*Stimmung*), 118
Moore, M. K., 109, 115, 144
morphe, 42
motion, 6, 8
multiple drafts (Dennett), 99, 186
Mundle, C. W. K., 17, 25, 27, 30, 38–39,
    51, 53–54, 60
music, 96–97
Myers, G., 27

narrative, 186–87, 193, 195–98
Natorp, 180–82
natural attitude, 92, 115
Neisser, U., 219n12
neonate imitation, 109–10, 113–14, 119,
    124–25, 144, 168
network, 155–58, 172, 174, 182, 214n5
neurological timing, 187–88
neural development, 114
neural functioning, 88, 161–62, 186
neuropsychology, 160–61, 164
neuroscience, 99, 114, 161, 199
Newman, B., 101
Newton, I., 173, 177, 179
Nietzsche, F., 117
noema, 45–46, 98, 104, 110, 121, 123,
    132–33, 140–42, 147–51, 168
noema as interpretation, 148
noematic content, 111, 150
noesis-noema distinction, 98, 155
noetic act (of consciousness), 47, 49,
    51–52, 55, 105, 130, 142, 150; having
    duration, 26, 28, 38–39; and LA1,
    22; and *Präsenzzeit* 35–36; and PSA,
    61–62; shaped by memory, 98; and the
    specious present, 18; structure of, 64
noetic apprehension; *see* apprehension
noetic schema (apprehension—content
    of apprehension), 44–46, 130, 131,
    134–35, 156, 168, 183
nonlinearity, 88, 99, 196
nonlinear neuronal processing, 3, 186

nonlinear (nonserial) temporality, 103,
    193
nonpresence, 5, 13, 80
non-self, 124; differentiation between self
    and non-self, 145
now, 36, 40, 47, 91, 96, 100, 111
now-phase of consciousness, 78, 79–80

Oatley, K., 191
obligation, 123
objective synthesis, 8, 10, 12, 18, 21, 76
objective time, 54–56, 66, 108, 118
Olson, D., 197, 218n11
operative intentionality, 131
organism-environment interaction, 182
otherness; *see* alterity
other(s), 106, 110–25, 144–46, 157, 160,
    168

pain, 137, 185
pairing (Husserl), 111
parallel processing, 88
parataxis, 100
Parfit, D., 214n4
passions, 83
past, 29, 95, 111; in the A-Series, 87;
    beyond the reach of memory, 101, 103,
    122, 169, 188–89; as constructed, 192;
    effect of, 97, 105, 190; in Heidegger,
    118; in Mead, 113; as prenoetic,
    174–75; presence of, 79; retention of,
    41–42, 48; in specious present, 17ff.
pathology, 92
Penrose, R., 3–4
perception, 6–7, 41–42, 44–45, 49–51, 56,
    64, 89, 132, 137, 147, 176, 187–88
perceptual masking, 94, 163, 208n9
personal identity, 8–13, 73–85, 152, 154
phase(s); *see* consciousness, phase of
phenomenal experience, 94
phenomenological method, 43, 54, 90,
    152–54
phenomenological reduction; *see epoche*
phenomenological reflection, 5, 62, 64,
    66, 69, 89, 92, 159–60
phi phenomenon, 3, 162, 164, 186, 201
phrase, 100, 104
physiological processes, 136, 183–85
physiological diplopia, 187
Plato, 207n6,

Plumer, G., 17, 23, 27, 29–31, 34, 37, 52–53, 55–60
philosophy of mind, 1–3
philosophy of the subject, 13
Pöppel, E., 161–63, 187, 215n10
possibilities, 113, 117–19, 123, 168, 171
post-Husserlian conception of intentionality, 133
poststructuralism, 1–2, 4, 12–13, 74, 81–84, 104
practical interests, 147, 193
practical schemas, 150
Präsensfeld, 97
Präsenzzeit, 32, 35–39, 49, 51–52, 64, 204n4
prenoetic, concept of the, 5, 119, 124
prenoetic community, 145
prenoetic effects, 104–6, 147, 151, 155–56, 174, 178, 190, 193, 198–99
prenoetic factors (forces, processes), 14, 85, 98, 148, 150–51, 157–59, 160, 164, 166, 172, 181–82, 188, 192, 198; and the body, 136–37; and history, 138; and identity, 152–53; and intentionality, 133ff., 148; as network (system), 154, 156
prenoetic temporality, 125; past, 74, 191–92
prepersonal, 83
prereflective, 92
presence, 5, 42, 44, 79, 91, 102–3, 121, 123
present, 95, 180; in the A-Series, 87; and alterity, 111, 167–69; in Augustine, 6; conscious, 11–12; informed by the past, 190; and intentionaltiy, 122; strict (real), 27; *see* specious present
present-at-hand, 116, 118
present moment of consciousness, 20
primal impression, 41, 46, 50–51, 64–65, 67–68, 76, 80, 101, 124, 131, 164, 167, 174
primary memory; *see* retention
primitive self-consciousness, 124
principle of non-contradiction, 176
principle of simultaneous awareness, 53, 60–64
proprioception, 124
Prior, A. N., 196
protention, 41, 46, 49–50, 57, 64ff., 80, 180; and alterity, 122ff.; as continuum, 68; death outstrips, 160; and dispersed identity, 154; as an imposition, 193; and integration, 67–68; in Lyotard, 101; as a primal expectation, 67; versus retention, 67–68; as unfulfilled intention, 52; *see* asymmetry of retention and protention
PSA; *see* principle of simultaneous awareness
psychologism, 56, 133, 173
pure experience (James), 155–56
psychopathology, 86, 184
psychopharmacology, 184
psychosomatic symptoms, 184

quantum theory, 4
quasi-temporal, 66, 103
Querintentionalität; see transverse intentionality
Querschnitt; see consciousness, phase of
Quinton, A., 73

radical empiricism (James), 99, 155–56, 214n3
real (*reell*) contents, 11, 44, 47–48, 51, 78, 98, 130–31, 135, 183; and intentional contents, 54; *also see* content, hyle, and consciousness, act of
reality of time, 56, 172, 174, 176–77; objective reality of time, 176; prenoetic reality of time, 176
recollection, 41–42, 94, 102, 139 , 189, 191; *also see* memory
reflection, 66, 77–78, 139, 186, 197, 200–201; dissociation in, 93–94; distortion in, 211n6; as hermeneutical, 160; hermeneutical constraints on 165; and hyle, 135; limitations of, 89ff.; as prenoetically constrained, 160; and the transcendental ego, 169–70; unitary reflective consciousness, 94
reference, 133, 135
Reid, T., 9
reification, 64–66, 68, 89
reell; see real
relation (intentional), 47; *also see* intentionality
re-presentation (*Vergegenwärtigung*), 40–41, 51, 66, 102, 122–23
representation, 110

representational content, 123
responsibility, 122–23, 125
retention, 5, 41, 46–48, 50ff., 55, 57ff., 76–77, 154, 168 , 188, 190; Derrida on, 79–80; involves double intentionality, 48; failure to retain, 100–102, 122; and forgetting, 97; and historical effect, 139; and integration, 67; and intentionality, 105; and the noetic schema, 130–31; and perceptual masking, 94; and reflection, 78; and temporal order, 87ff.; and the unconscious, 159–64; see asymmetry of retention and protention
retentional continuum, 50–51, 68, 76, 78, 80, 87, 102
retentional fading, 87, 102
retentional-protentional structure, 5, 13, 33, 35, 51ff., 101, 151; asymmetry in, 68; and content, 179–80; integration of, 67; and intentionality, 105; and Lotzean assumptions, 61; and prenoetic forces, 154
reversibility of time, 91, 95, 98, 102
Ricoeur, P., 197, 198
Ryle, G., 1

same, the, 121–22, 124, 168
Sartre, J.-P., 1, 105
Saussure, F. de, 88
Scheler, M., 136
schizophrenia, 185, 217n5
Schutz, A., 111–13, 204n2, 209n3
screen memory (Freud), 97–98, 103, 105
Searle, John, 3, 141, 190, 203n1
selectivity, 163, 218n9
self, 10, 110, 112–13, 116, 121, 124–25, 145; differentiation between self and non-self, 145; see personal identity
self-alienation, 116
self-consciousness, 78–79, 111; see primitive self-consciousness
self-constitution, 77, 81, 125, 158
self-presence, 79
self-understanding, 160
semantics, 181
sensation(s) (sense data, sense-contents), 51; and alterity, 124; at an instant, 31, 59; and LA2, 22, 37, 77; in noetic schema, 44, 47–48, 130–31; and the

past, 54; in specious present, 24, 37; see hyle
sense modalities, 30, 135; intermodal relations; see intersensory differences
serial order, 90, 99
seriality, 86, 88–96, 100–106, 124, 174–75, 185, 199–200
Serres, M., 209n13
significance (Bedeutsamkeit), 133, 151
simultaneity, 77; and cognitive paradox, 4, 6–7; in dreams, 193; and Lotzean assumptions, 61; and neural processing, 187
Sinn (meaning, sense), 44–45, 132–33, 135, 140–41, 148, 151; see noema
Smith, D. W., 140–42, 148, 150, 153
social class, 147
sociality, 108, 112–15
Sokolowski, R., 208n7
soul, 6, 8, 42, 100
space, 2, 84–85, 97
space-time, 3, 173
spacing (Derrida), 84, 85
spatializing time, 92, 197, 203n1
specious present, 60, 76, 91; and cognitive paradox, 4; contemporary terminology 203n4; diagram of, 19, 20, 24; and Locke, 9; German translation 205n1; Husserl's explanation, 49–52; in Husserl and James, 32–38, 63ff.; intentional status of, 54; intermodal/intersensory differences in, 30, 58; in the Jamesian tradition, 17–31; measurement of, 27ff., 54–55; in McTaggart, 29, 55ff.; in Mead, 111, 113, 122; neuronal explanation, 161; and objective synthesis, 10; perplexities of, 26ff., 53ff.; in radical empiricism, 155
speech, 143
speed of light, 56
Spiegelberg, H., 33
Stern, W., 32–35, 37–39, 48, 51–52, 62–63
Stevens, R., 33
Stoics, 177
Strawson, G., 195–96
stream (flow, flux) of consciousness 3, 53; content of, 179–81; as conversation (Mead), 112; diagram, 20; disruptions of, 184ff., 194; in Hume, 75–76; and

identity, 81; and Joycean machine, 104, 199–200; and language, 196; in Locke, 8; as metaphor 219n13; and personal identity, 11, 83–85; and the prenoetic, 152ff, 169ff.; as private, 110; quasi-temporal nature of, 67; reflective distortion of, 65, 90; self-unification of, 78; as a system of differences, 75–76; and temporal order, 87–88; in Woolf, 191
structuralism, 1
Stumpf, K., 33
subjectivity, 81, 83, 86, 89, 125, 134, 173
sublime, 102, 169
subpersonal processes, 99, 136, 161–64, 182–83, 188
subsumption, 121
succession, 53, 75; and cognitive paradox, 4, 6–7; and LA2, 37; and Lotzean assumptions, 61; neuronal explanation, 162; and noetic apprehensions, 47; of phrases, 100; and retention, 77; as seriality, 86ff.; in specious present, 38–39
suicide, 171
superpersonal, 182, 189
synaesthesia, 184
syncretic sociability (Wallon), 125
syncretism, 125
system of differences, 75, 81, 91, 99

temporal diplopia, 187
temporal fading, 59
temporal field (*Zeitfeld*), 54
temporal masking, 164
temporal order (sequence), 2, 7, 87, 182, 184, 188, 201
temporal signs, theory of (Lotze), 21
tense, 175–76, 178
textuality, 193, 195–97, 200–201
theater metaphor, 74, 83–84, 104ff., 112, 169
They, the; *see das Man*
thrownness, 118
time: backward referral, 3, 187, 201; diagrams, 19, 20, 24, 76–77, 188, 203n1, 204n3; linear, 3–4, 88, 90, 193; measure of motion, 6; Newtonian, 3; nonlinear, 3, 103, 193; objective, 18, 21; physical concept, 4; reversibility, 13; subjective

construction, 173; and subjectivity, 89; ubiquity of, 176, 178; universality of, 3
time-consciousness: and alterity, 108 167; in cognitive science, 2–4; in Derrida 79–81; and *differends* (Lyotard), 102–4; in Heidegger, 118; in Husserl, 2–4, 39ff., 53ff., 131; and integration, 67ff.; in James, 2–4, 17ff.; limitations of Husserl's analysis, 64ff.; in Merleau-Ponty, 88ff.; neuronal explanation, 161; and personal identity, 10–11, 73–74; post-Husserlian accounts, 12ff.; *see* retentional-protentional structure
time perception, 203n2
trace (Derrida), 80, 84, 101
transcendence, 121
transcendental, 67, 81, 112–13
transcendental ego; *see* ego, transcendental
transverse intentionality (*Querintentionalität*), 50–51, 77, 154

unconscious, 159, 160, 166; in Husserl, 182
unconscious affect (Freud), 102–3, 105

Varela, 161–62, 215n10
Vergegenwärtigung; see re-presentation
visual cortex, 92
Volkmann, W. V., 7, 19, 21, 33, 35, 37, 54
Voltaire, F., 75, 206n2
von Cramon, D., 92
von Neumann, J., 88

Wälde, M., 33
Wallon, H., 125
Ward, J., 7, 9, 20, 37, 54, 204n6
Watson, J., 1
Weiskrantz, L., 92
Whitehead, A. N., 87, 100, 194
Williams, D., 169
Wittgenstein, L., 190
Wood, D., 34, 180–82, 193–94, 196, 217n4
Woolf, V., 191, 200- 201
Woolfian consciousness, 191
Wundt, W. , 7, 18, 33, 37, 54, 63, 204n6
Wyschogrod, E., 172

Zeitstrecke, 35–36
Zihl, J., 92